SAYINGS
OF THE CENTURY

NIGEL REES

London
GEORGE ALLEN & UNWIN
Boston   Sydney

George Allen & Unwin (Publishers) Ltd,
40 Museum Street, London WC1A 1LU, UK

George Allen & Unwin Australia Pty Ltd,
8 Napier Street, North Sydney, NSW 2060, Australia

First published 1984

British Library Cataloguing in Publication Data

Rees, Nigel
  Sayings of the century.
1. Quotations, English
I. Title
080   PN6081
ISBN 0-04-808048-9

Set in 11 on 12 pt Plantin Light
Layout by Columns of Reading
and printed in Great Britain by
Mackays of Chatham

Contents

Preface	v
One Small Quote for Mankind	1
Royalty: We are Quite Amused	3
Exploration: Because It's There	11
Celebrities: Famous for Fifteen Minutes	15
1914 – 18: The First World War	26
Shaw: As GBS Once Said . . .	37
Famous Phrases	42
The Presidency: Where the Buck Stops	65
Literature: Phrasal Footnotes	89
Churchill: He Mobilised the English Language	98
Dentopedology: Foot in Mouth	110
Before the War: The Gathering Storm	115
1939 – 45: The Second World War	121
Catchphrases	134
Prime Ministers: A Word from No. 10	143
Media: The Clattering Train	155
Moi, General de Gaulle	164
Titles: Where the Kinquering Kongs Took Them From	168
Cinema: This is Where We Came In	176
Martin Luther King: I Have a Dream	187
Advertising: It Pays to Sloganise	193
Mao Tse-tung: His Little Red Book	205
Business: Do You Sincerely Want to be Rich?	208
1959 – 73: The Vietnam War	211
Protest: We're Against It	214
Sport: Winning Isn't Everything	219
Politics: The Art of the Possible	223
Sex: The Most Fun You Can Have Without Laughing	251
Last Words	254
Acknowledgements	257
Picture Credits	260
Index of Sayings	262

Preface

TO call a book *Sayings of the Century* and to describe it as an annotated collection of well-known phrases from the twentieth century when, at the time of publication, there are still seventeen years still to run, requires some explanation. Especially is this so when the casual dipper-in will exclaim that there are all kinds of omissions and that the choice of quotations dealt with appears highly subjective.

So, to begin with, let me say what this book is *not*. It is not a dictionary of quotations in the style of Bartlett or the Oxford. After all, what would be the point of duplicating those books, even with a special emphasis on the twentieth century? Additionally, within its chosen sphere, this book does not in any way seek to be comprehensive – how could it be? – though I suspect that it probably does include most of the significant sayings of the century and those which one might expect to find in a volume with this title.

But what does the book contain? My sole criterion for choosing the phrases and sayings has been *whether there is anything more to say about them*. Hence, if a famous remark does not require amplification, it is usually omitted. The reason for this approach stems from my own familiarity with numerous books of quotations over a period of some nine years since I started a BBC radio programme called *Quote . . . Unquote*. Whilst checking the origin and use of thousands of quotations for that programme I have been struck repeatedly by discrepancies between the versions given in different reference books, by inaccuracies and misattributions, and by the omission of phrases which I thought were significant and which I was curious to find out about. In other reference books, I have also felt a lack of background and contextual information necessary for the proper understanding and use of quotations.

To keep the present book within limits and to concentrate my own researches I have therefore restricted it – in a very subjective way – to well-known phrases and sayings which have arisen this century and in which I have acquired a special interest.

They are divided into major categories – like the remarks of American Presidents, British Prime Ministers, sayings of the First and Second World Wars, lines from films, advertisements, and show business. Then there are special chapters devoted to one or two interesting and quotable individuals, like Churchill, De Gaulle, and Shaw. Within the chapters the phrases are set out either in approximate chronological order, by surname of speaker, or by alphabetical order of key words.

The justification for launching this project in 1984, when the century has not run its course, must be that there is such a wealth of material already. I also hope that the book will be revised in future editions to take in new material. More importantly, some of the questions about phrase origins raised by this book will not be answered until it is published. Phrase-detection is a continuous process – and in some cases can literally never have an end – but the mere fact of this book's existence will lead to new information coming forward.

I have tried to correct some of the errors and misapprehensions surrounding some of the sayings of our time but I am conscious, too, that by supposition or sheer error I will start a few false hares myself. Where possible I have tried to go back to original sources and, where recordings exist, have checked text against delivery. Still, mistakes will have crept in and I will be more than pleased to be told of any, so that errors may be corrected in future editions.

Inevitably, in a work of this type, one is building on research already carried out by other authors. I feel that the best way of acknowledging particularly useful sources without overburdening the book with footnotes is to indicate by numbers in the text those books that are listed in the back of this volume.

My toils in the quotation field have led me to formulate two or three laws about the way people use and abuse quotations. My first law is: *When in doubt, ascribe all quotations to Bernard Shaw* – which I don't mean to be taken literally, but as a general observation of the habit people have of attaching remarks to the nearest obvious speaker. Churchill, Wilde, Orson Welles and Alexander Woollcott are other useful figures upon whom to father remarks when you don't know who really said them. Part of my job in this book has been to unscramble the results of this tendency.

My second law is that: *There's always an earlier use of a phrase, however far back you go.* It is only required of me to state that so-and-so was the first person to say something for a correspondent to point out that Herrick or the Bible or some Egyptian papyrus had an earlier formulation of the phrase. Hence, a certain circumspection will be apparent in this book as I say 'is associated with' or 'was popularised by' rather than 'was originated by'.

Having said that, I need to make another point. Although I have sometimes suggested that such and such a speechwriter coined a phrase, the important fact must always be: who gave the phrase currency or popularised it. This may appear somewhat ungrateful to the back-room boys but it is a fact of life.

The words 'quotation', 'catchphrase' and 'slogan' occur frequently in this book, so perhaps I should attempt to distinguish between terms not always distinctly used:

a *quotation*, in my book, is a saying that is capable of being traced to a particular source, be it speaker or book or film or show, even if this has not proved possible;

a *catchphrase* is simply a saying that has 'caught on' with the public and may not be capable of tracing to a precise source;

a *slogan* is a phrase designed to promote a product, idea or cause (I also feel that it should have been used with some consciousness of its being a slogan, rather than just occurring in conversation like a catchphrase).

There can be considerable overlap between these categories. Indeed, it is possible for a saying to be all three things simultaneously.

Do the sayings contained in this book have any particular twentieth-century quality about them? The day of the telling phrase, the jewelled epigram and the polished period is largely over. Most of the sayings I have selected have a colloquial quality, an informal bent. I suppose the eruption of the mass media during the century is largely responsible for this. Broadcasting, in particular, by demanding a more informal style has more or less put paid to political oratory. Lloyd George and Ramsay MacDonald, old-style orators, found it impossible to accommodate to the new medium. Stanley Baldwin took to it like a duck to water. It is said that at his first broadcast he struck a match and lit his pipe just before he began. Homeliness became the hallmark of most public speech. By way of compensation, I have chosen to print in full the abdication speech of King Edward VIII, President John F. Kennedy's inaugural address, Dr Martin Luther King Jr's 'I have a dream' speech, and a substantial portion of Winston Churchill's wartime 'blood, tears, toil and sweat' speech. These seem to hark back to an earlier period when greater emphasis was placed upon saying important things well and memorably.

The greatly quoted wits and personalities of the nineteenth century barely strayed into our own time – Mark Twain survived to 1910 as, curiously enough, did Tolstoy. Oscar Wilde just failed to qualify under this book's precise definition of the twentieth century which is January 1901 to 31 December 2000. He died on 30 November 1900. Queen Victoria just queezed in – she died on 19 January 1901.

This book has a bias towards phrases from politics, entertainment and popular speech and neglects to say very much about literature. This is partly because there is not always a great deal more to say about creatively honed remarks. Perhaps it also reflects a lack of mighty lines in the novels and poetry of the century.

I have been helped in my researches by many kind people. Perhaps I should dedicate this book, however, to the person who asked me whether I knew the origin of the phrase **dragged kicking and screaming into the twentieth century**. I had to tell him I did not, though I later come across a 1959 reference to a speech in which Adlai Stevenson used the expression about the Republican Party's need for such a manoeuvre. But the inquiry set me thinking, and this book is the result. I hope it will fascinate anyone who has the slightest feeling for language and for the excitement and terrible scope of an amazing century. May it constitute a small monument of verbal history as we move towards the day when we must drag and kick ourselves in to the twenty-first century.

Nigel Rees
London, 1984

ONE SMALL QUOTE FOR MANKIND

SIX hundred million television viewers round the world watched as Neil Armstrong (*b*.1930) became the first man to set foot on the moon. What were his first words going to be on this momentous occasion? It seemed to him that every person he had met in the previous three months had asked him what he was going to say or had made suggestions. Among the hundreds of sayings he was offered were passages from Shakespeare and whole chapters from the Bible.

'I had thought about what I was going to say, largely because so many people had asked me to think about it,' Armstrong reflected afterwards.[3] 'I thought about [it] a little bit on the way to the moon, and it wasn't really decided until after we got on to the lunar surface. I guess I hadn't actually decided what I wanted to say until just before we went out.'

As he stepped on to the surface what he *says* he said was: **That's one small step for a man, one giant leap for mankind.**

What the 600 million *heard* at 10.56 pm (EDT) on 20 July 1969 was another matter. Although the verbal formula of 'small steps' and 'giant leaps' soon passed into the language, a quick flip through several dictionaries of quotations reveals numerous variations. One has 'for *all* mankind', another 'one *big step*', but the most common version is 'One small step for (. . .) man.' This completely ruins the

1

nice contrast between 'a man' (one individual) and 'mankind' (all of us). However, this his how Armstrong's line was first reported and, indeed, exactly how it sounds on recordings. There is no perceptible gap between 'for' and 'man'.

When he returned to earth, the astronaut spotted the near-tautology in a transcript of the mission and tried to put over a correct version. It was explained that the indefinite article 'a' had not been heard because of static on the radio link or because 'tape recorders are fallible'. But, is it not possible that Armstrong fluffed his mighty line?

If the twentieth-century's most audible saying could result in such confusion, what hope was there for the rest?

ROYALTY

We Are Quite Amused

THE sayings of the British Royal Family have customarily been accorded attention out of all proportion to their intrinsic worth. It only needs a King to say 'Good morning, gentlemen' for the press to scribble it down in notebooks, or a Prince of Wales to make a light remark for it to be greeted by gales of thigh-slapping laughter. Yet why wonder? It is part of a magical charade which most people continue to enjoy playing

With commendable tidiness, Queen Victoria (*b*.1819) died during the first month of the new century – on 18 January 1901. To a new era she bequeathed much speculation as to whether she had ever made use of the put-down **We are not amused.** The subject was raised in the 1919 *Notebooks of a Spinster Lady* written by Miss Caroline Holland (1878–1903): '[The Queen's] remarks can freeze as well as crystallise . . . there is a tale of the unfortunate equerry who ventured during dinner at Windsor to tell a story with a spice of scandal or impropriety in it. "We are not amused," said the Queen when he had finished.'

The equerry in question appears to have been the Hon. Alexander Yorke. Unfortunately, the German he had told the story to laughed so loud that the Queen's attention was drawn to it. Another contender for the snub is Admiral Maxse whom she commanded to give his well-known imitation of her which he did by putting a handkerchief on his head and blowing out his cheeks. Interviewed in 1978, Princess Alice, Countess of Athlone, said she had once asked her grandmother about the phrase – 'I asked her . . . [but] she never said it' – and affirmed what many have held, that Queen Victoria was 'a very cheerful person'.

It might seem that the dying queen's last word – **Bertie!** – was an entirely-to-be-expected reference to her late and long-lamented consort, Prince Albert. Instead, it was the name of her son and heir, Albert Edward, who took the title of King Edward VII.

On 5 December 1901, the Duke of York – four days later to be created Prince of Wales and in 1910 to become King George V – gave a speech in the Guildhall to mark the recent completion of his tour round the Empire. He warned against taking the Empire for granted: 'To the distinguished representatives of the commercial interests of the Empire . . . I venture to allude to the impression which seemed generally to prevail among our brethren overseas, that the old country must wake up if she intends to maintain her old position of pre-eminence in her Colonial trade against foreign competitors.' This statement was encapsulated by the popular press in the phrase **Wake Up, England!**

George V (*b.*1865) is credited with two remarks on the more mundane aspects of kingship: **After you've met one hundred and fifty Lord Mayors, they all begin to look the same** and **Never miss an opportunity to relieve yourself; never miss a chance to sit down and rest your feet.** Later, the Duke of Windsor was to ascribe the second remark to 'an old courtier' but it seems likely he heard it from his father. A correspondent who wished to remain anonymous told me in 1981 that a naval officer of her acquaintance who was about to accompany Prince George, Duke of Kent, on a cruise, was asked by George V to make sure that the Prince was properly dressed before going ashore. He also advised: 'Always take an opportunity to relieve yourselves.' Another correspondent suggested that Edward VII was the first to say this when he was Prince of Wales. On the other hand, more than a century earlier, the Duke of Wellington had said: 'Always make water when you can.'

A rare example of a royal joke comes from the period just before George V's death. In December 1935 it was revealed that Sir Samuel Hoare, the Foreign Secretary, had come to an arrangement with M. Laval, his French counterpart, whereby Abyssinia was virtually to be consigned to the Italians behind the League of Nations' back. The Hoare–Laval Pact had been concluded in Paris when Sir Samuel was passing through on his way to a holiday in Switzerland. In the furore

4

that followed he had to resign. George V joked: **No more coals to Newcastle, no more Hoares to Paris.** He may just have been repeating a remark that was current anyway and is unlikely to have said it to Hoare himself, despite Lord Avon's recollection of what the King told him.[78]

On Monday 20 January 1936, a few members of the Privy Council gathered in the King's bedroom at Sandringham to witness the signing of a proclamation constituting a Council of State. The King was so weak it took a long time. To the Privy Councillors he murmured: **Gentlemen, I am sorry for keeping you waiting like this – I am unable to concentrate**. These are sometimes referred to as his last words.

At 9.25 pm, Lord Dawson of Penn, the King's doctor, issued a bulletin. It said: **The King's life is moving peacefully towards its close.** This was taken up by the BBC. All wireless programmes were cancelled and every quarter of an hour the announcer, Stuart Hibberd, read the medical bulletin until the King died just before midnight.

The following day, Stanley Baldwin, the Prime Minister, broadcast a tribute which included a different version of the deathbed words:

> There is one thing I can tell you without any impropriety, for though much, and most indeed, of what passes near the end is sacred . . . I think I may tell you this. The King was having brief intervals of consciousness, and each time he became conscious it was some kind enquiry or kind observation of someone, some words of gratitude for kindness shown. But he did say to his secretary [Lord Wigram] when he sent for him: **How is the Empire?** – an unusual phrase in that form. And the secretary said: 'All is well, sir, with the Empire,' and the King gave him a smile and relapsed once more into unconsciousness.

Other accounts make it clear that the wonderfully imperial inquiry arose *before* the privy council meeting. One of them suggests that only the word 'Empire' was audible and the rest of the inquiry merely assumed by the King's secretary.

There is, moreover, according to oral tradition, a third deathbed utterance, but I have been unable to find out how it originated. At some stage in his final illness the King was assured that he would soon be fit enough to visit his favourite watering place at Bognor. **Bugger Bognor!** he is supposed to have cried. Kenneth Rose in his biography[78] suggests, however, that the remark may date back to George V's recuperative visit to Bognor after his serious illness in the winter of 1928–9:

5

'A happier version of the legend rests on the authority of Sir Owen Morshead, the King's librarian. As the time of the King's departure from Bognor drew near, a deputation of leading citizens came to ask that their salubrious town should henceforth be known as Bognor Regis.

'They were received by Stamfordham, the King's private secretary, who, having heard their petition, invited them to wait while he consulted the King in another room. The sovereign responded with the celebrated obscenity, which Stamfordham deftly translated for the benefit of the delegation. His Majesty, they were told, would be graciously pleased to grant their request.'

King Edward VIII (1894 – 1972) reigned for less than a year. He abdicated in order to marry the American divorcee, Mrs Wallis Simpson. For most of 1936, the British public was kept in ignorance of the manoeuvres going on behind the scenes to resolve this crisis. Baldwin subsequently told his daughter of a meeting he had had with the new King's mother, Queen Mary, as the storm grew: 'I had a tremendous shock. For, instead of standing immobile in the middle distance, silent and majestic, she came trotting across the room exactly like a puppy dog: and before I had time to bow, she took hold of my hand in both of hers and held it tight. "Well, Prime Minister," she said **"here's a pretty kettle of fish."** '
Years later, meeting Queen Mary at a dinner party, Noel Coward boldly asked: 'Is it true, Ma'am, that you said, "Here's a pretty kettle of fish"?' She replied: 'Yes, I think I did.'[65]
In November, the King went to South Wales to tour the depressed areas and moved the public with his expressions of concern. At the Bessemer steel works at Dowlais where 9,000 men had been rendered unemployed, hundreds sang an old Welsh hymn. Afterwards the King was heard to say to an official: 'These works brought all these people here. **Something must be done**, to find them work.' Occasionally quoted as 'something ought to be done' and followed the next day by the promise 'You may be sure that all I can do for you, I will,' the King's words were taken as an indication of his concern for ordinary people and of his impatience with established authority.
Although distress at what he saw in South Wales was no doubt genuine, the King's assurances might look less hollow if we did not now know that by then he had already informed his family and the Prime Minister of his decision to abdicate.
Press comment on the Simpson affair finally burst through

following innocuous remarks made on 1 December by the Bishop of Bradford, Dr Alfred Blunt. Speaking at a diocesan conference, he was dealing with a suggestion that the Coronation should be secularised and with criticism that the King was not a regular churchgoer: 'The benefit of the King's Coronation depends under God upon . . . the faith, prayer and self-dedication of the King himself . . . We hope that he is aware of this need. Some of us wish that he gave more positive signs of such awareness.'

The *Yorkshire Post* linked the Bishop's words to rumours then in circulation. Dr Blunt claimed his address had been written six weeks earlier, without knowledge of the rumours, and added: 'I studiously took care to say nothing whatever of the King's private life, because I know nothing about it.'

So, apparently by chance, the matter became public. By lunchtime on 11 December, Edward VIII had ceased to be King. Mrs Alice Keppel, one-time mistress of Edward VII exclaimed: **Things were done better in my day.** That night, before he left the country, 'His Royal Highness Prince Edward' took the opportunity of broadcasting a message to his former subjects. Churchill growled Marvell's lines:

> He nothing common did or mean
> Upon that memorable scene.

Indeed, nothing in Edward's reign became him like the leaving it. He later commented:[98] 'It has become part of the Abdication legend that the broadcast was actually written by Mr Churchill. The truth is that, as he had often done before with other speeches, he generously applied the final brush strokes.' The phrases 'bred in the constitutional tradition by my father' and 'one matchless blessing . . . a happy home with his wife and children' are the two most obvious of such strokes. They were applied to a basic text drawn up by Edward's lawyer, Walter Monckton. Sir John Reith who introduced the broadcast noted that he had seen 'never so many alterations in a script'.

The moving speech, here quoted in full, could be heard by all his subjects over the wireless – a unique event. However relieved people may have been subsequently that Edward's reign was not prolonged, for the moment they were touched, if not reduced to tears, by the courageous tones in which the broadcast was delivered and by the protestations of love and duty it included:

At long last I am able to say a few words of my own. I have never wanted to withold anything, but until now it has not been

7

constitutionally possible for me to speak. A few hours ago I discharged my last duty as King and Emperor, and now that I have been succeeded by my brother, the Duke of York, my first words must be to declare my allegiance to him. This I do with all my heart.

You all know the reasons which have impelled me to renounce the throne. But I want you to understand that in making up my mind I did not forget the country or the Empire which as Prince of Wales, and lately as King, I have for twenty-five years tried to serve. But you must believe me when I tell you that **I have found it impossible to carry the heavy burden of responsibility and to discharge my duties as King as I would wish to do without the help and support of the woman I love.**

And I want you to know that the decision I have made has been mine and mine alone. This was a thing I had to judge entirely for myself. The other person most nearly concerned has tried up to the last to persuade me to take a different course. I have made this, the most serious decision of my life, only upon the single thought of what would in the end be best for all.

This decision has been made less difficult to me by the sure knowledge that my brother, with his long training in the public affairs of this country and with his fine qualities, will be able to take my place forthwith, without interruption or injury to the life and progress of the Empire. And he has one matchless blessing, enjoyed by so many of you and not bestowed on me – a happy home with his wife and children.

During these hard days I have been comforted by Her Majesty my Mother and by my Family. The Ministers of the Crown, and in particular Mr Baldwin, the Prime Minister, have always treated me with full consideration. There has never been any constitutional difference beween me and them and between me and Parliament. Bred in the constitutional tradition by my Father, I should never have allowed any such issue to arise.

Ever since I was Prince of Wales, and later on when I occupied the Throne, I have been treated with the greatest kindness by all classes of the people, wherever I have lived or journeyed throughout the Empire. For that I am very grateful.

I now quit altogether public affairs, and I lay down my burden. It may be some time before I return to my native land, but I shall always follow the fortunes of the British race and Empire with profound interest, and if at any time in the future I can be found of service to His Majesty in a private station I shall not fail. And now we all have a new King. I wish him, and you, his people,

8

happiness and prosperity with all my heart. God Bless you all. God Save the King.

King George VI (1895–1952), hampered by a speech impediment, was scarcely noted for what he said. Yet in his Christmas broadcast of 1939 he quoted an obscure poet with such success that he captured the public imagination as few other Royals have done. He quoted Miss Minnie Louise Haskins (1875–1957), a retired lecturer at the London School of Economics, who had written these words as the introduction to a poem called *The Desert* in 1908:

I said to the man who stood at the Gate of the Year, 'Give me a light that I may tread safely into the unknown.' And he replied, 'Go out into the darkness, and put your hand into the Hand of God. That shall be to you better than light, and safer than a known way.'

Miss Haskins did not hear the broadcast but found herself inundated with writing offers. Her reprinted poem sold 43,000 copies, she was included in *Who's Who* and merited an obituary in *The Times* – testimony to the power of being quoted by the right person at the right time.

Though noted in private for a lively sense of humour, Queen Elizabeth II (*b.*1926) has made little impression as a speaker in public. Initially, the cut-glass delivery of platitudes in her Christmas broadcasts fuelled the attacks on the monarchy launched by Lord Altrincham and Malcolm Muggeridge in 1958. In a magazine article, Altrincham said the Queen's style of speaking (*not* her voice) was 'frankly a pain in the neck' and what she was given to say suggested 'a priggish school girl, captain of the hockey team, a prefect and a recent candidate for confirmation'. He was slapped in the face by a member of the League of Empire Loyalists for his pains. Muggeridge weighed in shortly afterwards calling the Queen 'frumpish and banal' in an American magazine. As a result, he was banned from broadcasting for a while by the BBC.

The Queen's style was encapsulated in the phrase **My husband and I.** Her father had quite naturally spoken the words 'The Queen and I' but something in the Queen's drawling delivery turned her version into a joke catchphrase. It first appeared during her second Christmas broadcast (made from New Zealand) in 1953 – 'My husband and I left London a month ago' – and still survived in 1962: 'My husband and I are greatly looking forward to visiting New Zealand and Australia in the New Year.' By 1967, the phrase had become 'Prince Philip and I'. At a Silver Wedding banquet in 1972, the Queen allowed herself a little joke: 'I think on this occasion I may be forgiven for saying "My husband and I".'

A cliché often falling from Royal lips has been **You must have seen a lot of changes in your time?** – a conversational device when chatting to people not known to one and perhaps of no great interest. Such is the aura surrounding British royalty that even such plonking remarks can reduce grown men to twirps. In 1969 Walter Annenberg went to present his credentials as US Ambassador to the Court of St James. Unfortunately for him, a TV crew was hovering at his elbow making the film *Royal Family*. Consequently, millions were able to hear the peculiarly orotund remarks he thought appropriate for the occasion. When asked by the Queen about the state of his official residence, he said: 'We're in the Embassy residence, subject, of course, to some of the discomfiture as a result of a need for, uh, elements of refurbishing and rehabilitation.'

Cutting through such flummery, Prince Philip (*b*.1921) obtained a reputation for blunt speaking. 'Just at the moment we are suffering a national defeat comparable to any lost military campaign,' he told businessmen on 17 October 1961, 'and what is more, it is self-inflicted . . . **I think it is about time we pulled our finger out.**' Such language frequently led to what the Prince styled 'dentopedology – the science of opening your mouth and putting your foot in it' and a need for retractions or further elaboration. His 1962 remark, **I never see any home cooking – all I get is fancy stuff**, had to be qualified lest it reflect badly on the Buckingham Palace chefs. He had been referring to meals consumed *away* from the Palace. **The *Daily Express* is a bloody awful newspaper** (said at a 1962 press reception in Rio de Janeiro) was later qualified in answer to a question from Willie Hamilton MP:[32] 'I was having a private conversation with a journalist who claimed that the *Daily Express* was a splendid newspaper. My reply was spontaneous and never intended for publication . . . I can say that the reasons [for my remark] no longer exist.'

Of the next generation of Royals, it can only be hoped that quotability will depend not so much on *who* is speaking as on *what* is said. When the Princess of Wales (*b*.1961) was asked in 1981 what her first impression of Prince Charles had been, she replied: **Pretty amazing!** This innocuous verdict on their encounter in a freshly ploughed field during 1977 briefly achieved catchphrase status.

EXPLORATION

Because It's There

THE restless urge to discover new things, to go to
unexplored places and take part in daring exploits was well
demonstrated in the early part of the century by the mountaineer,
George Leigh Mallory (1886–1924). He disappeared in 1924 on his
last attempt to scale Mount Everest. The previous year, during a
lecture tour of the US, he had frequently been asked why he wanted
to achieve this goal. He replied: **Because it's there.**

In 1911, at Cambridge, A. C. Benson had urged Mallory to read
Carlyle's life of John Sterling – a book that achieved high quality
simply 'by being *there*'. Perhaps that is how the construction entered
Mallory's mind. There have been many variations (and misattri-
butions) since. Richard Ingrams of *Private Eye* once invented for the
Duke of Edinburgh a reply to the question why he had married
Queen Elizabeth: 'Because she was there.'

More intrepid utterances from those who have ventured into the
unknown:

When Captain Lawrence Oates (nicknamed 'Titus') (1880–1912)
walked to his death on Scott's 1912 polar expedition, in the vain hope
of saving his companions, he defined courage for a generation of
Englishmen. Beaten to the South Pole by the Norwegian explorer,
Amundsen, the small party fell victim to terrible weather conditions

11

on the return journey to its ship. One man died and Oates, suffering from scurvy, frostbitten and gangrenous feet, and an old war wound, realised that he would be next. Without him slowing them down, the remaining three might stand a better chance of survival. With classic stiff upper lip understatement, Oates was reported by Scott as having said: **I am just going outside, and I may be some time.** He did not bother to spend the couple of hours' painful effort needed to put on his boots. He went out in his stockinged feet and did not return. Scott wrote: 'We knew that poor Oates was walking to his death, but though we tried to dissuade him, we knew it was the act of a brave man and an English gentleman. We all hope to meet the end with similar spirit, and assuredly the end is not far.' His Antarctic epitaph, composed by E. L. Atkinson and Apsley Cherry Garrard, was: 'Hereabouts died **a very gallant gentleman**.'

It was inevitable in time that iconoclasts would review the evidence and wonder, in the light of Oates's expressed criticisms of Scott, whether his action was truly voluntary or whether it was the result of silent hints from the expedition leader that he should take this course. As the only record of what Oates said was contained in Scott's diary, it has even been suggested that the words were Scott's invention and never actually said by Oates. But opinion suggests that it was an act perfectly in character and there would have been no need to invent anything.

Captain Robert Falcon Scott (1868–1912) did, however, contrive masterly epitaphs for himself and his companions by keeping at his diary as he slowly froze to death: 'Great God! This is an awful place and terrible enough for us to have laboured without the reward of priority' (he wrote on reaching the Pole). Towards the end, he addressed a message to the public:

> We are showing that Englishmen can still die with a bold spirit, fighting it out to the end . . . **Had we lived, I should have had a tale to tell of the hardihood, endurance, and courage of my companions which would have stirred the hearts of every Englishman. These rough notes and our dead bodies must tell the tale**.

The last entry in his diary, with the writing tapering away, was for 29 March 1912: 'It seems a pity, but I do not think I can write more. R. SCOTT. **For God's sake look after our people**.'

The most exciting archaeological find of the century was that of the tomb of Tutankhamun in November 1922. The British archaeologist,

Howard Carter (1873–1939), backed by his patron, the fifth Earl of Carnavon, had been digging fruitlessly for many years in Egypt's Valley of the Kings. Then he hit upon a flight of steps beneath the ruins of old workmen's huts. Carter wired for Carnavon to join him. Three days of digging were needed to clear the entrance passage. On 26 November another sealed door appeared. It was through the hole which he made in this door that Carter glimpsed the treasure. He described the moment in a thrilling passage:[38]

> I inserted the candle and peered in, Lord Carnavon, Lady Evelyn and Callender standing anxiously beside me to hear the verdict. At first I could see nothing, the hot air escaping from the chamber causing the candle flame to flicker, but presently, as my eyes grew accustomed to the light, details of the room within emerged slowly from the mist, strange animals, statues and gold – **everywhere the glint of gold**. For the moment – an eternity it must have been to the others standing by – I was struck dumb with amazement, and when Lord Carnavon, unable to stand the suspense any longer, inquired anxiously, 'Can you see anything?' it was all I could do to get out the words, 'Yes, **wonderful things**.' Then, widening the hole a little further so that both could see, we inserted an electric torch.

The first two climbers to reach the summit of Mount Everest, the world's highest mountain, in the Himalayas, were the New Zealander, Edmund Hillary (*b.*1919) and his Sherpa guide, Tenzing Norgay. They were members of a British-led expedition in 1953. In his autobiography,[35] Hillary described what happened when he came down from the summit:

> George (Lowe) met us with a mug of soup just above camp, and seeing his stalwart frame and cheerful face reminded me how fond of him I was. My comment was not specially prepared for public consumption but for George . . .'Well, **we knocked the bastard off!**' I told him and he nodded with pleasure . . . 'Thought you must have!'

The Apollo XI space mission which first put a man on the surface of the moon in July 1969 provided two other phrases in addition to Neil Armstrong's famous first words. As the lunar module touched down, Armstrong announced: **Tranquillity Base here – the Eagle has landed.** Nobody at Mission Control had known that Armstrong would call it that, although the name was logical enough. The

13

landing area was in the Sea of Tranquillity; 'Eagle' was the name of the craft (referring to the American national symbol). Confusingly, the writer Jack Higgins later used the phrase *The Eagle Has Landed* as the title of a 1975 thriller set in the Second World War.

The Apollo XI astronauts carried with them, and left behind on the moon, not only an American flag but also a plaque saying:

HERE MEN FROM THE PLANET EARTH
FIRST SET FOOT UPON THE MOON
JULY, 1969 AD
WE CAME IN PEACE FOR ALL MANKIND.

This ensured that 'for all mankind' became a stockphrase from then on, although the conjunction of 'all' and 'mankind' was already well established.

The Apollo 13 space mission took off at 13.13 Houston time on 11 April 1970. Two days into the moon mission – i.e. on the 13th – and 200,000 miles from earth, an oxygen tank exploded seriously endangering the crew. James Lovell (*b*.1928), the commander, noted with considerable understatement: **OK, Houston, we have had a problem here . . . Houston, we have a problem.** In fact, it is hard to decipher precisely what was said. *The Times* (15 April) had: 'Hey, we've got a problem.' Asked to repeat this, Lovell said: 'Houston, we've had a problem. We've had a main bus interval' (indicating a fault in the electrical system). Emergency procedures allowed the crew a safe return to earth. John L. Swigert Jr, another crew member, has also been credited with the words.

CELEBRITIES
Famous for Fifteen Minutes

THE artist Andy Warhol (*b. c.*1930) predicted in the 1960s that: **In the future everyone will be famous for fifteen minutes.** He was referring to the opportunities for easy notoriety afforded by the mass media.

To be famous for having said something requires a modicum of effort – though often circumstances can give the most mundane words an element of memorability. Here are some 'celebrities' talking and providing a mixture of things worth saying – and things that were remembered anyway:

Kingsley AMIS (*b.*1922)

Novelist Amis wrote an article in *Encounter* (July 1960) in which he discussed the expansion of higher education and drew attention to 'the delusion that there are thousands of young people who are capable of benefiting from university training but have somehow failed to find their way there.' He concluded: **More will mean worse.**

When *The Times* misquoted this as 'more means worse', Mr Amis fired off a broadside (22 February 1983):

I think the difference is substantial, but let that go for now. You show by your misquotation that you couldn't be bothered to look up the reference, thereby ignoring the context, any arguments or evidence put forward, etc.

Having garbled my remark you say roundly that in the event I was wrong. Not altogether perhaps. Laziness and incuriosity about sources are familiar symptoms of academic decline.

Amis's phrase should not be confused with the **Less is more** philosophy of the architect Ludwig Mies van der Rohe (1886–1969). Mies meant that less visual clutter makes for a more satisfying living environment.

Margot ASQUITH (1865–1945)

The wife of the Liberal Prime Minister, H. H. Asquith, was noted for the sharp remarks she made about people. I am going to suggest, however, that her most famous shaft was said by someone else in a notable demonstration of my two laws of quotation.

The story goes – and I have told it many times myself since first hearing it in 1968 – that Margot Asquith went on a visit to the United States (*that* is not in dispute) where she met Jean Harlow. The film actress inquired whether the first name of the Countess (which she was by this time – the 1930s) was pronounced 'Margo' or 'Margott'. ' "Margo",' replied the Countess, **'The "T" is silent – as in Harlow**.'

I have always had a lingering doubt about this story as I never came across a reputable source. Then, quite recently, I was given a much more convincing version of its origin.

Margot *Grahame* (1911–82) was an English acress who, after stage appearances in Johannesburg and London, went to Hollywood in 1934. Her comparatively brief career as a film star included appearances in *The Informer*, *The Buccaneer* and *The Three Musketeers*, in the mid-1930s.

It was when she was being built up as a rival to the likes of Harlow (who died in 1937) that Grahame later claimed the celebrated exchange had occurred. She added that it was not intended as a put down. She did not realise what she had said till afterwards.

Grahame seems a convincing candidate for speaker of the famous line. I suspect she *did* say it and when her star waned people attributed the remark to the other, better-known and more quotable source.

W. H. AUDEN (1907–73)

No, it was not said *about* Auden but *by* Auden: the poet remarked to a reporter: 'Your cameraman might enjoy himself, because **my face**

looks like a wedding-cake left out in the rain.'

Tallulah BANKHEAD (1903–68)

A frequently employed critical witticism is **there's less in this than meets the eye**. Its modern popularity stems from the use made of the words by the actress Tallulah Bankhead. She said them to Alexander Woollcott *à propos* the play *Aglavaine and Selysette* by Maurice Maeterlinck on 3 January 1922.

But it is an old formula. James Boswell attributed a version to Richard Burke, son of Edmund (1 May 1783): 'I suppose here *less* is meant than meets the ear.'

Robert BENCHLEY (1889–1945)

I must get out of these wet clothes and into a dry Martini – who said it? For a while it was pinned upon Alexander Woollcott but it now seems likely that if Woollcott said it he obtained the remark from Robert Benchley who in turn heard it from his press agent. Benchley is the man with whom the line is associated, however, because he liked it and used it when playing opposite Ginger Rogers in the film *The Major and the Minor* (1942).

Ronald BRITTAIN (*c*.1899–1981)

As Regimental Sergeant-Major Brittain, he was reputed to have the loudest voice in the British Army. As his obituary in *The Times* put it:

> With his stentorian voice and massive parade ground presence [he] came to epitomise the British Army sergeant. Though he himself denied ever using it, he was associated with the celebrated parade ground expression **You 'orrible little man** – in some quarters, indeed, was reputed to have coined it . . . His **Wake Up There!** to the somnolent after a command had in his opinion been inadequately executed was legendary – doubtless the ancestor of all the Wake Up Theres which have succeeded it.

G. K. CHESTERTON (1874–1936)

This writer was noted for being disorganised. He is reputed to have sent a telegram to his wife saying: **Am in Market Harborough. Where ought I to be?** According to one biographer, Maisie Ward, a hundred different places have been substituted for 'Market Harborough' – most obviously, Crewe and Wolverhampton. But Market Harborough it was.

Chesterton's wife, Frances, on this occasion cabled the answer:

'Home' – because, as she explained, it was easier to get him home and start him off again.

Agatha CHRISTIE (1891–1976)

The crime writer was married to an archaeologist, Sir Max Mallowan, and so it seemed quite feasible when she was quoted as saying: '**An archaeologist is the best husband** any woman can have; the older she gets, the more interested he is in her.' However, she vehemently denied having said it and thought it a very silly remark for anyone to have made.

Noel COWARD (1899–1973)

If the many people who have tried to imitate Noel Coward's clipped delivery over the years were to be believed, the words he uttered most often in his career as actor and playwright were **Dear boy**. His friend Cole Lesley claimed:[45] 'He rarely used this endearment, though I expect it is now too late for me to be believed.' William Fairchild who wrote dialogue for the part of Noel Coward in the film *Star* was informed by the Master: 'Too many Dear Boys, dear boy.'

Coward's witticisms and anecdotes were numerous and, as is the way with such things, much mangled by way of repetition – and, rather less often, attributed to others. Bartlett, for example, attributes **Just know your lines and don't bump into the furniture** to Spencer Tracy. I have also seen it attributed to Alfred Lunt, but it was probably Coward's most famous piece of theatrical advice.

Coward noted in his diary for April 1955:[63] 'The only thing that really saddens me over my demise is that I shall not be here to read the nonsense that will be written about me . . . There will be lists of apocryphal jokes I never made and gleeful quotations of words I never said. *What* a pity I shan't be here to enjoy them!'

The archetypal Coward lines occur in his play *Private Lives* (1930): 'Very flat, Norfolk', 'Certain women should be struck regularly like gongs', 'Moonlight can be cruelly deceptive', 'You are looking very lovely in this damned moonlight, Amanda', and, most notably, **Strange how potent cheap music is.** Some texts of the play (as quoted by Bartlett and the ODQ, for example) employ 'extraordinary' instead of 'strange' but Gertrude Lawrence used the latter in the famous gramophone recording she made with Coward in 1930. The line may be popular for two reasons. Coward's voice can be heard quite clearly in it and there is an in-joke – he, as playwright or actor, was referring to one of his own compositions ('Someday I'll Find You').

Although Coward often recycled witticisms from his conversation in plays, there is one firm example of a borrowing. *Come Into the Garden, Maud* (1966) included the line: **She could eat an apple through a tennis racquet.** However, a diary note for 10 December 1954[63] stated: 'Lunched and dined with Darryl Zannuck who, David Niven wickedly said, is the only man who can eat an apple through a tennis racquet!'

A peculiar musical version of *Gone with the Wind* presented at the Drury Lane Theatre prompted two typical Coward observations. When a horse messed up the stage and juvenile actress Bonnie Langford burst upon an unsuspecting public, Coward said: **If they'd stuffed the child's head up the horse's arse, they would have solved two problems at once,** and **Two things should be cut: the second act and the child's throat.**

As an example of how Coward stories tend to get rearranged somewhat haphazardly, I might mention one that was told to me (by an actress) in 1979. Diana Wynyard was supposed to have told Coward: 'I saw your *Private Lives* the other night. Not very funny.' He: 'I saw your Lady Macbeth the other night – very funny!' In fact, this dates back to a 1920s dinner party when Lady Diana Cooper told Coward that she had not laughed once at his early comedy *The Young Idea.* 'How strange,' Coward replied, 'when I saw you acting in *The Glorious Adventure* [a film about the Great Fire of London], I laughed all the time!'[63]

Posthumously, on 30 April 1979, Coward had the somewhat dubious privilege of having a speech from his play *Cavalcade* (1931) smuggled unacknowledged into a party political broadcast by Margaret Thatcher on the eve of her General Election win. The much-quoted toast: 'That one day **this country of ours, which we love so much, will find dignity and greatness and peace again**,' became the Thatcher peroration: 'There is another Britain . . . which each one of us knows . . . It's message is quiet but insistent . . . And it says, above all, may this land of ours, which we love so much, find dignity and greatness and peace again.'

At the first night of *Cavalcade*, Coward made a celebrated curtain speech – this was at Drury Lane, too – which he ended by saying: 'In spite of the troublous times we are living in, **it is still pretty exciting to be English.**'

Howard DIETZ (1896–1983)

The librettist and writer went straight from Columbia University to Goldwyn Pictures and shortly after became director of publicity and advertising. When asked to design a trademark *c*.1916, he based it on the university's lion and added the Latin words meaning 'Art for

Art's Sake' underneath: **Ars Gratia Artis.** (There has been a suggestion that the more correct Latin would be: *Ars artis gratia* – though one wonders whether any arrangement of these words would really be appropriate for a Hollywood company.) The trademark and motto were carried over when Samuel Goldwyn retired to make way for the merger of Metropolitan with the interests of Louis B. Mayer in what has become known since as MGM or Metro-Goldwyn-Mayer.

Dietz also came up with a memorable slogan for Metro-Goldwyn-Mayer: **More Stars than in Heaven**.

W. C. FIELDS (1880–1946)

To start at the end: the last words of the great comedian were not: **On the whole I'd rather be in Philadelphia**, nor are these words written on his tombstone (all it bears is his name and dates). The joke was merely suggested during a craze for asking film stars what they thought would be suitable epitaphs for themselves. It is an extension, anyway, of an older expression: 'Sooner dead than in Philadelphia' and probably came from *Vanity Fair* magazine in the 1920s.

Fields's mockery of the Pennsylvania capital also occurred in: **I went to Philadelphia and found that it was closed.** This saying was later more often applied to New Zealand (by Anna Russell in the 'fifties and the Beatles in the 'sixties, for example).

The nearest to a memorable deathbed utterance Fields produced before his demise on Christmas Day 1946 was when the actor Thomas Mitchell, to his amazement, found the comedian thumbing through a Bible. When Mitchell asked him what he was doing, Fields answered: 'Looking for loopholes.' His actual last words were: 'Goddamn the whole friggin' world and everyone in it but you, Carlotta' (a reference to his mistress).

Never give a sucker an even break has been attributed to various people but has become largely associated with Fields. He is believed to have ad-libbed it in the musical *Poppy* (1923) and certainly spoke it in the film version (1936). Barlett attributes the saying to Edward Francis Albee (1857–1930).

Any man who hates dogs and babies can't be all bad has also come to be associated with Fields. In fact, it was said by Leo Rosten (*b*.1908) *of* Fields at a Masquers' Club dinner on 16 February 1939. Usually 'children' is substituted for 'babies'.

F. Scott FITZGERALD (1896–1940)

Tom Burnam[10] has neatly established the facts about a famous exchange said to have occurred between Scott Fitzgerald and Ernest Hemingway: **The very rich are different from you and me. Yes, they have more money.**

The facts are these: in his short story 'The Rich Boy' (1926), Fitzgerald wrote: 'Let me tell you about the very rich. They are different from you and me.' Ten years later in *his* short story 'The Snows of Kilimanjaro', Hemingway had the narrator remember 'poor Scott Fitzgerald', his awe of the rich, and that 'someone' had said, 'Yes, they have more money.'

When Fitzgerald read this story he protested to Hemingway who dropped Fitzgerald's name from further printings of the story. In any case, the put-down was not original to Hemingway. It had been made by a woman in response to Hemingway's own observations on the rich. In 1936, Hemingway said at a lunch with the critic Mary Colum: 'I am getting to know the rich.' She replied: 'The only difference between the rich and other people is that the rich have more money.'

Henry FORD (1863–1947)

In the course of a libel action against the *Chicago Tribune* which came to court in the spring of 1919 – an editorial had described him as an 'anarchist' and an 'ignorant idealist' – the motor magnate found himself as much on trial as the defendant. Cross-examined for no less than eight days, Ford was continually tripped up by his ignorance. He could not say when the United States came into being. He suggested 1812 before 1776. He was asked about a statement reported by Charles N. Wheeler in an interview with Ford of 25 May 1916: 'History is more or less bunk. It's tradition.' Ford explained: 'I did not say it was bunk. It was bunk to me . . . but I did not need it very bad.' This is popularly remembered as **History is bunk**.

The *Tribune* was found guilty of libel – and fined six cents.

Afterwards, Ford declared: 'You know, I'm going to . . . give the people an idea of real history. I'm going to start a museum. We are going to show just what actually happened in years gone by.' And so indeed he did.

A rather more felicitous saying of Ford's was: **People can have [the Model T in] any colour – so long as it's black.** However, the company had to bow to the inevitable in 1925 and offer a choice of colours.[36]

Mervyn GRIFFITH-JONES (1909–79)

When Penguin Books Ltd were tried at the Old Bailey in October 1960 for publishing an unexpurgated edition of D. H. Lawrence's novel *Lady Chatterley's Lover*, the jury and the public at large were amused by the social attitudes revealed in the questioning of Mr Griffith-Jones, the senior prosecuting counsel. In his opening address to the jury on the first day, he said:

> You may think that one of the ways in which you can test this book, and test it from the most liberal outlook, is to ask yourselves the question, when you have read it through, would you approve of your young sons, young daughters – because girls can read as well as boys – reading this book. Is it a book that you would have lying around in your own house? **Is it a book that you would even wish your wife or your servants to read?**

The jury was visibly amused at this quaint and patronising approach. Gerald Gardiner, in his closing speech for the defence, commented:

> I cannot help thinking that this was, consciously or unconsciously, an echo from an observation which had fallen from the Bench in an earlier case: 'It would never do to let members of the working class read this.' I do not want to upset the Prosecution by suggesting that there are a certain number of people nowadays who as a matter of fact don't *have* servants. But of course that whole attitude is one which Penguin Books was formed to fight against . . .

The publishers were found not guilty of having published an obscene book and from the trial may be dated the permissive revolution in British sexual habits.

John LENNON (1940–80)

In March 1966, John Lennon of the Beatles gave an interview to Maureen Cleave of the London *Evening Standard* in which he said: 'Christianity will go. It will vanish and shrink. I needn't argue about that. I'm right and I'll be proved right. **We're more popular than Jesus now**. I don't know which will go first – Rock and Roll or Christianity.'

The remark lay dormant for several months but when the Beatles paid a visit to the USA, it was reprinted and caused an outcry. The Beatles were burned in effigy and their records banned by radio stations in Bible-belt states.

Lennon subsequently withdrew the remark and tried to explain how it had arisen:

If [I] had said television is more popular than Jesus, I might have got away with it. As I just happened to be talking to a friend, I used the word 'Beatles' as a remoter thing – not what I think, but Beatles as those other Beatles like other people see us. And I said that they were having more influence on kids and things than anything else including Jesus. But I said it in that way. I'm not saying that we're better or greater or comparing us with Christ as a person, or God – as a thing, or whatever it is, you know. I just said what I said – and I was wrong. (Press conference, Chicago, 11 August 1966.)

Not only did Lennon and the Beatles get misunderstood, they also attracted some of the most overblown critical praise of the century. In the *Sunday Times* for 29 December 1963, ballet critic Richard Buckle called Lennon and McCartney: 'The greatest composers since Beethoven.' When the 'Sgt. Pepper' album was released in 1967, Langdon Winner said: 'The closest western civilisation has come to unity since the Congress of Vienna in 1815 was the week the "Sgt. Pepper" album was released . . . for a brief while the irreparably fragmented consciousness of the West was unified, at least in the minds of the young.'

William Mann, music critic of *The Times* compared the Beatles to Schubert and noted their 'pandiatonic clusters' and 'flat sub-mediant key switches'. When the so-called 'White Album' was released in 1968, Tony Palmer jumped on the bandwagon in the *Observer* and called them 'the greatest songwriters since Schubert'.

LIBERACE (*b*.1919)

The flamboyant American pianist, Liberace, discussed reviews of his shows in an autobiography (1973):[46]

I think the people around me are more apt to become elated about good reviews (or depressed by bad ones) than I am. If they're good I just tell them, 'Don't let my success go to your head.' When the reviews are bad I tell my staff that they can join me as **I cry all the way to the bank**.

Liberace gave currency to this saying long before 1973, however.'

Alice Roosevelt LONGWORTH (1884–1980)

The words 'If you haven't anything nice to say about anyone, come and sit by me' were embroidered on a cushion at the Washington DC home of Alice Roosevelt Longworth, daughter of President Theodore

Roosevelt. She spent a lifetime making caustic remarks about American political figures. 'Just a slob' was how she described President Harding; 'a poor boob', Eisenhower. 'One-third sap, two-thirds Eleanor' was Alice's comment on her cousin Franklin. The two barbs for which she was most famous, however, she admitted picking up from others.

Calvin Coolidge 'looked as if he had been **weaned on a pickle**. Mrs L. told William Safire: 'I heard that in my dentist's office. The last patient had said it to him. I didn't originate it – but didn't it describe him exactly?'

A description that helped destroy Thomas E. Dewey when he stood against Truman came from one Grace Hodgson Flandrau: 'Dewey looks like **the bridegroom on the wedding cake**.' Mrs L. admitted: 'I thought it frightfully funny and quoted it to everyone. Then it began to be attributed to me.' (It is often remembered as 'The Man on the Wedding Cake'.)

Groucho MARX (1895–1977)

The lines that were written for him in the movies and the things that he said himself coalesce. Never mind where they originated – they all ended up coming out of Groucho's mouth.

Here, however, is his most famous utterance. But is there any firm basis for it? His brother Zeppo recalled:

> The Friars Club in this country is a theatrical club and most performers belong to it, but Groucho never spent much time there, he didn't have much use for it. So he wrote them a letter, and he said: 'Dear Friars, please accept this letter of resignation as I don't have any use for the club and, furthermore, **any club that would have me as a member, I don't want to belong to**.'

Hector Ace recalled it this way: 'He had some misgivings about the quality of the members, doubts verified a few years later when an infamous card-cheating scandal erupted there. "Gentlemen, please accept my resignation. I don't care to belong to any social organisation that will accept me as a member." '

His friend, Arthur Sheekman, put it this way in his introduction to *The Groucho Letters* (1967): 'Please accept my resignation. I don't care to belong to any club that will have me as a member.'

Bartlett has: 'I wouldn't want to belong to any club that would accept me as a member.'

If nothing else, these versions show how many different ways you can tell a joke. But wouldn't it be good to see the original letter?

Vivian NICHOLSON (*b*.1936)

Viv Nicholson and her husband Keith, a trainee miner, were bringing up three children on a weekly wage of £7 in Castleford, Yorkshire. Then in September 1961 they won £152,000 on Littlewoods football pools. Arriving by train to collect their prize, as Viv recalled in her autobiography,[56] they were confronted by reporters. One asked: 'What are you going to do when you get all this money?' Viv said: **I'm going to spend, spend, spend**, that's what I'm going to do.' She says it was just an off the cuff remark, but it made newspaper headlines and was later used as the title of her book and of a TV play.

The win was the prelude to tragedy: Keith died in a car crash and Viv worked her way through a succession of husbands until the money had all gone.

John OSBORNE (*b*.1929)

As is the way, the writer who started a theatrical revolution with his play *Look Back in Anger* in 1956 and who was a principal 'angry young man' mellowed in time and became a benign old English gentleman. In August 1961, however, he was still breathing fire and let fly in a letter to the left-wing periodical *Tribune* from an address in Valbonne, France:

> This is a letter of hate. It is for you my countrymen – I mean those men of my country who have defiled it. The men with manic fingers leading the sightless, feeble, betrayed body of my country to its death . . . There is murder in my brain, and I carry a knife in my heart for every one of you. Macmillan, and you, Gaitskell, you particularly . . . I only hope [my hate] will keep me going. I think it will. I think it may sustain me in the last few months. Till then, **Damn you, England**. You're rotting now, and quite soon you'll disappear. My hate will outrun you yet if only for a few seconds. I wish it could be eternal.

Rebecca WEST (1892–1983)

Although I have seen it attributed to Alexander Woollcott, it was Rebecca West who characterised the novelist Michael Arlen with the phrase: **Every other inch a gentleman.** Despite his polished manners Arlen was skewered thereafter by this slur. The format was used by actress Beatrice Lillie (Lady Peel) for the title of her 1973 autobiography: *Every Other Inch a Lady*.

1914–1918

The First World War

IT was known at first as 'The European War', following the assassination of Archduke Franz Ferdinand. The heir to the Austrian throne was shot by a Serbian nationalist at Sarajevo on 28 June 1914. His Britannic Majesty's Consul sent a cable to London stating: 'Heir apparent and his consort assassinated this morning by means of an explosive nature.' This incident led Austria–Hungary to declare war on Serbia and by the end of August most of the rest of Europe had joined in.

Then, quite rapidly, it became known as 'The Great War'. By 10 September 1918, Lieut-Colonel C. A. Court Repington was describing it in his diary as the 'First World War': 'I saw Major Johnstone, the Harvard Professor who is here to lay the bases of an American History. We discussed the right name of the war. I said that we called it now *The* War, but that this could not last. The Napoleonic War was *The Great War*. To call it *The German War* was too much flattery for the Boche. I suggested *The World War* as a shade better title, and finally we mutually agreed to call it the **First World War** in order to prevent the millennium folk from forgetting that the history of the world was the history of war.' Repington's book entitled *The First World War 1914–18* was published in 1920,[75] ominously suggesting that the Great War had been merely the 'first' of what might turn into a series.

Just before Great Britain entered the fray, Sir Edward Grey (1862–1933), the Foreign Secretary, tolled the knell for the era that was about to pass. He later described what took place:[29]

A friend came to see me on one of the evenings of the last week – he thinks it was on Monday August 3. We were standing at a window of my room in the Foreign Office. It was getting dusk, and the lamps were being lit in the space below on which we were looking. My friend recalls that I remarked on this with the words: **The lamps are going out all over Europe; we shall not see them lit again in our lifetime**.

Field Marshal Lord Kitchener was appointed Secretary of State for War on 6 August 1914, two days after the outbreak. He set to work immediately, intent on raising the 'New Armies' required to supplement the small standing army of the day which he rightly saw would not be adequate for a major conflict.

In fact, work on advertising for recruits had started the year before and with some success. Towards the end of July 1914, Eric Field of the Caxton Advertising Agency received a call from a Colonel Strachey who 'swore me to secrecy, told me that war was imminent and that the moment it broke out we should have to start at once.' That night Field wrote an advertisement headed **Your King and Country need you** with the royal coat of arms as its only illustration. The day after war was declared – 5 August – this appeared prominently in the *Daily Mail* and other papers.

The appeal took various forms but Kitchener preferred this first version and insisted on finishing every advertisement with 'God Save the King'. The famous drawing by the humorous artist Alfred Leete was added when the advertisement appeared on the cover of *London Opinion* (5 September) and was taken up by the Parliamentary Recruiting Committee for poster use (issued 14 September). Kitchener was shown with staring eyes and pointing finger and the slogan was altered to: **Your Country Needs You!** (Margot Asquith later commented: 'If Kitchener was not a great man, he was, at least, a great poster.')

The idea was widely imitated abroad. In the USA, James Montgomery Flagg's poster of a pointing Uncle Sam bore the legend 'I want *you* for the US Army'. 'Your country needs you' became a catchphrase used in telling a man he had been selected for a dangerous or disgusting task. 'For King and Country' was the official reply to the question: 'What are we fighting for?' (According to Partridge,[61] the unofficial reply was: 'For King and Cunt.')

The linking of 'king' and 'country' was traditional. Bacon (1625) wrote: 'Be so true to thyselfe, as thou be not false to others; specially to thy King, and Country.' In 1913 J. M. Barrie included in his play *Quality Street*: 'If . . . death or glory was the call, you would take the shilling, ma'am . . . For King and Country.' The phrase echoed on after the First World War. 'For King and Country' was quoted on the tomb of the Unknown Warrior in Westminster Abbey, Rothermere newspapers carried it on their mastheads for a while after the 1926 General Strike, it featured in the motion for the Oxford Union debate of 1933, and a 1964 film about a First World War deserter was called *King and Country*.

Initially, it was not thought that the war would last very long, It would be 'Over by Christmas', hence the anti-German slogan **Berlin by Christmas**. The fact that this promise was not fulfilled in 1914 did not prevent Henry Ford from saying, as he tried to stop the war a year later: 'We're going to try to get the boys out of the trenches before Christmas. I've chartered a ship, and some of us are going to Europe.' He was not referring to American boys because the United States had not joined the war at that stage. The *New York Tribune* announced: 'GREAT WAR ENDS CHRISTMAS DAY. FORD TO STOP IT.'

After the war, in the period 1919–24, there was a German nationalist cry, 'Auf nach Berlin' ('On to Berlin').

There then took place what Churchill called 'upon the whole the greatest battle ever fought in the world'. On 5 September, General Joseph Jacques Césaire Joffre (1852–1931), the French Commander-in-Chief, issued his order for the start of the first battle of the Marne. In his memoirs,[44] Joffre recalled that his staff was installed in an ancient convent of the Order of Cordeliers, 'and my own office was in what had formerly been a monk's cell. It was from here that I directed the battle of the Marne and it was in this room that, at half-past seven the next morning, I signed the following order addressed to the troops':

> We are about to engage in a battle on which the fate of our country depends and it is important to remind all ranks that the moment has passed for looking to the rear; all our efforts must be directed to attacking and driving back the enemy. **Troops that can advance no farther must**, at any price, **hold on to the ground they have conquered and die on the spot rather than give way**. Under the circumstances which face us, no act of weakness can be tolerated.

The French and British managed to push the Germans back along the 200-mile front of the Marne river, preventing the enemy from reaching Paris as it had threatened to do.

A rumour spread during September 1914 that a million Russian troops had landed at Aberdeen and passed through England on their way to the Western Front. As if to give more credence to the rumour, it was stated that they were **Russians with snow on their boots**. Arthur Ponsonby[65] said that 'Nothing illustrates better the credulity of the public mind in wartime and what favourable soil it becomes for the cultivation of falsehood.'

Several suggestions have been made as to how this false information caught hold: that the Secret Service had intercepted a telegram to the effect that '100,000 Russians are on their way from Aberdeen to London' (without realising that this referred to a consignment of Russian eggs); that a tall, bearded fellow had declared in a train that he came from 'Ross-shire', and so on.

In fact, the British Ambassador to Russia *had* requested the despatch of a complete army corps but the request was never acceded to. Ponsonby commented: 'As the rumour had undoubted military value, the authorities took no steps to deny it . . . [but] an official War Office denial of the rumour was noted by the *Daily News* on September 16, 1914.'

Later in the war, in a 1917 speech to the US Senate, Senator Hiram Johnson (1866–1945) commented: **The first casualty when war comes is truth.**

In Britain, an advertising man called H. E. Morgan promoted the slogan **Business as usual** – as a shopkeeper might do after a fire. This had quite a vogue until it was proved to be manifestly untrue. Morgan was a consultant to H. Gordon Selfridge, the London store owner, who consequently also became associated with the phrase. On 26 August 1914, Selfridge said: ' "Business as usual" must be the order of the day.' In a speech at the Lord Mayor's Banquet in the Guildhall on 9 November, Winston Churchill, First Lord of the Admiralty, said:

The British people have taken for themselves this motto – 'Business carried on as usual during alterations on the map of Europe' [*Laughter and cheers*]. They expect the navy, on which they have lavished so much care and expense, to make that good, and that is what, upon the whole, we are actually achieving at the present time.

The Government's critics looked askance at this attitude.

The greatest canard of the First World War was that Kaiser Wilhelm II had described the 1914 British Expeditionary Force as 'a contemptibly little army' (referring to its size rather than its quality). The British press was then said to have mistranslated this so that it made him appear to have called the BEF a **contemptible little army**. Rank and file thereafter styled themselves 'The Old Contemptibles'.

The truth, as again revealed by Arthur Ponsonby, is that the whole episode was a propaganda ploy masterminded by the British. The BEF Routine Orders for 24 September 1914 contained what was claimed to be a copy of Orders issued by the German Emperor on 19 August:

> It is my Royal and Imperial command that you concentrate your energies for the immediate present upon one single purpose, and that is that you address all your skill and all the valour of my soldiers to exterminate first, the treacherous English [and] walk over General French's contemptible little army . . .

The Kaiser's alleged words became widely known but an investigation during 1925 in the German archives failed to produce any evidence of the order ever having been issued. The ex-Kaiser himself said: 'On the contrary, I continually emphasised the high value of the British Army, and often, indeed, in peace-time gave warning against underestimating it.' It is now accepted that the phrase was devised at the War office by Sir Frederick Maurice.

'Arf a mo, Kaiser! became a catchphrase after a recruiting poster had shown a British 'Tommy' lighting his pipe prior to going into action. (The phrase surfaced again in the Second World War as 'Arf a mo, 'itler!')

The war's distinctive contribution to modes of battle was the trench. The expression **Over the top** was used for charging over the parapet and out of the trenches on the attack. In a curious transition, this phrase was later adopted by show business people when describing a performance that goes beyond the bounds of restraint. In 1982, a controversial British television series used the initials *OTT*.

In France, Parliament had suspended its sittings at the outbreak of hostilities and the conduct of the war had been entrusted to the Government and to Joffre and the General Staff. By 1915, however, opinion was changing. It may have been about this time that Georges Clemenceau (1841–1929), who became French Prime Minister again in 1917, uttered his most famous witticism: **War is too serious a business to be left to the generals** ('La guerre, c'est une chose trop grave pour la confier à des militaires'). This notion has also been attributed to Talleyrand (Briand quoted his version to Lloyd George during this war) and, indeed, Clemenceau may have said it himself much earlier (*Bartlett*, 1968, cites an 1886 source). Whatever the case, Clemenceau launched one of those phrase-formats which is capable of many variations. De Gaulle followed with 'Politics is too important to be left to the politicians.' Tony Benn, the British Labour Minister of Technology, seeking greater control over the media in 1968, came up with: 'Broadcasting is really too important to be left to the broadcasters and somehow we must find some new way of using radio and television to allow us to talk to each other.' Akin to the format is Shaw's: 'Youth is a wonderful thing; what a crime to waste it on children.'

Edith Cavell (1865–1915) was a British Red Cross nurse who, without question, broke the rules of war by using her job to help Allied prisoners escape from German-occupied territory. She was condemned by a Germany court-martial for 'conducting soldiers to the enemy' and shot. Her message to the world: 'This I would say, standing as I do in view of God and Eternity: I realise that **patriotism is not enough; I must have no hatred and bitterness towards anyone**.' These were not in the form of 'last words' spoken before the firing squad but were said the previous day to an English chaplain, the Revd Stirling Gahan, who visited her in prison.

Bernard Shaw complained in his Preface to *Saint Joan* (1923): 'Her countrymen, seeing in [her death] a good opportunity for lecturing the enemy on his intolerance, put up a statue to her, but took particular care not to inscribe on the pedestal [these words], for which omission, and the lie it implies, they will need Edith's intercession when they are themselves brought to judgement.' This was true at the time Shaw wrote it but subsequently the words were carved beneath the statue that stands opposite the National Portrait Gallery in London. (It was at the unveiling of this not very great likeness that the artist James Pryde exclaimed: 'My God, they've shot the wrong person!')

Daddy, what did *you* do in the Great War? – accompanied by the picture of an understandably appalled father puzzling over what to reply to the daughter on his knee – was a recruiting slogan that became a catchphrase in the form 'What did you do in the Great War, Daddy?' Partridge[62] recalled that it gave rise to such responses as: 'Shut up, you little bastard. Get the Bluebell and go and clean my medals.'

Another enduring phrase from the very early stages of the First World War was: **Are we downhearted? – No!** – though Partridge suggests it had earlier political origins. Indeed, Joseph Chamberlain (1838–1914) said in a 1906 speech: 'We are not downhearted. The only trouble is, we cannot understand what is happening to our neighbours.' The day after he was defeated as a candidate in the Stepney Borough Council election of 1909, Clement Attlee, the future Prime Minister, was greeted by a colleague with the cry: 'Are we downhearted?' Attlee, being the person he was, responded: 'Of course we are.'

On 18 August 1914 the *Daily Mail* reported: 'For two days the finest troops England has ever sent across the sea have been marching through the narrow streets of old Boulogne in solid columns of khaki, thousands upon thousands of them, waving as they say that new slogan of Englishmen: "Are we downhearted? . . . Nooooo!" "Shall we win? . . . Yessss!" ' Lawrence Wright incorporated the phrase in a song.

Churchill was still using the phrase at the end of the Second World War. Addressing crowds on V-E Day 1945, he asked: 'Did anyone want to give in?' The crowd shouted: 'No.' Then he asked 'Were we downhearted?' The crowd again shouted 'No!'

The phrase **They shall not pass** ('Ils ne passeront pas') was popularly supposed to have been coined by Marshal Henri Philippe Pétain (1856–1951), who defended Verdun with great tenacity in 1916. He is said to have uttered it on 26 February that year. However, the first official record of the expression appears in the Order of the Day for 23 June 1916 from General Robert Nivelle (1856–1924) to his troops at the height of battle. His words were: 'Vous ne les laisserez pas passer' ('You will not let them pass'). Alternatively, Nivelle is supposed to have said these words to General de Castelnau on 23 January 1916. To add further to the mystery, the inscription on the Verdun medal was 'On ne passe pas.'[5] I suspect that the slogan was coined by Nivelle and was used a number of times by him but came to be associated more with Pétain, the more famous 'Hero of Verdun'.

Even so, the phrase did not stop with Pétain. Later, as 'No pasarán', it was used on the Republican side during the Spanish Civil War.

Also during Verdun, on 9 April, Pétain released an order of the day which concluded: 'Without a doubt the Germans will attack again. Let every one of us work and watch to obtain the same success as yesterday. Courage! We shall have them yet!'

'We shall have them' (**On les aura!**) was by then already a popular slogan and one that was to be made much use of later in a recruiting poster by Abel Faivre.

The Battle of Jutland on 31 May/1 June 1916 was not only the first naval engagement of the twentieth century but also the only major sea battle of the First World War. It was, on the face of it, an indecisive affair. The British Grand Fleet under its Commander-in-Chief, Sir John Jellicoe, failed to secure an outright victory. Admiral Sir David Beatty (1871–1936), commanding a battle cruiser squadron, saw one ship after another sunk by the Germans. At 4.26 on the afternoon of 31 May, the *Queen Mary* was sunk with the loss of 1,266 officers and men. This was what led Beatty to comment calmly to his Flag Captain, Ernle Chatfield: **There seems to be something wrong with our bloody ships today.** Sometimes the words 'and with our system' have been added to the remark, as also 'Turn two points to port' (i.e. nearer the enemy), but Chatfield denied that anything more was said.[59] Ultimately, the battle marked the end of any German claim to naval control of the North Sea and, in that light, was a British victory, but Jutland was a disappointment at the time and has been chewed over ever since as a controversial episode in British naval history.

Nine days after the American Expeditionary Force landed in France, Colonel Charles E. Stanton (1859–1933), a member of General Pershing's staff, stood at the tomb of Lafayette in the Picpus cemetery, Paris, and declared: 'Here and now, in the presence of the illustrious dead, we pledge our hearts and our honour in carrying this war to a successful issue. **Lafayette, we are here**.' This graceful tribute to the Marquis de Lafayette who enlisted with the American revolutionary armies in 1777 and forged a strong emotional link between the United States and France was delivered by Stanton on 4 July 1917 and repeated on 14 July. As *Bartlett*[5] points out, the remark has also been attributed to Pershing though he disclaimed having said 'anything so splendid'. There is evidence, however, that he may have pronounced the phrase before Stanton and that Stanton merely picked it up.

On 21 March 1918, the Germans launched their last great offensive.

Sir Douglas Haig (1861–1928), the British Commander-in-Chief on the Western Front, issued an order for his troops to stand firm on 12 April:

> Every position must be held to the last man: there must be no retirement. With our **backs to the wall**, and believing in the justice of our cause, each one of us must fight on to the end. The safety of our Homes and the Freedom of mankind alike depend on the conduct of each one of us at this critical moment.

A. J. P. Taylor[91] commented: 'In England this sentence was ranked with Nelson's last message. At the front, the prospect of staff officers fighting with their backs to the walls of their luxurious chateaux had less effect.'

As the war moved to its end, valiant cries proliferated. American Marine Sergeant Daniel Daly is remembered for having shouted during the Battle of Belleau Wood in June 1918: **Come on, you sons of bitches! Do you want to live forever!**

Marshal Ferdinand Foch (1851–1929) remarked to General Joffre during the second battle of the Marne (July/August 1918): 'Mon centre cède, ma droite recule, **situation excellente. J'attaque!**' ('My centre gives way, my right retreats; situation excellent. I shall attack.')

The Armistice was signed at 5 am on 11 November 1918 and came into force at 11 am – **At the eleventh hour on the eleventh day of the eleventh month.** This curious coincidence of time and date gained further resonance from the use of the phrase 'at the eleventh hour' from the parable of the labourers (of whom the last 'were hired at the eleventh hour' – St Matthew 20:9).

In the afternoon, Lloyd George announced the terms of the Armistice to the House of Commons and concluded: 'I hope we may say that thus, this fateful morning, came to an end all wars.' H. G. Wells had popularised the notion of **the war to end wars** in a book he had brought out in 1914: *The War That Will End War*. This, however, was not an original cry: it had been raised in other wars. Later, Wells commented ruefully: 'I launched the phrase "the war to end war" and that was not the least of my crimes.'

On the evening of 11 November, Clemenceau said to General Mordacq: **'We have won the war: now we have to win the peace,** and it may be more difficult.'

On 24 November, Lloyd George gave a speech at Wolverhampton

in which he asked: 'What is our task? To make Britain a fit country for heroes to live in.' This became well known as **a land fit for heroes** or, occasionally, 'A country fit for heroes'. By 1921, with wages falling in all industries, the sentiment was frequently recalled and mocked.

Calls for retribution soon followed. Sir Eric Geddes (1875–1937), a Conservative politician who had lately been First Lord of the Admiralty, said of Germany in an electioneering speech at the Guildhall, Cambridge, on 9 December:

> I have personally no doubt we will get everything out of her that you can squeeze out of a lemon and a bit more . . . I will squeeze her until you can hear the pips squeak . . . I would strip Germany as she has stripped Belgium.

The next night at the Beaconsfield Club he rearranged the words:

> The Germans, if this Government is returned, are going to pay every penny; **they are going to be squeezed as a lemon is squeezed – until the pips squeak**. My only doubt is not whether we can squeeze hard enough, but whether there is enough juice.

During the Versailles Peace Conference and for some time afterwards, Northcliffe newspapers and others kept up the cry **Hang the Kaiser!** Candidates at the 1918 General Election were said to have lost votes if they had not subscribed to this policy. The Allies committed themselves to try the ex-Kaiser in the Treaty of Versailles (28 June 1919) but the Government of the Netherlands refused to hand him over for trial in January 1920. Arthur Ponsonby[65] argued that casting the Kaiser as the villain of the piece had been a put-up job anyway. He concluded:

> When, as months and years passed, it was discovered that no responsible person really believed, or had ever believed, in [the Kaiser's] personal guilt, that the cry, 'Hang the Kaiser,' was a piece of deliberate bluff, and that when it was over and millions of innocent people had been killed, he, the criminal, the monster, the plotter and initiator of the whole catastrophe, was allowed to live comfortably and peacefully in Holland, the disillusionment to simple, uninformed people was far greater than was ever realised. It was the exposure of this crude falsehood that first led many humble individuals to inquire whether, in other connections, they had not also been duped.

The ex-Kaiser died in 1941.

Rudyard Kipling was invited by the Imperial War Graves Commission to devise memorial texts for the dead. He admitted to 'naked cribs of the Greek anthology'. He also reworked biblical lines. The inscription carved over lists of the dead in every war cemetery – **Their Name Liveth for Evermore** – echoed Ecclesiasticus 44:14: 'Their bodies were buried in peace, And their name liveth to all generations.'

Over the graves of the unknown dead was put the simple description:

A Soldier of the Great War
Known unto God

SHAW

As GBS Once Said...

ODDLY, for someone whose writings do not lend themselves to brief quotation, George Bernard Shaw (1856–1950) is frequently given as the source of sayings – including many he never said. Clearly, his reputation as one who held forth in an entertaining way on any number of subjects has brought this about. But what did he actually say?

Shaw's play *Pygmalion* is about the conversion of an illiterate, ill-spoken flower-girl by a professor of phonetics and uses the same theme as Smollett's novel *Peregrine Pickle*. In that book, Pickle trains the girl and then introduces her into exclusive and elegant circles:

But one evening, being at cards with a certain lady whom she detected in the very act of unfair conveyance, she taxed her roundly with the fraud, and brought upon herself such a torrent of sarcastic reproof as overbore all her maxims of caution, and burst open the floodgates of her own natural repartee, twanged off with the appellation of b***** and w*****, which she repeated with great vehemence, to the terror of her antagonist and the astonishment of all present: Nay, to such an unguarded pitch was she provoked, that starting up, she snapt her fingers, in testimony of disdain, and, as she quitted the room, applied her hand to that part which was the last of her that disappeared, inviting the company to kiss it, by one of its coarsest denominations.

Here, obviously, is the origin of the celebrated tea-party scene in Act III of *Pygmalion* in which Eliza Doolittle, having successfully taken part in polite conversation, is asked by a young man, on leaving, if she is walking across the Park. She replies: 'Walk? **Not bloody likely!** I am going in a taxi.'

The audience for the first performance in London on Saturday 11 April 1914 had been prepared by that morning's edition of the *Daily Sketch*:

> *PYGMALION* MAY CAUSE SENSATION!! Mr Shaw introduces a certain forbidden word. WILL MRS PATRICK CAMPBELL SPEAK IT? Has the censor stepped in or will the word spread? If he does not forbid it then anything might happen!! It is a word which the *Daily Sketch* cannot possibly print and tonight it is to be uttered on the stage. There can be little doubt of the word actually used by the author. And this evening the most respectable audience in London is to hear this appalling word fall with bombshell suddenness from Mrs Pat's lips. This audience has been brought up on Shakespeare but they are not yet accustomed to Shaw . . . It will come as a shock to the Upper Circle if they hear Mrs Pat uttering a word that has never been heard except from Covent Garden porters and never before read except in the poetry of Mr John Masefield.
>
> But if the censor does pass the word and if the audience at His Majesty's does approve it, then it will become the catchword of the season. And girls from Golders Green, young ladies from Lewisham, maidens from Maidstone will all pick up this revolting epithet like the suburban girl in the play. She shocks and distresses her mother. So will they.

When the phrase was finally uttered, the audience gasped – 'their intake of breath making a sound that could have been mistaken for a protracted hiss', according to Shaw's biographer, Hesketh Pearson. 'This never happened again because all future audiences knew what was coming and roared with laughter.' Then there was laughter which continued for a minute and a quarter according to the stage manager's stopwatch.

Although the play was well received by the critics, the press rumbled on about the language it used. *The Times* (13 April 1914), in its review of the play, said:

O, greatly daring Mr Shaw! You will be able to boast you are the first modern dramatist to use this word on the stage! But really, was it worth while? There is a whole range of forbidden words in the English language; a little more of your usage and we suppose that they will be heard, too. And then goodbye to the delights of really intimate conversation.

The *Daily Mirror* sought the views of a number of bishops. Sydney Grundy, theatre critic of the *Daily Mail*, said there was no harm in Shaw's 'incarnadine adverb' when informed by genius but 'on his pen it is poison'.

The Theatrical Managers' Association wrote to Sir Herbert Beerbohm Tree, who was presenting the play as well as playing Professor Higgins, saying that a member had complained of the phrase and that 'with a view to retaining the respect of the public for the theatre' they wanted him to omit the words. He declined.

A review opened at the Alhambra shortly afterwards with the title *Not ****** Likely*. In time the euphemistic alternative 'Not Pygmalion likely!' emerged.

Shaw concluded: 'By making a fashionable actress use bad language in a fashionable theatre, I became overnight more famous than the Pope, the King, the Kaiser and the Archbishop of Canterbury.'

Pygmalion was filmed with Leslie Howard and Marie Lohr in 1938, and thus the word 'bloody' was heard for the first time in the cinema *before* Clark Gable's celebrated 'damn' in *Gone with the Wind* (1939). By the time *My Fair Lady* – the musical version of *Pygmalion* – was filmed in 1964, the shock effect of 'bloody' was so mild that Eliza was given the line 'Come on, Dover, move your ruddy arse!' in the Ascot racing sequence – which, I suppose, takes us right back to *Peregrine Pickle* . . .

There is some truth in the story that Shaw was once approached by a woman who thought herself to be a fine physical specimen and suggested that they combine to make a baby, saying: 'You have the greatest brain in the world and I have the most beautiful body; so we ought to produce the most perfect child.' His reply? **What if the child inherits my beauty and your brains?**

Alas, this was not said to Isadora Duncan or any of the other women who have been woven into the tale. Hesketh Pearson said the request came from 'a woman in Zurich', though no trace of a letter containing it has ever been found.

Blanche Patch, Shaw's secretary, gave the definitive version of another story. **One look at you, Mr Shaw, and I know there's famine in the land**, the film director, Alfred Hitchcock, commented. **One look at you, Mr Hitchcock**, replied Shaw, **and I know who made it.** (Lord Northcliffe is one of the other people inserted into this story.)

The saying that 'dancing' or 'the waltz' (and later, incredibly, 'the twist') is **a perpendicular expression of a horizontal desire** is sometimes attributed to Shaw. Until we turn up the proof, it is perhaps safest to say it came from Anon. On the other hand, I'll give my vote to Shaw for **England and America are two countries separated by the same language** rather than to Oscar Wilde or anyone else.

The sweeping statement **All Americans are deaf, dumb and blind** *is* from Shaw but in a different context from that sometimes suggested. He did not say it when Helen Keller – who was deaf, dumb and blind – was announced as a visitor. According to Hesketh Pearson, he paid her the compliment: 'I wish all Americans were as blind as you.'[10]

A saying that is quite often wrongly ascribed to John or Robert Kennedy because they both used it in numerous political speeches is, in fact, also from Shaw. Spoken by the Serpent in *Back to Methuselah* in an attempt to seduce Eve, it goes: **You see things; and you say 'Why?' But I dream things that never were; and I say 'Why not?'** President Kennedy quoted it correctly in his address to the Irish Parliament in Dublin in June 1963. Robert's version tended to be: 'Some men see things as they are and say "Why?" I dream things that never were and say, "Why not?" ' In this form it was attributed to RFK (Shaw going unmentioned) in the address delivered by Edward Kennedy at RFK's funeral service in 1968.

So frequently was this saying invoked by Robert Kennedy as a peroration that, on the campaign trail, the words 'As George Bernard Shaw once said . . .' became a signal for reporters to dash for the press bus. Once he forgot to conclude with the Shaw quote, according to Arthur M. Schlesinger,[83] and several reporters missed the bus. On another occasion it came on to rain and Kennedy told the crowd: 'It's silly for you to be standing in the rain listening to a politician . . . As George Bernard Shaw once said, "Run for the buses." '

Neil Armstrong: 'One small step . . .'

King Edward VIII's abdication speech available on record.

we shall stick it out
to the end but we
are getting weaker of
course and the end
cannot be far.
It seems a pity but
I do not think I can
write more —
R Scott

Last Entry.

For Gods Sake look
after our people

The last page, *left*, of Captain R. F. Scott's diary.

Noel Coward, *top*, (with Gertrude Lawrence) in *Private Lives*: 'Strange how potent cheap music is . . .'

Admiral Beatty: (*far right*): 'Something wrong with our bloody ships . . .'

Groucho Marx: 'Any club that would have me as a member, I don't want to belong to.'

W. C. Fields, *left*: 'Any man who hates dogs and babies can't be all bad.'

John Osborne, *above*: 'Angry young man'

George Bernard Shaw, *left*: 'I dream things that never were; and I say "Why not?" '

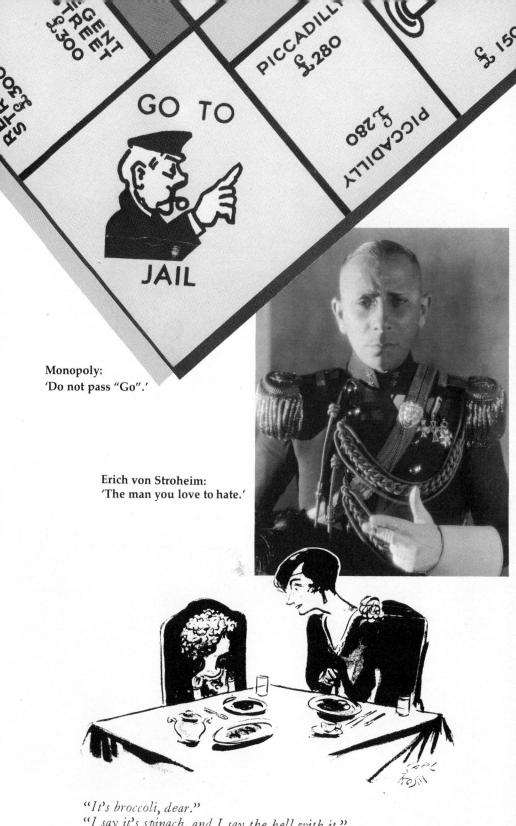

Monopoly:
'Do not pass "Go".'

Erich von Stroheim:
'The man you love to hate.'

"*It's broccoli, dear.*"
"*I say it's spinach, and I say the hell with it.*"
From the *New Yorker*, 1928.

Malcolm Fraser, Prime Minister of Australia (1975–83), was known for his political catchphrase 'Life wasn't meant to be easy.' As he had the grace to admit, however, he traced this fairly commonplace thought to the character of the He-Ancient in *Back to Methuselah*: '**Life is not meant to be easy**, my child; but take courage: it can be delightful.'

Fraser told *The Times* (16 March 1981): 'A friend who I was visiting in hospital asked me why I didn't give up politics and return to the good life at [my sheep farm in Victoria]. I said life wasn't meant to be like that. That would be too easy. So that's what it grew from. I wouldn't mind a cent for every time it's been quoted or misquoted. It's the best thing I ever said.'

Presumably, Shaw would agree.

FAMOUS PHRASES

THIS book is concerned, on the whole, with quotations – that is to say, with what specific people have said. In this chapter, however, we turn to some well-known phrases and sayings that are probably better known in their own right and not linked to any source. Where it is possible to point to a precise source, this is done:

The AFFLUENT society

The economist John Kenneth Galbraith (*b.*1908) popularised this term when he used it as the title of his 1958 book about the effects of high living standards on economic theories which had been designed to deal with scarcity and poverty. The resulting 'private affluence and public squalor' stemmed from an imbalance between private and public sector output. For example, there might be more cars and TV sets but not enough police to prevent them from being stolen.

Dr Martin Luther King Jr, in a letter from gaol in 1963, used the phrase thus: 'When you see the vast majority of your twenty million Negro brothers smouldering in an airtight cage of poverty in the midst of an **affluent society** . . . then you will understand why we find it difficult to wait.'

The notion was not new to the mid-twentieth century: Tacitus in his *Annals* (*c.*AD 115) said that 'many, amid great affluence, are utterly miserable' and Cato the Younger (95 – 46 BC), when denouncing the contemporary state of Rome, said: 'Habemus publice egestatem, privatim opulentiam.'

. . . is ALIVE and well and living in . . .

This format-phrase probably began in a perfectly natural way – 'What's happened to old so-and-so?' 'Oh, he's **alive and well and living in** Godalming.' In the Preface to *His Last Bow* (1917) Conan Doyle wrote: 'The Friends of Mr Sherlock Holmes will be glad to learn that he is still alive and well . . .' But the extended form was given a tremendous fillip when the Belgian-born song-writer and singer Jacques Brel (1929–78) was made the subject of an off-Broadway musical entertainment entitled *Jacques Brel is Alive and Well and Living in Paris* (1968–72). Quite why M. Brel should have merited this 'Where is he now?' treatment, I have no idea. But the format caught on. It was used as part of genuine religious sloganeering – 'God is not dead . . . he is alive and well and living in your heart', etc. – and in graffiti additions: 'God is not dead – he is alive and well and working on a much less ambitious project' (quoted 1979); 'Jesus is not dead – he is alive and well and signing copies of the Bible in Foyles' (quoted 1980).

ANGRY young man

Following the success of John Osborne's play *Look Back in Anger* which was produced at the Royal Court Theatre, London, in May 1956 and which portrayed an anti-hero called Jimmy Porter, the term **angry young man** was applied to a group of writers in their twenties and thirties, like Osborne, who expressed dissatisfaction with conventional values. Kingsley Amis and Colin Wilson were among the motley crew so dubbed. The phrase did not occur in Osborne's play but was applied to the playwright by George Fearon in the theatre's publicity material. Fearon told the *Daily Telegraph* (2 October 1957): 'I ventured to prophesy that this generation would praise his play while mine would, in general, dislike it . . . "if this happens," I told him, "you would become known as the Angry Young Man". In fact, we decided then and there that henceforth he was to be known as that.'

Kenneth Tynan commented:[93]

There is nothing new in young men being angry: in fact, it would be news if they were anything else. Byron and Shelley were classically angry young men . . . The very phrase was used in 1951 by an English social philosopher named Leslie Paul as the title of his autobiography; it is the story of a devout left-wing agitator who lost his faith in Russia during the 1930s and turned, like so many others, to a vague sort of Christian humanism. What distinguishes the modern English 'young angries' is that they all came of age around the time that their elders invented the hydrogen bomb. How could they revere 'civilisation as we know it' when at any moment it might be transformed into 'civilisation as we knew it'? . . . These unanswerable questions set up feelings of uselessness and impotence, which led some to apathy, in others to a sort of derisive detachment, and in still others to downright rage.

The Big APPLE

As a name for New York City, **Big Apple** seems to have arisen in the 1930s – but for what reason? Take your pick: the Spanish word for a block of houses between two streets is 'manzana', which is also the word for apple; in the mid-1930s there was a Harlem night club called 'The Big Apple' which was a mecca for jazz musicians; there was also a jitterbugging dance from the swing era *c*.1936 which took its name from the nightclub; 'big apple' was race-track argot and New York City had a good reputation in this field.

William Safire[82] plumps for the jazz version, recalling a 1944 jive 'handbook' defining 'apple' as: 'the earth, the universe, this planet. Any place that's large. A big Northern city.' Hence, you called New York the Big Apple if you considered it to be the centre of the universe. It was, if you like, a place full of opportunity and ripe for plucking.

In the eighteenth century, Horace Walpole called London 'The Strawberry' because of its freshness and cleanliness in comparison with foreign cities.

BELIEVE it or not!

Believe it or not! was reinforced as an exclamation through its use as the title of a long-running syndicated newspaper feature, radio and TV series, in the US. Robert Leroy Ripley (1893–1949) created and illustrated a comic strip *Ripley's Believe It or Not* from *c*.1923 onwards. The researcher on the strip until 1975 was Norbert Pearlroth (who died aged 89 in 1983). Believe it or not, he spent seven days a week in the New York Public Library unearthing 62,192 amazing facts and anecdotes.

I am getting BETTER and better

Every day and in every way I am getting better and better was a translation of 'Tous les jours, à tous les points de vue, je vais de mieux en mieux', a kind of mantra devised by the French psychologist Emile Coué (1857–1926). He was the originator of a system of 'Self-Mastery Through Conscious Auto-suggestion' which had a brief vogue in the 1920s. His patients had to repeat this phrase over and over and it became a popular catchphrase of the time, thought physical and mental improvement did not noticeably follow. 'Couéism' died with its inventor.

In the country of the BLIND . . .

The saying **In the country of the blind the one-eyed man is king** has become associated with the name of H. G. Wells because of its use by him in the story *The Country of the Blind* (1904) – though he quite clearly labelled it as an 'old proverb.' Indeed, it is that, and occurs in the proverbs of many languages.[18] An early appearance is in a book of *Adages* by Erasmus (*d.*1536): 'In regione caecorum rex est luscus.' Other early sixteenth-century uses of the saying include John Palsgrave's translation of Fullmin's *Comedy of Acolastus* and John Skelton's 'An one eyed man is Well syghted when he is amonge blunde men' (1522).

The BUTLER did it!

I have drawn a complete blank over the origins of the phrase **the butler did it!** as a solution for detective stories of the – I would suppose – 1920s and 30s, although a correspondent recalled hearing it spoken by a member of the audience after a showing of the last episode of the film series *The Exploits of Elaine* at a London cinema in *c.*1916. Joseph R. Sandy told me (1983): 'The detective was called Craig Kennedy and the butler's name was Bennet. I do not remember who played the parts (except the heroine, who was Pearl White) or anything much more about the serial.'

So perhaps the phrase was current by that date. Quite why it has entered common parlance, I have no idea. One of the conventions of crime writing of the period was that the butler or servants rarely if ever did 'do' it. Father Ronald Knox, compiling a list of rules for this kind of writing in his introductions to *The Best Detective Stories of the Year, 1928*, noted: 'The only person who is really scratch on morals is the aged butler; I cannot off-hand recall any lapse of virtue on the part of a man who has been with the family for sixteen years. But I may be wrong; I have not read all the detective stories.'

The earliest use of the phrase I can give chapter and verse for is the film *My Man Godfrey* (1957 – not the 1936 original) which is not even a whodunnit: 'The butler did it! He made every lady in the house, oh, so very happy!'

Alan Melville remembered (1983):

Years ago, a repertory actor up in Scotland ruined every available Agatha Christie or other crime drama by saying the line straight out to the audience when he was slightly pissed – 'no need to wait to the end, the butler did it.' He was sacked, poor soul, but the sad thing is that the week he got his cards the play he was appearing in, however unsteadily, was one in which the butler really did do it.

The police CAUTION

Anything you say will be taken down and may be given in evidence. The police caution in the UK is not fixed in form. The version that one might expect from fictional use is something like: 'You are not obliged to say anything unless you wish to do so but I must warn you that whatever you do say will be taken down in writing and may be given in evidence against you.' But this is wrong. The police are advised that care should be taken to avoid any suggestion that evidence might only be used *against* a person, as this could prevent an innocent person making a statement which might help clear him of the charge.

In the US, on the other hand, things are different. G. Gordon Liddy[47] described a March 1966 raid on Dr Timothy Leary's house in connection with drugs charges:

'Doctor, my name is G. Gordon Liddy and I'm assistant district attorney of Dutchess County. I want to question you about what's been going on here, but first I want you to understand that you don't have to make any statement, and any statement you do make may be used against you in a court of law. You also have the right to a lawyer. You understand?'

The law of the state of New York did not then require that these warnings be given prior to interrogation. They were, however, the standard prelude to questioning by special agents of the FBI. As a former FBI agent, I gave them as a matter of routine and had advised the sheriff's officers to do the same.

No COMMENT

This useful phrase when people in the news are being hounded by journalists has never quite achieved cliché status. After all, why should people in such a position have to find something original to say? Nevertheless, it has become used as a consciously inadequate form of evasion, often in an obviously jokey way (cf. 'We are just good friends' when evading questions on the degree of intimacy between two people).

I suspect that it arose by way of reaction to the ferretings of Hollywood gossip columnists in the 1920s and 30s, though perhaps it was simply a reaction to the popular press in general in the first half of the century.

Winston Churchill appeared to come across it for the first time in 1946, so perhaps it was not generally known before then, at least outside the USA. After a meeting with President Truman, he said: 'I think **No comment** is a spendid expression. I got it from Sumner Welles.'

A good example of its use can be found in a terse broadcast interview conducted with Kim Philby on 10 November 1955 after he had been cleared of being the 'third man' in the Burgess/Maclean spy case. He later defected to Moscow in 1963 and was shown to have been a liar all along. The interview went like this:

'Mr Philby, Mr Macmillan, the Foreign Secretary said there was no evidence that you were the so-called "third man" who allegedly tipped off Burgess and Maclean. Are you satisfied with that clearance that he gave you?'

'Yes, I am.'

'Well, if there was a "third man", were you in fact the "third man"?'

'No, I was not.'

'Do you think there was one?'

'No comment.'

Full marks should be given to anyone who can devise a more sparkling alternative. British TV executive Desmond Wilcox evaded questions about his ousting from the BBC in 1980 with: 'Sorry, your camera's run out of film.'

Martha 'The Mouth' Mitchell, wife of President Nixon's disgraced Attorney-General and the blabber who helped get the Watergate investigations under way, once declared: 'I don't believe in that "no comment" business. I always have a comment.'

DEEP Throat

Deep Throat was the most fashionable American porno movie of the late 1960s. The censor would not allow it to be shown in Britain but everyone knew that it concerned a woman, played by Linda Lovelace, whose clitoris was placed in the back of her throat enabling her to engage in a very special form of oral sex. It is said that the film grossed $600 million. I saw it once in a seedy cinema in Times Square and cannot remember anything about it at all, not least because the film-stock was so murky.

The name lived on, however, because of the Watergate scandal. *Washington Post* reporters Carl Bernstein and Bob Woodward, who unearthed the scandal, starting in 1972, relied for some of their information on an anonymous Executive Branch informant. They never revealed who it was – indeed, some have suggested that 'Deep Throat' did not exist but was a cover for unjustified suppositions. As the reporters explained:[7]

> Woodward had promised he would never identify him or his position to anyone. Further, he had agreed never to quote the man, even as an anonymous source. Their discussions would be only to confirm information that had been obtained elsewhere and to add some perspective. In newspaper terminology, this meant the discussions were on 'deep background'. Woodward explained the arrangement to managing editor Howard Simons one day. He had taken to calling the source 'my friend', but Simons dubbed him **Deep Throat**, the title of a celebrated pornographic movie. The name stuck.

DESIDERATA

There can have been few bedroom walls during the great wall-poster craze of the late 1960s which did not bear a copy of a text called 'Desiderata' ('desirable things'), reputedly found in Old St Paul's Church, Baltimore and dating from 1692. It began: '**Go placidly amid the noise and haste**, and remember what peace there may be in silence. As far as possible without surrender be on good terms with all persons. Speak your truth quietly and clearly; and listen to others, even the dull and ignorant; they too have their story. Avoid loud and aggressive persons, they are vexations to the spirit . . .'

Les Crane spoke the words on a hit record in 1972. However, 'Desiderata' had nothing to do with Old St Paul's. That was a fanciful idea incorporated in the first US edition of the poster. Nor did 1692 come into it. The words were written by Max Ehrmann in 1927 and copyright was renewed in 1954 by Bertha K. Ehrmann.[9] In 1983, the poster was still on sale as 'from 1692' but carrying the copyright lines.

All DRESSED up and nowhere to go

This phrase began life in a song by G. Whiting (1912): 'When You're All Dressed Up and No Place to Go':

When you're **all dressed up and no place to go**,
Life seems dreary, weary and slow.
My heart has ached as well as bled
For the tears I've shed,
When I've had no place to go
Unless I went back to bed. . . .

The song was popularised by the American comedian Raymond Hitchcock *c*.1915 but the phrase gained further emphasis when it was used by William Allen White (1868–1944) in 1916 to describe the Progressive Party following Theodore Roosevelt's decision to retire from Presidential competition. He said they were: 'All dressed up with nowhere to go.'

The ESTABLISHMENT

In September 1955, Henry Fairlie was writing a series of articles for the *Spectator* and wanted to describe why it had taken the British Foreign Office four years to admit that the spies Burgess and Maclean had defected to Moscow. It was, he said, **The Establishment** keeping quiet. By this, he meant a conservative, partly hereditary, secretive, self-perpetuating ruling class. 'I do not mean only the centres of official power – though they are certainly part of it – but rather the whole matrix of official and social relations within which power is exercised.'

Hugh Thomas, editing a book about the phenomenon,[92] stated: 'The word was, however, in use among the thoughtful at least a year previously; I recall myself employing it while passing the Royal Academy in a taxi in company with Mr Paul Johnson of the *New Statesman* in August 1954.' Thomas defined 'Establishment' as 'the English constitution and the group of institutions and outlying agencies built round it to assist in its protection' – i.e. the Crown, City, Church, Civil Service, Armed Forces, BBC (as it used to be), and so on.

Since then the phrase has been used whenever a speaker has sought to invoke a sinister ruling clique. When a nightclub was set up at the start of the British 'satire' boom in the early 1960s, it was inevitably called 'The Establishment'.

In much the same sense, however, the phrase had been used in America by Ralph Waldo Emerson during the last century. It was also applied to a powerful clique in the US from the 1960s onwards – the power brokers of corporate society, sometimes better known as the Eastern Establishment. The coining of the acronym 'WASP', standing for White Anglo-Saxon Protestant, to describe it, has been attributed to Professor J. Digby Baltzell. Art Buchwald commented: 'In this country when you attack The Establishment, they don't put you in jail or a mental institution. They do something worse. They make you a member of the Establishment.'

EVERYTHING you always wanted to know

Everything you always wanted to know about sex but were afraid to ask was the self-explanatory title of a book (published 1970) by David Reuben MD (*b*.1933). It gave to the language a format-phrase (compounded by its use as a film title by Woody Allen in 1972 – in fact, Allen simply bought the title of the book and none of its contents).

Subsequently, almost any subject could be slotted into the sentence. An advertisement for the UK *Video Today* magazine (December 1981) promised: 'All you ever wanted to know about video but were afraid to ask.'

The FAMILY that prays together . . .

A religious slogan familiar from bumper-stickers and elsewhere in the 1960s and 70s has a somewhat longer history. **The family that prays together stays together** was devised by Al Scalpone, an advertising copywriter, for Father Patrick Peyton of the Roman Catholic Rosary Crusade in the USA. This crusade started in 1942 and the slogan was first broadcast on 6 March 1947 during radio's *Family Theater of the Air*.[18]

Among graffiti variants (quoted 1974) are: 'The family that shoots together, loots together', 'The family that flays together, stays together' and an addition (quoted 1981): 'Thank heavens my mother-in-law's an atheist.'

Inside every FAT man . . .

In *The Unquiet Grave* (1944), Cyril Connolly wrote: **Imprisoned in every fat man a thin one is wildly signalling to be let out.**

But, five years before, George Orwell in *Coming Up for Air* had written: 'I'm fat, but I'm thin inside. Has it ever struck you that there's a thin man inside every fat man, just as they say there's a statue inside every block of stone?'

Not to be outdone, Kingsley Amis twisted the idea round in *One Fat Englishman* (1963): 'Outside every fat man there was an even fatter man trying to close in.'

And Timothy Leary was quoted in 1979 as having said: 'Inside every fat Englishman is a thin Hindu trying to get out.'

Do not FOLD, spindle or mutilate

In the USA, when punched cards and computer cards began to accompany bills and statements in the 1950s, computerisation was looked on as a harbinger of the Brave New World (though Bartlett[5] dates use of the bossy injunction from the 1930s). By the 1960s, the words evoked a machine age that was taking over.

A slogan of the student revolution was: 'I am a human being. **Do not fold, spindle or mutilate**.'

A graffito (quoted 1974) read: 'I am a masochist – please spindle, fold or mutilate.'

Fifty million FRENCHMEN

A good deal of confusion surrounds the phrase **Fifty million Frenchmen can't be wrong**. As a slightly grudging expression it appears to have originated with American servicemen during the First World War, justifying support for their French allies. The precise number of millions was variable. A song with the above title (by Rose, Raskin & Fisher) was recorded by Sophie Tucker on 15 April 1927. Cole Porter's musical *Fifty Million Frenchmen* opened in New York on 27 November 1929.

Where the confusion has crept in is that Texas Guinan (1884–1933) – the New York nightclub hostess famous for greeting clients with the phrase **Hello, sucker!** – was refused entry into France with her girls in 1931 and said: 'It goes to show that fifty million Frenchmen *can* be wrong.' She returned to America and renamed her show *Too Hot for Paris*.

Shaw also held out against the phrase. He insisted: 'Fifty million Frenchmen can't be right.'

God protect me from my FRIENDS

The ethics of Sicilian banditry caused Gavin Maxwell to call his 1956 book about Salvatore Giuliano, *God Protect Me From My Friends*. In full the expression is: 'I can look after my enemies, but **God protect me from my friends**.' In fact, a proverb along these lines is common to many languages. Another frequently cited English language form is: 'With friends like these, who needs enemies?' This compares with the saying: 'With a Hungarian for a friend, who needs enemies?'

The Morrises[55] cite Maréchal Villiers leaving Louis XIV: 'Defend me from my friends; I can defend myself from my enemies.' And George Canning:

Give me the avowed, the erect, the manly foe,
Bold I can meet – perhaps may turn his blow!

But of all plagues, Good Heaven, thy wrath can send,
Save, save, Oh, save me from the candid friend!

Charlotte Brontë also used the idea in a letter about a patronising review of one of her books.

Do not pass 'GO'

A *Sunday Mirror* editorial (3 May 1981) stated: 'The laws of contempt are the ones under which editors and other media folk can be sent straight to jail without passing Go.' A businessman said to a woman who had paid for her husband to be duffed up (report of trial, *The Times*, 30 November 1982): 'If the police find out you are paying, you will go to jail, directly to jail, you will not pass "go" or collect £200.'

These two citations are testimony to the enduring use of Monopoly phraseology. Monopoly is the name of a board game invented by an unemployed salesman, Charles Darrow, in Johnstown, Pa. It was created in 1929 – the year of the Wall Street crash – and so the game was based on fantasies of owning real estate. The properties that players could buy, rent or sell according to the throw of a dice and thus move towards a monopoly position were named after places in Atlantic City – hence New York Avenue, Park Place, Mediterranean Avenue, and Marvin Gardens (although it should have been 'Marven').

The hugely popular game – 85 million sets sold up to 1982 – was patented by Parker Bros Inc. in 1935 and sixteen different language versions followed. Hence, the UK version in which players begin on the square marked 'Go', in due course may come back to that square and 'collect £200 salary as you pass', land on the 'Go to jail' square, or draw a 'Chance' card with the penalty:

GO TO JAIL
MOVE DIRECTLY TO JAIL
DO NOT PASS 'GO'
DO NOT COLLECT £200.

The GREEKS had a word for it

For seemingly so venerable a phrase, it may come as a surprise to learn that **the Greeks had a word for it** dates back no further than 1929 when the words were used as the title of a play by Zoe Akins (1856–1958). Although, as she said, 'the phrase is original and grew out of the dialogue', it does not appear anywhere in the text. The 'it' refers to love.

HAPPINESS is . . .

Samuel Johnson declared in 1766: 'Happiness consists in the multiplicity of agreeable consciousness.'

However, it was Charles M. Schulz (*b*.1922), creator of the 'Peanuts' comic strip, who launched the **Happiness is . . .** format. In *c*.1957 he had drawn a strip 'centring around some kid hugging Snoopy and saying in the fourth panel that "Happiness is a warm puppy." ' This became the title of a best-selling book in 1962 and let loose a stream of promotional phrases using the format, including: 'Happiness is egg-shaped', 'Happiness is a cigar called Hamlet' (UK advertising slogans), 'Happiness is being elected team captain – and getting a Bulova watch', 'Happiness is a $49 table' (US advertising slogans), 'Happiness is being single' (US bumper-sticker), 'Happiness is seeing Lubbock, Texas in the rear view mirror' (song title), and many, many more.

No wonder Lennon and McCartney wrote a song called 'Happiness is a Warm Gun' (1968).

The man you love to HATE

Coming across a 1979 film tribute to the Hollywood director Erich von Stroheim with the title **The man you love to hate**, I fell to wondering where it came from. In fact, it was a billing applied to von Stroheim in the 1918 propaganda film *The Heart of Humanity* in which he played an obnoxious German officer who not only attempted to violate the leading lady but nonchalantly tossed a baby out of the window. At the film's première in Los Angeles, von Stroheim was hooted and jeered at when he walked on stage. He had to explain that he was only an actor – and was himself an Austrian, not a German.

Eat your HEART out

As a swanking exultation – a minor singer having just finished a powerful ballad might exclaim, '**Eat your heart out**, Frank Sinatra!' – this saying acquired a show business popularity in mid-century. The original phrase 'to eat one's heart out' meant 'to pine' and Leo Rosten convinced me[79] that the injunction comes from the Yiddish: 'Es dir oys s'harts'.

ILLEGITIMI non carborundum

The cod-Latin phrase **Illegitimi non carborundum** for 'Don't let the bastards grind you down' was used by General 'Vinegar Joe' Silwell as his motto during the Second World War, though it is not suggested he devised it. Partridge[62] gave it as 'Illegitimis' and its origins in British army Intelligence very early on in the war. 'Carborundum' is the trade name for a very hard substance called silicon carbide, used in grinding.

Some of my best friends are JEWS

A self-conscious (occasionally jokey) disclaimer of prejudice. In a May 1946 letter, Somerset Maugham replied to charges of being anti-Semitic and said: 'God knows I have never been that; **some of my best friends** both in England and America **are Jews** . . .' So, clearly, at that date the phrase could be uttered straight. However, I think it had been rejected as a cartoon caption by the *New Yorker* prior to the Second World War and presumably dates, in any case, from the Hitlerite repression of the Jews from the 1930s on.

The Russian Prime Minister, Alexei Kosygin, was presumably not aware of any irony in 1971 when he said: 'There is no anti-semitism in Russia. Some of my best friends are Jews.'

JUSTICE should not only be done . . .

The origin of this well-known sentiment is contained in a ruling by Lord Chief Justice Hewart (1870–1943). A man named McCarthy had been accused at Hastings of dangerous driving. There had been an accident in which people were injured. He was convicted, but it was later discovered that a partner in the firm of solicitors who had demanded damages was clerk to the Hastings justices. As Robert Jackson noted,[41] no one believed that the clerk had acted improperly during the case but the circumstances warranted an application by McCarthy's solicitor for the conviction to be quashed in a Divisional Court. McCarthy's appeal succeeded. Hewart ruled in the case of Rex *v.* Sussex Justices (9 November 1923): 'A long line of cases shows that it is not merely of some importance, but it is of fundamental importance, that **justice should not only be done, but should manifestly and undoubtedly be seen to be done**.'

When a fellow judge jokingly suggested that the word 'seen' was a misprint for 'seem', Hewart made it clear that justice must always be 'seen' to be done in the view of the defendant and of the world.

Subsequently at a dinner a lawyer replied to a toast by saying: 'It is not only of some importance, but of fundamental importance, that the Lord Chief Justice should have a good dinner, but manifestly and undoubtedly should be seen to have had it. And he has and it is!'

'Beachcomber' commented that 'Justice must not only be seen to be done, it has to be seen to be believed.'

KILROY was here

Partridge[61] quoted a clipping from the *San Francisco Chronicle* of 2 December 1962:

> Two days before the Japanese attack on Pearl Harbor, an unimposing, bespectacled, 39-year-old man took a job with a Bethlehem Steel Company shipyard in Quincy, Mass. As an inspector . . . James J. Kilroy began making his mark on equipment to show test gangs he had checked a job – the mark: **Kilroy was here**. Soon the words caught on at the shipyard, and Kilroy began finding the slogan written all over the installation.
>
> Before long, the phrase spread far beyond the bounds of the yard, and Kilroy – coupled with the sketch of a man, or at least his nose peering over a wall – became one of the most famous names of the Second World War. When the war ended a nation-wide contest to discover the real Kilroy found him still employed at the shipyard. And last week, James Kilroy . . . died in Boston's Peter Bent hospital, at the age of 60.

I suppose that is the most likely explanation for what must be the most widely known graffito of all, but I am not entirely convinced. Flexner[24] stated confidently that the phrase had begun to appear in a few docks and ports and on ships in late 1939 and was well established by 1942. Partridge also offered a rival theory, quoting from another (1945) newspaper clipping: 'The phrase originated in the fact that a friend of Sgt Francis Kilroy thought him a wonderful guy and scrawled on the bulletin board of a Florida air base, "Kilroy will be here next week." The phrase took the fancy of army fliers and it spread across the world.'

There is little doubt that Kilroy was of American origin. The name became synonymous with American G.I.'s who took it with them wherever they went during the Second World War.

LIFE begins at forty

In 1932, William B. Pitkin (1878–1953), Professor in Journalism at Columbia University, published a book called *Life Begins at Forty* in which he dealt with 'adult reorientation' at a time when the problems of extended life and leisure were beginning to assert themselves. Based on lectures Pitkin had given, the book was a hearty bit of uplift: 'Every day brings forth some new thing that adds to the joy of life after forty. Work becomes easy and brief. Play grows richer and longer. Leisure lengthens. Life's afternoon is brighter, warmer, fuller of song; and long before shadows stretch, every fruit grows ripe . . . **Life begins at forty**. This is the revolutionary outcome of our new Era . . . Today it is half a truth. Tomorrow it will be an axiom.' It is certainly a well-established catchphrase. Helping it to take hold was a song with this title (by Yellen and Shapiro) recorded by Sophie Tucker in February 1937.

LIVE now, pay later

The 'now/later' format phrase had its beginnings, I am sure, in advertisements either for travel ('Go now, pay later') or for goods on hire purchase ('Buy now, pay later'). However, the format was given renewed popularity when it was used as the title of Jack Trevor Story's screenplay **Live Now, Pay Later** (1962). This was based on Jack Lindsay's novel *All on the Never Never*. Incidentally, I wonder whether that term for hire purchase has any connection with the 'Never-never Land' in J. M. Barrie's *Peter Pan* (1904)?

Numerous uses could be cited of what became a cliché: 'Book now, pay later' (Covent Garden opera programme, 1977); 'Our layaway plan – die now, pay later' (graffito on US funeral parlour ad, quoted 1974).

The LOST Generation

This refers to the large number of promising young men who gave their lives in the First World War. The ideal figure was that of the dashing poet Rupert Brooke (who was not actually killed in battle, as it happens). Numerically, it is not an accurate description from the British point of view. 750,000 men from the UK were killed. France, with a smaller population, lost twice as many.

An extension of the phrase arose from a remark by a French garage owner in the Midi just after the war. He rebuked an apprentice who had made a shoddy repair to Gertrude Stein's car, saying that 'all of you young people who served in the war' were from **a lost generation** ('une generation perdue'). Ernest Hemingway used this as the epigraph to his novel *The Sun Also Rises* (1926) and referred to it again in *A Moveable Feast* (1964). Thus, the term came to be applied to people like Hemingway and Scott Fitzgerald who were not killed in the war but who were part of a generation thought to have lost its values.

MURPHY'S Law

Most commonly known as Murphy's Law (and indistinguishable from Sod's Law) the saying **If anything can go wrong, it will** dates back to the 1940s. The *Macquarie Dictionary*[49] suggests that it was named after a character who always made mistakes in a series of educational cartoons published by the US Navy. The *Concise Oxford Dictionary of Proverbs*[18] suggests that it was invented by George Nichols, a project manager for Northrop, the Californian aviation firm, in 1949. He developed the idea from a remark by a colleague, Captain E. Murphy of the Wright Field-Aircraft Laboratory.

The best-known demonstration of Murphy's Law is that a piece of bread when dropped on the floor always falls with its buttered side facing down (otherwise known as the Law of Universal Cussedness). This idea, however, pre-dated the promulgation of the Law. In 1867, A. D. Richardson wrote in *Beyond Mississippi*: 'His bread never fell on the buttered side.' In 1884, James Payn composed the lines:

> I never had a piece of toast
> Particularly long and wide,
> But fell upon the sanded floor,
> And always on the buttered side.

The corollary of this aspect of the Law is that bread always falls buttered-side down *except* when demonstrating the Law.

Some would argue that Murphy's Law was originally designed to be constructive and not defeatist – that it was a prescription for avoiding mistakes in the design of a valve for an aircraft's hydraulic system. If the valve could be fitted in more than one way, then sooner or later someone would fit it the wrong way. The idea was to design it so that the valve could only be fitted the right way.

. . . is the NAME of the game

A cliché phrase from the mid-1960s, meaning: 'That's what it's really all about.' US National Security Adviser McGeorge Bundy talking about foreign policy goals in Europe (1966) said: 'Settlement **is the name of the game**.' In time, everything seemed to be 'the name of the game', following the title of an American TV movie called *Fame Is The Name of the Game* (1966). Then followed several series of *The Name of the Game* (1968–71). The expression was replaced for a while by 'That's where it's at . . .'

Have a NICE day

William Safire traced the origins of this pervasive American greeting in his book *On Language*.[81] Beginning with an early flourish in Chaucer's *The Knight's Tale* ('Far wel, have good day') it then jumped to 1956 and the Carson/Roberts advertising agency in Los Angeles. 'Our phone was answered "Good morning, Carson/Roberts, have a happy day",' recalled Ralph Carson. 'We used the salutation on all letters, tie tacks, cuff buttons, beach towels, blazer crests, the works.' Shortly after this, WCBS-TV weather-girl, Carol Reed, would wave goodbye with 'Have a happy'.

In the 1960s, 'Have a good day' was revived. Then, the early 1970s saw **Have a nice day** push its insidious way in, although Kirk Douglas had got his tongue round it in the 1948 film *A Letter to Three Wives*. 'Have a nice city' was a slogan in the 1970 Los Angeles mayoral election.

From all this, it may be understood that the usage is a Californian imposition upon the rest of the USA.

What's a NICE girl like you . . .?

A chat-up line taking various forms and which, I suspect, may have arisen in Hollywood Westerns of the 1930s is **What's a nice girl like you doing in a joint like this?** It was certainly established as a film cliché by the 1950s when Muir and Norden included this version in a BBC radio *Take It from Here* parody: 'Thanks, Kitty. Say, why does a swell girl like you have to work in a saloon like this?'

In 1973, *Private Eye* carried a cartoon of a male weed-smoker saying to a female: 'What's a nice joint like you . . .?'

The OPERA isn't over . . .

A rather elaborate expression for 'Don't count your chickens' or 'The fight isn't over yet' which perhaps deserves somewhat wider circulation is **The opera isn't over till the fat lady sings.** The *Washington Post* (13 June 1978) described its genesis, thus: 'One day three years ago, Ralph Carpenter, who was then Texas Tech's sports information director, declared to the press box contingent in Austin, "The rodeo ain't over till the bull riders rides." Stirred to top that deep insight, San Antonio sports editor Dan Cook countered with, "The opera ain't over till the fat lady sings." '

Sick as a PARROT

In the UK, alternative expressions of dismay or pleasure at the outcome of a football match – **Sick as a parrot** or **Over the moon** – became a cliché in the late 1970s. It probably all began because of the remorseless post-game analysis by TV football commentators and the consequent need for players and managers to provide pithy comments. Liverpool footballer Phil Thompson said he felt 'Sick as a parrot' after his team's defeat in the 1978 Cup Final. *Private Eye* fuelled the cliché by constant mockery, to such an extent that by 1980 an 'instant' BBC radio play about the European Cup Final, written on the spot and developed according to the outcome, was given the alternative titles *Over the Moon/Sick as a Parrot*. The writer was Neville Smith.

Some failed to note the cliché. *The Times* (21 January 1982) reported the reaction of M. Albert Roux, the London restaurateur, on gaining three stars in the Michelin Guide: ' "I am over the moon", M. Roux said yesterday . . . He quickly denied, however, that his brother (another celebrated restaurateur) would be "sick as a parrot".'

'Over the moon' is probably the older of the two phrases. Indeed, in the diaries of May, Lady Cavendish (published 1927) there is an entry for 7 February 1857 saying how she broke the news of her youngest brother's birth to the rest of her siblings: 'I had told the little ones who were first utterly incredulous and then over the moon.' The family of Catherine Gladstone (née Gwynne), wife of the Prime Minister, is said to have had its own idiomatic language and to have originated the phrase. The nursery rhyme 'Hey diddle diddle/ The cat and the fiddle,/ The cow jumped over the moon' dates back to at least 1765, however.

What may be an early version of 'Sick as a parrot' appears in Robert Southey's Cumbrian dialect poem 'The Terrible Knitters e' Dent' (1834). There, 'Sick as a peeate' (pronounced 'pee-at') means a feeling akin to a heavy lump of peat in the stomach.

Be PREPARED

The motto of the Boy Scout movement was based on the initials of its founder, Sir Robert Baden-Powell (1857–1941), who was frequently referred to by its members as 'B-P'. The words first appeared in the handbook *Scouting for Boys*, published in 1908. They mean: 'You are always in a state of readiness in mind and body to do your DUTY.' Winston Churchill wrote in *Great Contemporaries*:[15] 'It is difficult to exaggerate the moral and mental health which our nation had derived from this profound and simple conception. In those bygone days the motto **Be Prepared** had a special meaning for our country. Those who looked to the coming of a great war welcomed the awakening of British boyhood.'

PUBLIC Enemy No. One

John Dillinger (1903–34) was the first officially designated **Public Enemy Number One**. He robbed banks and killed people in Illinois, Indiana and Ohio during 1933–4 to such an extent that the Attorney General, Homer Cummings, called him this. In fact, he was the only person ever to be so named. The FBI's Ten Most Wanted Men list did not give a ranking. Dillinger's exploits and his escape from captivity caused great public interest. He was shot dead by FBI agents outside a cinema in Chicago.

The coining of the term 'Public enemy' in this context has been attributed to Frank Loesch, President of the Chicago Crime Commission, who had to try to deal with Al Capone's hold over the city in 1923. The idea was to try and dispel the romantic aura such gangsters had been invested with by the popular press. James Cagney starred in a gangster film called *The Public Enemy* in 1931.

The phrase soon passed into general speech: in June 1934, P. G. Wodehouse referring in a letter to difficulties with US income tax officials, said: 'I got an offer from Paramount to go to Hollywood at $1,500 a week and had to refuse as I am Public Enemy No 1 in America, and can't go there.'

The words were subsequently applied to other forms of undesirables, while Raymond Postgate, founder of the British *Good Food Guide* was dubbed 'Public Stomach No 1' and Beverley Nichols, the author and journalist, called himself 'Public Anemone No 1'.

Any PUBLICITY is good publicity

I would date **Any publicity is good publicity** from the 1960s but probably it's as old as the public relations industry. Alternative forms include: 'There's no such thing as bad publicity' and 'I don't care what the papers say about me as long as they spell my name right'. The latter saying has been attributed to the American Tammany leader, 'Big Tim' Sullivan.

Innocence RULES, OK?

In 1975, a Londoner, George Davis, was given a seventeen-year prison sentence for taking part in a robbery and for wounding with intent to avoid arrest. Those who believed in his innocence launched a vigorous campaign to get this conviction quashed. They dug up a Test cricket pitch, for example, but chiefly they wrote the slogan **George Davis is innocent, OK** all over the East End of London (not always getting the spelling of his name right, as it happens). The campaign was taken up elsewhere and in May 1976 Davis was released from prison, but not pardoned.

The use of the curious affirmative 'OK' at the end of the sentence was apparently inherited from gang usage of the late 1960s in Scotland and Northern Ireland (some would have it that it dates back to the 1930s). Either a gang or football team or the Provisional IRA would be said to **rule OK**. Later this was turned into a joke with numerous variations – 'Queen Elizabeth rules UK', 'Rodgers and Hammerstein rule OK, lahoma' and so on.

The Davis slogan took on an importance out of all proportion to the case (and could still be seen painted up in 1983). In July 1978 Davis was sentenced to fifteen years gaol for his part in a subsequent bank robbery.

They SHOOT horses, don't they?

Said by or to an exhausted person, **They shoot horses, don't they?** implies that he ought to be put out of his misery. Writing in 1951, critic Kenneth Tynan suggested that it would make a better title for an adaptation of Molière's *Le Malade Imaginaire* which had been called instead *The Gay Invalid.* in 1969 there was a film, based on Horace McCoy's 1935 novel with this title, portraying the dance hall marathons of the Depression years. Perhaps it was an expression dating from the old days of the West.

The greatest thing since SLICED bread

A 1981 ad in the UK stated: 'Sainsbury's bring you **the greatest thing since sliced bread**. Unsliced bread' – neatly turning an old formula on its head. Quite when the idea that pre-sliced bread was one of the landmark inventions arose, I am not sure. Sliced bread had appeared on the market by the 1920s – so any time after that, I suppose.

From the *Observer* (22 May 1983):

> At the last minute a Conservative Party election slogan in Punjabi was withheld from distribution when a spot check revealed the dangers of instant translation. In its English version, the slogan said Conservative policies were the country's most important discovery since the invention of sliced bread. Translated into Punjabi, the slogan read: 'Conservative policies are the country's most important discovery since the advent of circumcised nans (Indian bread).

I say it's SPINACH

A caption devised by Elwyn Brooks White (*b.*1899) for a cartoon by Carl Rose passed into the language. It appeared in the issue of the *New Yorker* of 8 December 1928 and showed a mother at table saying: 'It's broccoli, dear,' Her pretty little daughter replies: '**I say it's spinach**, and I say the hell with it.'

Herbert Ross, then editor of the magazine, remembered that when White asked his opinion of the caption the writer was clearly uncertain that he had hit on the right idea. 'I looked at the drawing

61

and the caption and said, "Yeh, it seems okay to me," but neither of us cracked a smile.'

The use of 'spinach' for 'nonsense' stems from this, as in the title of *Fashion is Spinach* by Elizabeth Dawes (1933).

Long Hot SUMMER

'It looks as if it will be a **long, hot summer** for the dons of Christ's College, Cambridge, who are once again faced with the tricky business of electing a master' (Lady Olga Maitland, *Sunday Express*, 11 July 1982). This bright phrase had rapidly turned into a journalist's cliché following the 1967 riots in the black ghettos of eighteen US cities, notably Detroit and Newark. In June of that year, the Revd Dr Martin Luther King Jr warned: 'Everyone is worrying about the long hot summer with its threat of riots. We had a long cold winter when little was done about the conditions that create riots.'

The Long Hot Summer had been the title of a 1958 film based on the stories of William Faulkner (using a phrase he had formulated in 1928) and also of a spin-off TV series (1965–6).

TALL, dark and handsome

Partridge hesitantly dates this cliché description of a romantic hero's qualities from women's fiction *c*.1910. Flexner[24] puts it in the late 1920s as a Hollywood term referring to Rudolph Valentino (though he was not particularly tall). Caesar Romero played the lead in the 1941 film called **Tall, Dark and Handsome** which no doubt helped fix the phrase in popular use.

TODAY is the first day

Today is the first day of the rest of your life is a saying that straddles the media. My belief was that it had first appeared as a piece of graffiti in the late 1960s, had then been incorporated in a commercially produced wall-poster (appealing to the hippy mood of the time) and had then been taken up by Madison Avenue. It may well have had a more precise origin, however. Charles Dederich, founder of Synanon anti-heroin centres in California used it as a slogan in *c*.1969. But he may have popularised a saying that was current anyway.

If it's TUESDAY . . .

The title of a 1969 film about a group of American tourists rushing around Europe was **If It's Tuesday, This Must Be Belgium**. It established a phrase which people could use when they were in the midst of some hectic activity, whilst also reflecting on the confused state of many tourists superficially 'doing' the sights without really knowing where they are.

UGANDAN affairs

Since its inception in 1961, the British satirical magazine *Private Eye* has created any number of nicknames for people in the public eye and several distinctive phrases that have caught on with its readership.

Two phrases stand out. The euphemism **tired and emotional** for being drunk arose at the time when George Brown was Labour's Foreign Secretary (1966–8). Following one or two expansive incidents – and mindful that British libel laws make it unwise to suggest that anyone is ever drunk – the *Eye* ran a spoof memo under the headline 'BROWN – FO ACTS'. It had been 'dispatched by the FO to embassies and consulates abroad' and was 'intended as a guide to ambassadors and embassy spokesmen when dealing with the Foreign press.' The document gave French, Italian, German and Russian equivalents for Tired, Overwrought, Expansive, Over-worked, Colourful, and Emotional.

In *Eye* no. 293 (9 March 1973), there appeared a gossip item which launched another euphemism – this time for sexual intercourse:

> I can reveal that the expression 'Talking about Uganda' has acquired a new meaning. I first heard it myself at a fashionable party given recently by media-people Neal and Corinna Ascherson. As I was sipping my Campari on the ground floor I was informed by my charming hostess that I was missing out on a meaningful confrontation upstairs where a former cabinet colleague of President Obote was 'talking about Uganda'.
>
> Eager, as ever, to learn the latest news from the Dark Continent I rushed upstairs to discover the dusky statesman 'talking about Uganda' in a highly compromising manner to vivacious former features editor Mary Kenny . . . I understand that 'Long John' and Miss Kenny both rang up later to ascertain each other's names.

Later, the phrases 'Ugandan practices' or 'Ugandan discussions' or **discussing Ugandan affairs** came to be used more frequently. As always, the idea was not without precedent: in April 1928 Miss Irene Savidge was accused of indulging in something similar with the economist, Sir Leo Chiozza Money, a former junior minister in Lloyd George's government, on a bench in Hyde Park. They were charged with indecent behaviour. In court, Money said he had been advising her on her career and she said: 'We sat down for a while to discuss matters of industrial economics.' The court believed them and they were acquitted. (On a later occasion he did not get away with it.)

Like a VICARAGE tea-party

They may be verging on the cliché, but such critical comparisons can still be fun. One which lingers in my memory is from a *Daily Telegraph* review of Alan Sillitoe's novel *Saturday Night and Sunday Morning* (1958): 'A novel of today, with a freshness and raw fury that makes *Room at the Top* look **like a vicarage tea-party**.' The quote was used on the cover of the paperback edition of the Sillitoe novel.

THE PRESIDENCY

Where the Buck Stops

THE American Presidency, like British Royalty, is always getting quoted – even when it has nothing to say. But unlike British Royalty, it is usually *trying* to say something. By the second half of the century, there was little that an incumbent President said which went unrecorded. Relentless monitoring by the media exposed every kind of remark, both intentional and unintentional. Richard Nixon was not the only president who added to this process by having his private conversations recorded. From a mountain of material, I have chosen these nuggets – presented according to the order in which the presidents held office:

In September of the century's first year, President McKinley was assassinated. Speaking at the Minnesota State Fair a few days before that event, Vice-President Theodore Roosevelt supported the idea of backing negotiations with threats of military force when said: 'There is a homely adage which runs, **"Speak softly and carry a big stick** – you will go far."** If the American nation will speak softly and yet build and keep at a pitch of the highest training a thoroughly efficient navy, the Monroe Doctrine will go far.' (Note that he did not claim the remark to be original.)

Theodore Roosevelt (1858–1919) withdrew from Republican politics after two terms as President and unsuccessfully tried to make a comeback in 1912 as a Progressive ('Bull Moose') candidate. The popular name given to the Progressives stemmed from a remark of Roosevelt's when he was standing as Vice-President in 1900. Writing to Mark Hanna, he said: '**I am as strong as a bull moose** and you can use me to the limit.'

In 1913, Roosevelt was the first to say, 'Every reform movement has a **lunatic fringe**.' Even more use has been made over the years of another of his phrases. Visiting Joel Cheek, perfector of the Maxwell House coffee blend, in 1907, the President had a cup and said it was **Good . . . to the last drop.** This slogan has been in use ever since, despite those who have inquired, 'What's wrong with the last drop, then?' Professors of English have considered the problem and ruled that 'to' can be inclusive and need not mean 'up to but not including'.

Woodrow Wilson (1856–1924) was re-elected for a second term in 1916 by using the slogans **Wilson's Wisdom Wins Without War** and **He Kept Us Out of War**. The latter slogan derived from a speech by Martin H. Glynn (1891–1924), Governor of New York, at the Democratic National Convention in St Louis on 15 June 1916. In 1917, however, Wilson did take the USA into the First World War. His address to Congress on 2 April asking for a declaration of war included the words: '**The world must be safe for democracy**. Its peace must be planted upon trusted foundations of political liberty.' This is commonly rendered as 'the world must be made safe for democracy.' (The words might never have been remembered had not Senator John Sharp Williams of Mississippi started clapping and continued until everyone joined in.) In 1937, James Harvey Robinson commented: 'With supreme irony, the war to "Make the world safe for democracy" ended by leaving democracy more unsafe in the world than at any time since the collapse of the revolutions of 1848.'

After the war, **Back to Normalcy** and **Return to Normalcy with Harding** were slogans effectively used in the Republican campaign which brought Warren G. Harding (1865–1923) to the White House. Both were based on a word extracted from a speech he made in Boston during May 1920: 'America's present need is not heroics but healing, not nostrums but normalcy, not revolution but restoration, not agitation but adjustment, not surgery but serenity, not the dramatic but the dispassionate, not experiment but equipoise, not submergence in internationality but sustainment in triumphant nationality.' Out of such an alliterative bog stuck the word, 'normalcy' – a perfectly good Americanism, though it has been suggested that Harding was actually mispronouncing the word 'normality.' He himself claimed that 'normalcy' was what he had meant to say, having come across it in a dictionary.

Calvin Coolidge (1872–1933) has proved remarkably quotable, despite his nickname 'Silent Cal'. Elected in 1924 with the slogan **Keep Cool with Coolidge** – Will Rogers later added 'And do nothing . . .' – the taciturn President became famous for monosyllabic replies. A story from the twenties has Mrs Coolidge asking him about the subject of a sermon he had heard. 'Sin,' he answered. When prompted to elaborate on the clergyman's theme, Coolidge is said to have replied: **He was against it.** Coolidge later remarked that this story would have been funnier if it had been true.

Many of his sayings are true and memorable, however. **There is no right to strike against the public safety by anybody, anywhere, at any time** comes from a telegram he sent to the President of the American Federation of Labor during the Boston police strike of 1919 when Coolidge was Governor of Massachusetts. **The chief business of the American people is business** has become almost a national motto as 'the business of America is business.' He said it originally to a group of newspaper editors in 1925. Still, myths die hard and when Dorothy Parker was told of Coolidge's death in 1933 she came up with one of her most celebrated quips: **How can they tell?**

'We are challenged with a peacetime choice between the American system of **rugged individualism** and a European philosophy of diametrically opposed doctrines – doctrines of paternalism and state socialism.' So said Herbert Hoover (1874–1964), running for the Presidency in October 1928. Six years later he commented: 'While I can make no claim for having introduced the term "rugged individualism", I should have been proud to have invented it. It has been used by American leaders for over half a century in eulogy of those God-fearing men and women of honesty whose stamina and character and fearless assertion of rights led them to make their own way in life.'

In a less happy moment, Hoover declared: **When a great many people are unable to find work, unemployment results.**

Four times elected President, Franklin D. Roosevelt (1882–1945) may be criticised on the score of his achievements but not on his skills as a communicator. Running for the New York State Senate in

1910, he acquired the salutation **My friends** from Richard Connell who was running for the US Congress at the same time. Abraham Lincoln had also used this form of address on occasions. To the 1932 Democratic Convention which had just nominated him, FDR said:

> I pledge you, I pledge myself to a **New Deal** for the American people. Let us all here assembled constitute ourselves prophets of a new order of competence and of courage. This is more than a political campaign; it is a call to arms. Give me your help, not to win votes alone, but to win in this crusade to restore America to its own people.

The slogan 'New Deal' became the keynote of the election campaign but it was not new to politics. David Lloyd George had talked of a 'New deal for everyone' in 1919, Woodrow Wilson had had a 'New Freedom' slogan, and Teddy Roosevelt talked of a 'Square Deal'. The FDR use was engineered by either Samuel Rosenman or Raymond Moley. 'I had not the slightest idea that it would take hold the way it did,' Rosenman said later, 'nor did the Governor [Roosevelt] when he read and revised what I had written . . . It was simply one of those phrases that catch public fancy and survive.' On the other hand, Moley claimed: 'The expression "new deal" was in the draft I left at Albany with Roosevelt . . . I was not aware that this would be the slogan for the campaign. It was a phrase that would have occurred to almost anyone . . .'

Roosevelt took the presidential oath of office on 4 March 1933 and then delivered his first inaugural address:

> This is pre-eminently the time to speak the truth, the whole truth, frankly and boldly. Nor need we shrink from honestly facing conditions in our country today. This great nation will endure as it has endured, will revive and will prosper. So, first of all, let me assert my firm belief that **the only thing we have to fear is fear itself** – nameless, unreasoning, unjustified terror which paralyses needed efforts to convert retreat into advance.

The classic phrase did not appear in Roosevelt's first draft but appears to have been inserted by him the day before the speech was delivered. A copy of Thoreau's writings was with him at this time containing the line 'Nothing is so much to be feared as fear' but Raymond Moley asserted later that it was Louis Howe who contributed the 'fear' phrase, having picked it up from a newspaper advertisement for a department store. In fact, any number of precedents could be cited – the Duke of Wellington ('the only thing I am afraid of is fear'), Montaigne, Bacon, the Book of Proverbs – but in the end what matters is that Roosevelt had the wit to utter it on this occasion.

Like Churchill, Roosevelt quoted others as well as being quotable himself. In January 1941, before the USA had entered the Second World War, the President sent a letter to the British Prime Minister containing this extract from an 1893 poem by Longfellow (slightly adapted), accompanied by the comment 'I think this verse applies to your people as it does to us':

> Sail on, O Ship of State!
> Sail on, O Union, strong and great!
> Humanity with all its fears,
> With all the hope of future years,
> Is hanging breathless on thy fate!

Churchill responded in a broadcast on 3 May 1941, hinting at future American involvement, by quoting from 'Say Not the Struggle Naught Availeth' by the nineteenth-century poet, Arthur Hugh Clough. 'I have some other lines which are less well known but which seem apt and appropriate to our fortunes tonight, and I believe they will be so judged wherever the English language is spoken or the flag of freedom flies':

> For while the tired waves, vainly breaking,
> Seem here no painful inch to gain,
> Far back, through creeks and inlets making,
> Comes silent, flooding in, the main.
> And not by eastern windows only,
> When daylight comes, comes in the light,
> In front the sun climbs slow, how slowly,
> But westward, look, the land is bright.

Then came Pearl Harbor. 'Yesterday, December 7th 1941, a date which will live in world history, the United States of America was simultaneously and deliberately attacked by naval and air forces of the Empire of Japan' – such would have been Roosevelt's opening sentence when he spoke to Congress the day after if he had stuck to his first draft. Instead, FDR himself substituted **a date which will live in infamy** and put 'suddenly' in place of 'simultaneously'. With such strokes did he make his speech seeking a declaration of war against Japan the more memorable.

Catapulted into the presidency by Roosevelt's death in 1945, Harry S Truman (1884–1972) said to newspapermen: 'Boys, if you ever pray, pray for me now. I don't know whether you fellows ever had a load of hay fall on you, but when they told me yesterday what had happened, **I felt like the moon, the stars, and all the planets had fallen on me.**' Briskly, Truman set about doing the job, his style typified by two mottoes displayed on his Oval office desk. One was taken from Mark Twain – 'Always do right; this will gratify some people and astonish the rest' – the other was apparently his own invention: **The buck stops here.** 'Passing the buck' is a poker players' expression. It refers to a marker that can be passed on by someone who does not wish to deal. Later, Jimmy Carter restored this motto to the Oval office. When ex-President Nixon published his memoirs, people opposed to their sale went round with buttons saying: 'The book stops here.'

Truman's other most famous expression, **If you can't stand the heat, get out of the kitchen**, also appears to be original. 'Some men can make decisions and some cannot,' he wrote in 1960. 'Some men fret and delay under criticism. I used to have a saying that applies here, and I note that some people have picked it up.' *Time* (28 April 1952) reported that Truman gave a down-to-earth reason for his retirement quoting the line and calling it 'a favourite expression of his military jester Major General Harry Vaughan'. It seems likely, however, that on this occasion the President was mischievously fathering his own aphorism on the Major General.

Truman's language was notably salty for the period. His wife had to reprimand him for frequent recourse to 's.o.b's'. In 1951, Truman sacked General Douglas MacArthur from his command of UN forces in Korea for repeatedly criticising the administration's policy of non-confrontation with China. Truman added – lest the General hear of the decision and jump the gun – **The son of a bitch isn't going to resign on me, I want him fired.**

Even so, following the dismissal, Truman had to allow MacArthur a hero's return home. Given the opportunity to address Congress on 19 April 1951, MacArthur wrote his own speech – most of which was seen by Truman in advance. It ended:

I am closing my fifty-two years of military service. When I joined the Army, even before the turn of the century, it was the fulfilment of all my boyish hopes and dreams. The world has turned over many times since I took the oath on the Plain at West Point, and the hopes and dreams have long since vanished. But I still remember the refrain of one of the most popular barrack ballads of that day, which proclaimed, most proudly, that **Old soldiers never die. They just fade away.** And like the old soldier of that ballad, I now close my military career and just fade away – an old soldier who tried to do his duty as God gave him the light to see that duty. Goodbye.

The origins of the ballad quoted by MacArthur lie in a British army parody of the gospel hymn 'Kinds Words Can Never Die' which came out of the First World War. J. Foley copyrighted a version of the parody in 1920. The more usual form of the words is: 'Old soldiers never die/ They simply fade away'. One Representative said after hearing the speech: 'We heard God speak here today, God in the flesh, the voice of God!' Truman called it 'nothing but a bunch of bullshit'.

When the President's daughter, Margaret, gave a vocal recital in Washington she was criticised by Paul Hume in the *Post*: 'She is flat a good deal of the time . . . she cannot sing with anything approaching professional finish . . . she communicates almost nothing of the music she presents.' The President immediately fired off a handwritten note:

> I have just read your lousy review buried in the back pages. You sound like a frustrated old man who never made a success, **an eight-ulcer man on a four-ulcer job and all four ulcers working**. I never met you, but if I do you'll need a new nose and a supporter below. Westbrook Pegler, a guttersnipe, is a gentleman compared to you. You can take that as more of an insult than a reflection on your ancestry.

Subsequently, Truman asserted that he really told Hume he would 'kick his balls in' but the published versions of the letter (of which there was only one copy) do not bear him out, understandably perhaps. Truman worked on the assumption that 'every man in the United States that's got a daughter will be on my side' – and it turned out he was right.

This blast at the press, however, could hardly match Truman's triumphant waving of the *Chicago Daily Tribune* for 2 November 1948 when he had convincingly won re-election against the expectations of the pundits. The headline read **DEWEY DEFEATS TRUMAN**.

The slogan **I Like Ike** began appearing on buttons as early as 1947 when Second World War General Dwight David Eisenhower

(1890–1972) was being spoken of as a possible presidential nominee (initially as a Democrat). The three sharp monosyllables and the effectiveness of the repeated 'i' sound, stemming from Eisenhower's nickname 'Ike', helped create an enduring slogan. In July 1948, Irving Berlin wrote a song called 'They Like Ike' to give support to Eisenhower as a Republican presidential candidate. In the end Dewey won the nomination but by 1950 Berlin had put the song into his musical *Call Me Madam*. The same year, 15,000 people at a rally in Madison Square Gardens were urging Ike to return from his military sojourn in Paris and run in 1952, with the chant 'We Like Ike'. It worked.

During the campaign, Eisenhower promised '**I shall go to Korea** and try to end the war.' Between his election and inauguration, he did make a three-day visit to Korea as promised but had no discernible effect on the negotiations towards a truce.

Eisenhower's presidency was characterised by dull speech-making and convoluted extempore remarks. The only phrase for which he is remembered, if at all, occurred in his farewell address, delivered on 17 January 1961:

> This conjunction of an immense military establishment and a large arms industry is new in the American experience . . . In the councils of government, **we must guard against the acquisition of unwarranted influence**, whether sought or unsought, **by the military-industrial complex.** The potential for the disastrous rise of misplaced power exists and will persist.

The political scientist Malcolm Moos helped formulate this passage. Harry Truman, never able to say anything good about his successor, commented: 'Yes, I believe he did say something like that. I think somebody must have written it for him, and I'm not sure he understood what he was saying. But it's true . . .'

Three days after Eisenhower's farewell, John F. Kennedy's inaugural ushered in a brief period when the presidency aspired to excellence in the expression of its goals and managed to do many things with a certain style and wit. Apart from being a spontaneously witty man himself, Kennedy (1917–63) knew how to make use of the verbal powers of others. Long before running for the White House he had begun to carry round a stock of quotations in notebooks and in his head. Indeed, as a Senator, he tended to overwhelm his listeners with erudition. This tendency showed, however, a fondness for fine phrases and a genuine interest in communication.

President Theodore Roosevelt: 'Speak
softly and carry a big stick.'

President Calvin Coolidge:
'. . . He was against it.'

President Franklin D. Roosevelt:
'The only thing we have to fear is
fear itself.'

President Harry S Truman: 'The buck stops here.'

President John F. Kennedy: 'Let the word go forth from this time and place . . .'

President Lyndon B. Johnson, *top*: 'I shall not seek, and I will not accept . . .'

Richard M. Nixon, *centre*, (with family and 'Checkers'): 'Regardless of what they say about it, we are going to keep it.'

Ronald Reagan, *left*, (with Ann Sheridan) in *King's Row*: 'Randy – where's the rest of me?'

Marlon Brando in *The Godfather*: 'An offer he can't refuse.'

Kennedy's senate speeches benefited from thorough research by his staff. One of these was Theodore C. Sorensen who stayed with him till the end. In his book *Kennedy*,[87] Sorensen described in detail the composition of the inaugural speech and others that he worked on. In 1960, he had had a hand in coining the slogan for the forthcoming administration. Accepting the Democratic nomination in the Los Angeles Coliseum, Kennedy ringingly declared:

We stand today on the edge of a New Frontier – the frontier of the 1960s, a frontier of unknown opportunities and perils, a frontier of unfulfilled hopes and threats. Woodrow Wilson's New Freedom promised our nation a new political and economic framework; Franklin Roosevelt's New Deal promised security and succour to those in need. But the New Frontier of which I speak is not a set of promises – it is a set of challenges. It sums up not what I intend to offer the American people, but what I intend to ask of them.

Sorensen prepared this acceptance speech and claimed that the concept of the New Frontier – and the term itself – were new: 'I know of no outsider who suggested that expression, although the theme of the Frontier was contained in more than one draft.' A number of possible sources have been suggested but the likelihood is that Sorensen drew in a phrase that was in the air anyway at that time.

The last sentence of the speech quoted above is a clear pre-echo of a theme in the inaugural. Before looking in detail at some of the by now famous phrases in that speech, it is surely worth printing in full. Although at the time it seemed a touch self-consciously well-wrought and would-be Churchillian, in retrospect the speech stands out as one of the century's noblest pieces of rhetoric:

We observe today not a victory of party but a celebration of freedom, symbolising an end as well as a beginning, signifying renewal as well as change. For I have sworn before you and Almighty God the same solemn oath our forebears prescribed nearly a century and three-quarters ago.

The world is very different now. For man holds in his mortal hands the power to abolish all forms of human poverty and all forms of human life. And yet the same revolutionary beliefs for which our forebears fought are still at issue around the globe, the belief that the rights of man come not from the generosity of the state but from the hand of God.

We dare not forget today that we are the heirs of that first

73

revolution. **Let the word go forth from this time and place, to friend and foe alike, that the torch has been passed to a new generation of Americans, born in this century, tempered by war, disciplined by a hard and bitter peace, proud of our ancient heritage, and unwilling to witness or permit the slow undoing of those human rights to which this nation has always been committed, and to which we are committed today at home and around the world.**

Let every nation know, whether it wishes us well or ill, that we shall pay any price, bear any burden, meet any hardship, support any friend, oppose any foe to assure the survival and the success of liberty.

This much we pledge – and more.

To those old allies whose cultural and spiritual origins we share, we pledge the loyalty of faithful friends. United, there is little we cannot do in a host of co-operative ventures. Divided, there is little we can do, for we dare not meet a powerful challenge at odds and split asunder.

To those new states whom we welcome to the ranks of the free, we pledge our word that one form of colonial control shall not have passed away merely to be replaced by a far more iron tyranny. We shall not always expect to find them supporting our view. But we shall always hope to find them strongly supporting their own freedom, and to remember that, in the past, those who foolishly sought power by riding the back of the tiger ended up inside.

To those people in the huts and villages of half the globe struggling to break the bonds of mass misery, we pledge our best efforts to help them help themselves, for whatever period is required, not because the Communists may be doing it, not because we seek their votes, but because it is right. If a free society cannot help the many who are poor, it cannot save the few who are rich.

To our sister republics south of our border, we offer a special pledge: to convert our good words into good deeds, in a new **alliance for progress**, to assist free men and free governments in casting off the chains of poverty. But this peaceful revolution of hope cannot become the prey of hostile powers. Let all our neighbours know that we shall join with them to oppose aggression or subversion anywhere in the Americas. And let every other power know that this hemisphere intends to remain the master of its own house.

To that world assembly of sovereign states, the United Nations, our last best hope in an age where the instruments of war have far outpaced the instruments of peace, we renew our pledge of support: to prevent it from becoming merely a forum for invective, to strengthen its shield of the new and the weak, and to enlarge the area in which its writ may run.

Finally, to those nations who would make themselves our adversary, we offer not a pledge but a request: that both sides begin anew the quest for peace, before the dark powers of destruction unleashed by science engulf all humanity in planned or accidental self-destruction.

We dare not tempt them with weakness. For only when our arms are sufficient beyond doubt can we be certain beyond doubt that they will never be employed.

But neither can two great and powerful groups of nations take comfort from our present course – both sides overburdened by the cost of modern weapons, both rightly alarmed by the steady spread of the deadly atom, yet both racing to alter that uncertain balance of terror that stays the hand of mankind's final war.

So let us begin anew, remembering on both sides that civility is not a sign of weakness, and sincerity is always subject to proof. **Let us never negotiate out of fear, but let us never fear to negotiate.**

Let both sides explore what problems unite us instead of belabouring those problems which divide us.

Let both sides, for the first time, formulate serious and precise proposals for the inspection and control of arms, and bring the absolute power to destroy other nations under the absolute control of all nations.

Let both sides seek to invoke the wonders of science instead of its terrors. Together let us explore the stars, conquer the deserts, eradicate disease, tap the ocean depths and encourage the arts and commerce.

Let both sides unite to heed in all corners of the earth the command of Isaiah to 'undo the heavy burdens . . . [and] let the oppressed go free.'

And if a beachhead of co-operation may push back the jungle of suspicion, let both sides join in creating a new endeavour, not a new balance of power, but a new world of law, where the strong are just and the weak secure and the peace preserved.

All this will not be finished in the first one hundred days. Nor will it be finished in the first one thousand days, nor in the life of this Administration, nor even perhaps in our lifetime on this planet. But let us begin.

In your hands, my fellow citizens, more than mine, will rest the final success or failure of our course. Since this country was founded, each generation of Americans has been summoned to give testimony to its national loyalty. The graves of young Americans who answered the call to service surround the globe.

Now the trumpet summons us again – not as a call to bear arms, though arms we need; not as a call to battle, though embattled we are; but a call to bear the burden of a long twilight struggle, year in and year out, 'rejoicing in hope, patient in tribulation' a struggle against the common enemies of man: tyranny, poverty, disease and war itself.

Can we forge against these enemies a grand and global alliance, North and South, East and West, that can assure a more fruitful life for all mankind? Will you join in that historic effort?

In the long history of the world, only a few generations have been granted the role of defending freedom in its hour of maximum danger. I do not shrink from this responsibility; I welcome it. I do not believe that any of us would exchange places with any other people or any other generation. The energy, the faith, the devotion which we bring to this endeavour will light our country and all who serve it, and the glow from the fire that can truly light the world.

And so, my fellow Americans, ask not what your country can do for you; ask what you can do for your country.

My fellow citizens of the world, ask not what America will do for you, but what together we can do for the freedom of man.

Finally, whether you are citizens of America or citizens of the world, ask of us here the same high standards of strength and sacrifice which we ask of you. With a good conscience our only sure reward, with history the final judge of our deeds, let us go forth to lead the land we love, asking His blessing and His help, but knowing that here on earth God's work must truly be our own.

As part of the preparation for this speech, Kennedy told Sorensen to read all the previous inaugural addresses (hardly an inspiring task) and suggestions were solicited from the likes of Adlai Stevenson, John Kenneth Galbraith, and Billy Graham. A good deal of unsolicited material also came in. Nevertheless, the speech was still Kennedy's. He pulled all the various strands together and laid down certain basic conditions which contributed to its success: it was to be as short as possible, to deal almost exclusively with foreign affairs, to leave out the pronoun 'I', and to emulate Lincoln's Gettysburg address by using one-syllable words wherever possible. A number of the phrases in the speech had been used by Kennedy before. The 'Ask not . . .' idea, for example, had been used three times during the election. In a TV address during September 1960, Kennedy had said: 'We do not campaign stressing what our country is going to do for us as a people. We stress what we can do for the country, all of us.'

Drafting did not begin until a week before delivery and Sorensen said that 'no Kennedy speech ever underwent so many drafts . . . Kenneth Galbraith suggested "co-operative ventures" with our allies in place of "joint ventures", which sounded like a mining partnership. Dean Rusk suggested that the other peoples of the world be challenged to ask "what together we can do for freedom" instead of "what you can do for freedom". Walter Lippmann suggested that references to the Communist bloc be changed from "enemy" to "adversary".'

The 43-year-old President delivered his speech in the frosty air of Washington on 20 January 1961. His voice was a trifle flat and on one note. For a moment, though, it was possible to have hope. Subsequently, the balanced sentences and stabbing words have often been quoted and pored over. Arthur M. Schlesinger, another Kennedy aide, who took the title of his memoir *A Thousand Days*[84] from the speech, traced JFK's interest in the 'Ask not' theme back to a notebook of the President's dating from 1945 which included the Rousseau quotation: 'As soon as any man says of the affairs of state, What does it matter to me? The state may be given up as lost.' Other antecedents that have been cited include the Mayor of Haverhill at the funeral of John Greenleaf Whittier: 'Here may we be reminded that man is most honoured, not by that which a city may do for him, but by that which he has done for the city.' Oliver Wendell Holmes's Memorial Day Address 1884 contains the words: 'It is now the moment when by common consent we pause to become conscious of our national life and to rejoice in it, to recall what our country has done for each of us, and to ask ourselves what we can do for our country in return.' Warren G. Harding said at the Republican National Convention in Chicago, 1916: 'We must have a citizenship less concerned about what the government can do for it and more anxious about what it can do for the nation.' Kennedy's inverted use of 'Ask not' made what was obviously not a new concept eminently memorable.

The sentence beginning 'Let every nation . . .' was later inscribed on the Kennedy memorial at Runnymede. The contrapuntal form of words, as in 'Let us never negotiate out of fear, but let us never fear to negotiate,' became a hallmark of Kennedy speech-making. The

'Alliance for Progress', used as the name for Kennedy's Latin American policy, had first been mentioned by him in October 1960. Speechwriter Richard Goodwin said he took it from the title of a Spanish–American magazine, *Alianza*. **Alianza para Progreso** was officially launched in March 1961.

Quite the most bizarre use to which the speech has been put was on an EP disc called 'Sing Along with JFK' (1963). George Atkins and Hank Levine edited clips from Kennedy's actual speech into musical compositions with titles like the 'Ask Not Waltz', the 'Alliance for Progress Bossa Nova', and the 'Let Us Begin Beguine'.

During his Presidency, three key phrases of an informal kind became associated with the Kennedy approach to life. **Forgive but never forget** was one attributed to the late President by Sorensen in a 1968 television interview. **Grace under pressure** – reminiscent of the Latin tag 'Fortiter in re, suaviter in modo' and used as a definition of 'guts' – was acquired from Ernest Hemingway (in the *New Yorker*, 1929) and used by Kennedy at the start of his book *Profiles of Courage*.

Halfway through his presidency Kennedy told a news conference, on the subject of reservists for the armed forces:

> There is always inequity in life. Some men are killed in a war, and some men are wounded, and some men never leave the country . . . It's very hard in military life or in personal life to assure complete equality. **Life is unfair.** Some people are sick and others are well.

Mort Sahl added: 'He said it often and always wistfully, recognising that America was full of people who weren't forty-two and President.'

JFK's ability to select the apt phrase to enliven his speeches can be illustrated any number of times. Following the Bay of Pigs disaster in April 1961, he said: 'There's an old saying that **victory has a hundred fathers but defeat is an orphan.**' The earliest example of this observation appears in the diaries of Count Ciano, Mussolini's foreign minister, in 1942.

Then, in the final months before he was assassinated, Kennedy came up with a string of memorable sayings. He paid tribute to the eloquence of Winston Churchill when the old man was granted honorary citizenship of the United States (9 April 1963). **He mobilised the English language and sent it into battle**, said Kennedy, but the phrase was not his own. In a broadcast to mark Churchill's eightieth birthday in 1954, Edward R. Murrow had said:

'He mobilised the English language and sent it into battle to steady his fellow countrymen and hearten those Europeans upon whom the long dark night of tyranny had descended.'

On 26 July 1963: **'Yesterday, a shaft of light cut into the darkness** . . . For the first time, an agreement has been reached on bringing the forces of nuclear destruction under international control' – the nuclear Test Ban Treaty had been initialled by the USA, the USSR and the UK.

A month to the day before this, Kennedy had proclaimed a stirring slogan in West Berlin. He had rejected State Department drafts for a speech to be delivered outside the City Hall and found something better of his own to say. Kennedy faced an enormous and enthusiastic crowd and came up with a memorable call for freedom. Schlesinger recorded that Kennedy was at first exhilarated, then disturbed by the crowd's hysterical reactions. The President remarked that if he had said 'March to the Wall – tear it down', his listeners would have marched. What he said was this:

Two thousand years ago the proudest boast was 'Civis Romanus sum'. Today, in the world of freedom, the proudest boast is **Ich bin ein Berliner.**

There are many people in the world who really don't understand, or say they don't, what is the great issue between the free world and the Communist world. Let them come to Berlin. There are some who say that Communism is the wave of the future. Let them come to Berlin . . . And there are even a few who say that it is true that Communism is an evil system, but it permits us to make economic progress. Lasst sie nach Berlin kommen.

Freedom has many difficulties and democracy is not perfect, but we have never had to put up a wall to keep our people in . . .

We . . . look forward to that day when this city will be joined as one – and this country, and this great continent of Europe – in a peaceful and hopeful globe. When that day finally comes, as it will, the people of West Berlin can take sober satisfaction in the fact that they were in the front lines for almost two decades.

All free men, wherever they may live, are citizens of Berlin, and, therefore, as a free man, I take pride in the words 'Ich bin ein Berliner'.

Ben Bradlee[8] noted that Kennedy had to spend 'the better part of an hour' with Frederick Vreeland and his wife before he could manage to pronounce the German phrases. It had been worth it.

Flying away from the country, Sorensen remembered, the President was glowing at the reception he had received. Weary but happy, he said: 'We'll never have another day like this one as long as we live.'

Catapulted into the presidency by Kennedy's murder, Lyndon B. Johnson (1908–73) spoke movingly to Congress on 27 November 1963: **All I have, I would have given gladly not to be standing here today.** The following year he began to establish his own policies under the slogan of the **Great Society**, a name suggested by Richard N. Goodwin. After a certain tentative use in over a dozen speeches, the phrase was first elevated to capital letters in a speech before the University of Michigan at Ann Arbor in May 1964: 'In your time we have the opportunity to move not only toward the rich society and the powerful society but upward to the Great Society.'

According to Hugh Sidey,[86] Goodwin stumbled on the phrase one midnight in early March 1964. He was the 32-year-old Secretary General of the International Peace Corps Secretariat and, at that stage, was writing for Johnson on an occasional basis. Even when Goodwin was taken on full-time, LBJ was reluctant to admit that he had a hand in the President's speeches. Goodwin, an ex-Kennedy aide, gave Johnson a touch of the Kennedy eloquence he sorely needed but LBJ told Sidey on one occasion: 'To the best of my knowledge, Goodwin has not written a single speech for me. As far as I know, he had nothing to do with the Ann Arbor speech.' A few weeks later, however, he was to be heard boasting: 'Goodwin can write a better speech than Sorensen and in one fifth the time.' From such peculiar behaviour, it is not hard to see how LBJ developed what became known as a credibility problem.

All the Way with LBJ was a Johnson slogan in the election that gave him a landslide victory over the Republican challenger, Barry M. Goldwater, in November 1964. It had first been used when Johnson was seeking the presidential nomination that eventually went to Kennedy in 1960. 'All through the fall and winter of 1959 and 1960,' wrote Theodore White, 'the noisemakers of the Johnson campaign . . . chanted "All the Way with LBJ" across the South and Far West, instantly identifiable by their Texan garb, their ten-gallon hats (and, said their enemies, the cowflap on their boots.)'

Indeed, LBJ will be remembered chiefly for the Southern earthiness of speech that he brought to his Administration. John Kenneth Galbraith recalled the President asking: 'Did y'ever think, Ken, that making a speech on ee-conomics is a lot like pissing down your leg? It seems hot to you, but it never does to anyone else.' Galbraith took pains to point out that Johnson did not, as often reported, say of Gerald Ford that he could not walk and chew gum at the same time. What he said was: 'That Gerald Ford . . . **he can't fart and chew gum at the same time.**'

Other examples of Johnson's barnyard phraseology include **I've got his pecker in my pocket** – much used when he was Senate Majority leader – and 'I don't want loyalty . . . I want *loyalty* . . . I want him to kiss my ass in Macy's window at high noon and tell me it smells like roses.' On deciding not to get rid of FBI director, J. Edgar Hoover, he said: 'It's probably better to have him inside the tent pissing out, than outside pissing in.'

No doubt this sort of talk in private was designed to cover up insecurity and to enhance Johnson's macho image, but he found no equivalent in his public utterances in the way that Harry Truman did. LBJ enjoined his speechwriters to read Churchill and he took a line from Isaiah 1.18 – **Come now, [and] let us reason together** – as his watchword, but he continued to browbeat his opponents and to grab them by the lapels. The image that he projected in his speeches was not the same LBJ as in private conversations and was not convincing.

Johnson inspired a memorable compliment, albeit from one of his flunkeys. Jack Valenti (*b*.1921), later President of the Motion Picture Association of America, was head of LBJ's speechwriting staff and tried to portray the President as a wonderful human being. Speaking to the Advertising Federation of America in Boston, Valenti said in June 1965: '**I sleep each night a little better**, a little more confidently, **because Lyndon Johnson is my President**. For I know he lives and thinks and works to make sure that for all America and, indeed, the growing body of the free world, the morning shall always come.'

Unable to cope with the Vietnam War, Johnson surprised everybody by announcing that he would not run in the 1968 election. On Sunday night 31 March he went on television to call a partial bombing halt over North Vietnam but even an hour before the broadcast he did not know whether he would use the extra portion about his retirement. Those who were in on the secret were also unsure until he actually said it, that he would go:

It is true that a house divided against itself cannot stand. There is a division in the American house now and, believing this as I do, I have concluded that I should not permit the Presidency to become involved in the particular divisions that are developing in this political year. Accordingly, **I shall not seek, and I will not accept, the nomination of my party for another term as your President**.

81

Apart from the biblical reference in 'a house divided' (St Mark 3:25 – which perhaps had come to Johnson by way of an Abraham Lincoln speech in 1858), there is also an echo of General Sherman's words to the Republican National convention in 1884: 'I will not accept if nominated and will not serve if elected.'

As long ago as 1950, Richard M. Nixon (*b*.1913) was dubbed 'Tricky Dicky' by Helen Gahagan Douglas, his opponent in a California election. By 1952, the joke question **Would you buy a used car from this man?** had begun to circulate (it has also been attributed to Mort Sahl). On 23 September, 1952, Nixon was having to appear on TV to rebut charges that he had accepted a 'secret fund' from wealthy California businessmen: 'I come before you tonight as a candidate for the Vice-Presidency and as a man whose honesty and integrity has been questioned.' (He stumbled over the word 'integrity'.) He denied that any of the money had been put to his personal use. Every penny had gone on campaign expenses. He then went on to throw dust in the eyes of the viewers:

> One other thing I probably should tell you – because if I don't they will probably be saying this about me, too. We did get something, a gift, after the nomination. A man down in Texas heard Pat on the radio mention the fact that our two youngsters would like to have a dog and, believe it or not, the day before we left on this campaign trip we got a message from Union Station in Baltimore, saying they had a package for us. We went down to get it. You know what it was? It was a little cocker spaniel dog – in a crate that he'd sent all the way from Texas – black and white, spotted, and our little girl Tricia, the six-year-old, named it Checkers. And you know, the kids, like all kids, loved the dog, and I just want to say this, right now, that **regardless of what they say about it, we are going to keep it**.

No matter that the problem was not the dog but the 'secret fund'. The so-called 'Checkers' speech saved the day for Nixon. Republican headquarters received 300,000 messages of support. He went on to become Eisenhower's Vice-President but lost when he ran against Kennedy for the Presidency in 1960. He also lost when he ran for the California Governorship against Edmund G. ('Pat') Brown on 5 November 1962. He was reluctant to appear and concede defeat before newsmen, feeling that they had given him a tough time during the campaign. But he did, and bade them what turned out to be a temporary farewell:

I leave you gentlemen now and you will now write it. You will interpret it. That's you're right. But as I leave you I want you to know – just think how much you're going to be missing. **You won't have Nixon to kick around any more** because, gentlemen, this is my last press conference . . . I hope that what I have said today will at least make television, radio and the press first recognise the great responsibility they have to report all the news and, second, recognise that they have a right and a responsibility, if they're against a candidate to give him the shaft, but also recognise if they give him the shaft, put one lonely reporter on the campaign who will report what the candidate says now and then. Thank you gentlemen, and good day.

President Kennedy's comment was that Nixon must have been 'mentally unsound to make this statement. Nobody could talk like that and be normal.' In 1982, John Erlichman attributed the Nixon performance to a 'terrible hangover'.

Eventually elected President in 1968, Nixon's communication skills scarcely improved. He talked in the verbal equivalent of Muzak and, given the opportunity for using a well-turned phrase, he always ducked it. Speaking, at his own suggestion, to the first men on the moon he said: 'Hello, Neil and Buzz, I am talking to you by telephone from the Oval Room at the White House. **And this certainly has to be the most historic phone call ever made.**' Three days later on 24 July 1969, Nixon greeted them aboard the USS *Hornet* with the words: **This is the greatest week in the history of the world since the Creation.** Billy Graham told him shortly afterwards.: 'Mr President, I know exactly how you felt, and I understand exactly what you meant, but, even so, I think you may have been a little excessive.'

By 3 November 1969, Nixon was still trying to extricate the US from Vietnam and gave a TV address designed to show it would be wrong to end the war on less than honourable terms or to be swayed by anti-war demonstrations. The previous month a 'peace moratorium' had been organised culminating in a march on Washington. Working on the speech throughout the night before delivery, at about 4 am he wrote some paragraphs calling for the support of a particular section of American opinion:

If a vocal minority, however fervent its cause, prevails over reason and the will of the majority, this Nation has no future as a free society . . . I have chosen a plan for peace. I believe it will succeed. If it does succeed, what the critics say now won't matter.

83

If it does not succeed, anything I say then won't matter . . . And so tonight – to you, the **great silent majority of my fellow Americans** – I ask for your support.

The notion of a large unheard body of opinion – sometimes called the 'silent centre' – was not new but Nixon's appeal ushered in a period of persecution of the 'vocal minority' and, as a result of unfavourable discussion of the speech on TV and in the press, of media-bashing, too. Ironically, the phrase 'silent majority' was used in the nineteenth century to describe the dead. On his way out in 1884, Lord Houghton quipped: 'Yes, I am going to join the Majority and you know I have always preferred Minorities.'

Nixon swept on to an enormous victory in the 1972 election. He never said **I have a secret plan to end the war** – as was supposed by some – but a strong feeling prevailed that the end of the Vietnam conflict was in sight. In the light of this victory, it is ironic that excessive zeal among some of those charged with ensuring the president's re-election eventually led to his downfall. Their efforts were totally unnecessary, quite apart from being underhand and bungled.

The whole tone of the Watergate operation was set by Nixon. From the transcripts of recordings he himself had ordered to be made of his day-to-day conversations it was possible to learn that the holder of tremendous office, indeed a Head of State, said things like: 'I don't give a shit what happens. **I want you all to stonewall it**, let them plead the Fifth amendment, cover-up or anything else, if it'll save it, save the plan' (22 March 1973). It was like hearing a sleazy racketeer at work.

Then, as he tried to extricate himself from the mire, his language was not capable of any dignity and relied upon corn and cliché. **There will be no whitewash in the White House,** he said on 17 April 1973. On 18 November that year, facing separate charges of tax avoidance, he told a press conference:

I made my mistakes, but in all of my years of public life, I have never profited, never profited from public service – I have earned every cent. And in all of my years of public life, I have never obstructed justice. And I think, too, that I could say that in my years of public life, that I welcome this kind of examination, because people have got to know whether or not their President is a crook. Well, **I am not a crook**. I have earned everything I have got.

Even in his farewell speech to the Cabinet and White House staff – a rambling, maudlin performance on 9 August 1974 – he was unable to resist an inept reference to 'plumbers', a code word for those who had broken into the Watergate building for espionage purposes and started off the whole tawdry affair:

> [People] get the impression that everybody is here for the purpose of feathering his nest . . . Not in this Administration: not one single man or woman. And I say to them. There are many fine careers. **This country needs** good farmers, good businessmen, **good plumbers,** good carpenters . . .

On the other hand, Nixon's unprecedented act of resignation, executed earlier that day, was matter-of-fact to the point of abruptness. He simply signed a letter to Secretary of State Henry Kissinger which stated: 'I hereby resign the Office of the President of the United States.'

Gerald R. Ford (*b*.1913) had been lined up the previous year to assume the presidency. When Nixon's Vice-President, Spiro Agnew, had to step down for accepting back-handers earlier in his career, Ford was brought in as a 'Mr Clean'. Taking the vice-presidential oath of office on 6 December, 1973 he stated:

> Together, we have made history here today. For the first time, we have carried out the command of the 25th Amendment. In exactly eight weeks, we have demonstrated to the world that our great Republic stands solid, stands strong upon the bedrock of the Constitution. **I am a Ford, not a Lincoln**. My addresses will never be as eloquent as Mr Lincoln's. But I will do my very best to equal his brevity and his plain speaking.

When he became President (9 August 1974), Ford continued the plain-speaking theme:

> I assume the Presidency under extraordinary circumstances never before experienced by Americans. This is an hour of history that troubles our minds and hurts our hearts. Therefore, I feel it is my first duty to make an unprecedented compact with my country-men. Not an inaugural address, not a fireside chat, not a campaign speech, just a little straight talk among friends . . . I believe that **truth is the glue that holds government together**, not only our government but civilisation itself. That bond, though strained, is

85

unbroken at home and abroad . . . My fellow Americans, **our long national nightmare is over**. Our Constitution works. Our great Republic is a government of laws and not of men. Here, the people rule . . .

Despite Ford's attempts at simple eloquence – his speechwriter was Robert Hartmann – he was best known for his verbal (as well as physical) ineptitude. He did actually say: 'If Lincoln were alive today, he'd roll over in his grave.' Proposing a toast to the Egyptian leader, Anwar Sadat, in December 1975, he said: 'To the great people and the Government of Israel . . . excuse me, of Egypt.' Saying he was a great fan of baseball, he added: 'I watch a lot of games on the radio. Er, I mean television.' But the clanger that finally scuppered his chances of a further term occurred in the 1976 television debates with his challenger, Jimmy Carter: **There is no Soviet domination of Eastern Europe and there never will be under a Ford administration.** Pressed to elaborate on this surprising view, he said: 'I don't believe . . . Romanians consider themselves dominated by the Soviet Union. I don't believe that the Poles consider themselves dominated by the Soviet Union. Each of those countries is independent, autonomous. It has its own territorial integrity. And the United States does not concede that those countries are under the domination of the Soviet Union.' After a couple of clarifying statements, he finally admitted: 'I was perhaps not as precise as I should have been.'

My name is Jimmy Carter and I'm running for President became a political rallying cry as James Earl Carter (*b*.1924) came from nowhere to challenge Ford in 1976. **Jimmy who?** was the initial response. His campaign slogan, used as the title of a book and a song, was **Why not the best?** and stemmed from an interview Carter had had with Admiral Hyman Rickover when applying to join the nuclear submarine programme in 1948. 'Did you do your best [at Naval Academy]?' Rickover asked him. 'No, sir, I didn't *always* do my best,' said Carter. Rickover stared at him for a moment and then said: 'Why not?'

In *Playboy* for November 1976, the month of his election, Carter attempted to show that he was fallible despite his holier-than-thou image. **I've looked on a lot of women with lust,** he said. **I've committed adultery in my heart many times. God recognises I will do this and forgives me.** The American electorate, perceiving a useful working relationship with the Almighty, duly elected Carter.

On a visit to West Germany in July 1978, he resisted a suggestion (allegedly from his aide, Gerald Rafshoon) that he should emulate John Kennedy's 'Ich bin ein Berliner' by declaring in Frankfurt 'Ich bin ein Frankfurter'. (In fact, some Germans had even been amused by Kennedy's ringing phrase – a 'berliner' is the name of a small fruitcake.) In December 1978 there were red faces anyway when an inadequate American interpreter on Carter's visit to Warsaw translated the President's words 'I have come to learn your opinions and understand your desires for the future' as **I desire the Poles carnally.**

As re-election time approached, Carter, like his predecessor, became more gaffe-prone. Accepting his party's nomination at the August 1980 convention in New York, Carter sought to evoke some of the Great Democrats of the past, like Hubert H. Humphrey, who had not made it to the White House. He mentioned a 'Great President who might have been – Hubert Horatio Hornblower'.

It is odd that as the century moved on, Presidents became more famous for what they did not mean to say than for their studied utterances. The latter may have been watered down in any case by the tendency to rely on committees of speechwriters and by the sheer amount of coverage afforded by the media. It became harder for a gaffe to blush unheard. Ronald Reagan (*b.*1911), as one would expect of a former actor, was outstanding at performing a set speech but often incomprehensible without a script.

When he first entered politics and it was announced he would run for the California governorship, Jack Warner, the film producer, is supposed to have said: 'All wrong – **Jimmy Stewart for Governor, Reagan for best friend**.' Indeed, it was never possible to forget Reagan's Hollywood career. On the campaign trail, his supporters used the slogan **Win this one for the Gipper** – a reference to a part he had played in *Knute Rockne – All-American* (1940). George Gipp was a real-life football star who died young. At half-time in a 1928 army game, Rockne recalled something Gipp had said to him: 'Rock, someday when things look real tough for Notre Dame, ask the boys to go out there and win one for me.'

Reagan's early autobiography was entitled *Where's the Rest of Me?* from a line in *King's Row* (1941). Waking up to discover that both his legs have been amputated by a sadistic doctor, Drake McHugh (Reagan) calls out to his girlfriend, Randy Monaghan (Ann Sheridan): **Randy – where's the rest of me?**

As President, Reagan continued to seem happier repeating other people's lines than minting his own. His inaugural in January 1981 contained allusions to Kennedy, Carter and Churchill. Churchill became something of an obsession. Addressing both Houses of Parliament at Westminster in June 1982, Reagan quoted him half a dozen times.

More excusably, after the attempt on his life on 30 March 1981, Reagan rattled out a series of one-liners and quotations to the admiration of all. To his wife, Nancy, he explained 'Honey – I forgot to duck' (Jack Dempsey). In a written note, coming out of an anaesthetic: 'All in all, I'd rather be in Philadelphia' (W. C. Fields). 'There's no more exhilarating feeling than being shot at without result' (Churchill again).

With Reagan up and about once more, the ramblings continued. On a visit to Brazil in December 1982, he proposed a toast: 'Now, would you join me in a toast to President Figueiredo, to the people of Bolivia – no, that's where I'm *going* – to the people of Brazil, and to the dream of democracy and peace here in the Western Hemisphere.' (In fact, he wasn't going to Bolivia either, but to Colombia.)

Presidential speech had reached an uninspiring low. It was a long way from FDR, JFK and – yes – Winston S. Churchill.

LITERATURE

Phrasal Footnotes

CLINGING steadfastly to the criterion expressed in the preface – that this book concerns itself with twentieth-century sayings about which there is something more to be said – means that literature is little represented because, on the whole, novels, poems and plays speak for themselves. However, here are one or two marginal comments or footnotes:

All animals are equal

George Orwell (1903–50) created two notable slogans. In *Animal Farm*, his commentary on the totalitarian excesses of communism (1945) he coined the much-quoted commandment: **All animals are equal, but some are more equal than others.** While not suggesting that Orwell in any way cribbed the idea, I think it is interesting to note an earlier version. Hesketh Pearson reported in his biography of the actor/manager Sir Herbert Beerbohm Tree that Tree wished to insert one of his own epigrams in a play by Stephen Phillips called *Nero*, produced in 1906. It was: 'All men are equal – except myself.'

A rather closer source of inspiration may be found for **Big Brother is Watching You** from *Nineteen Eighty-Four* (1949) – a prophetic novel envisaging a dictatorial state in which every citizen is regimented and observed by a spying TV set in his home. 'Big Brother is Watching You' became a catchphrase, especially following the BBC TV dramatisation of the novel in 1954 (which caused a sensation).

Aspects of the Ministry of Truth in the novel were derived not only from Orwell's knowledge of the BBC but also from his first wife Eileen's work at the Ministry of Food, preparing for 'Kitchen Front' broadcasts during the Second World War, *c.*1942–4. One campaign used the slogan: 'Potatoes are Good for You' and was so successful that it had to be followed by 'Potatoes are Fattening.'

An offer he couldn't refuse

In 1969, Mario Puzo (*b.*1920) published his novel about the Mafia called *The Godfather*. It gave to the language a new expression. Johnny Fontane, a singer, desperately wants a part in a movie and goes to see his godfather, Don Corleone, seeking help. All the contracts have been signed and there is no chance of the studio chief changing his mind. Still, the godfather promises Fontane he will get him the part. As he explains: 'He's a businessman. **I'll make him an offer he can't refuse**.'

In the 1971 film this exchange was turned into the following dialogue: 'In a month from now this Hollywood big shot's going to give you what you want.' 'Too late, they start shooting in a week.' 'I'm going to make him an offer he can't refuse.'

In *The Godfather Papers*,[66] however, Puzo pointed out what he thought was the most quoted line from the novel: 'A lawyer with his briefcase can steal more than a thousand men with guns.' 'I've had people in France, Germany, and Denmark quote that line to me with the utmost glee. And some of them are lawyers.' Puzo mentioned this to the head of the studio, the producer, director and everyone on the film. But it is not in the film. Perhaps he made the wrong offer.

A rose is a rose

Ogden Nash wrote:

> The fault I'm sure is solely mine,
> But I cannot root for Gertrude Stein.
> For Gertrude Stein I cannot root;
> I cannot blow a single toot.

There was no need to apologise. The poem 'Sacred Emily' by Gertrude Stein (1874–1946) is well-nigh impenetrable to the average reader but somehow it has managed to give a format phrase to the language. If something is incapable of explanation, one says, for example, 'a cloud is a cloud is a cloud'. What Stein wrote, however, is frequently misunderstood. She did not say 'A rose is a rose is a rose', as she might well have done, but **Rose is a rose is a rose is a rose** (i.e. no indefinite article at the start and three not two repetitions). The Rose in question was not a flower but an allusion to the English painter, Sir Francis Rose 'whom she and I regarded,' wrote Constantine Fitzgibbon, 'as the peer of Matisse and Picasso, and whose paintings – or at least painting – hung in her Paris drawing-room while a Gauguin was relegated to the lavatory.' (Letter to the *Sunday Telegraph*, 7 July 1978.)

Born with the gift of laughter

Over the inside gate at Yale University's Hall of Graduate Studies is inscribed the quotation: **Born with the gift of laughter and a sense that the world was mad.** It is the first line of *Scaramouche* by the popular novelist Rafael Sabatini (1875–1950) though, understandably, Yale savants did not immediately recognise it as such. How this not very highly regarded literary figure came to have his work displayed in such an illustrious setting was subsequently explained in a letter to the *New Yorker* (8 December 1934) from a young architect, John Donald Tuttle. He had chosen the line, he said, as a form of protest against the neo-gothic style he had been forced to use on the building – 'a type of architecture that had been designed expressly for allowing archers to shoot arrows from slits in its surface and to enable yeomen to pour molten lead through slots on their enemies below. As a propitiatory gift to my gods for this terrible thing I was doing, and to make them forget by appealing to their sense of humour, I carved the inscription over the door.'

Catch-22

Few ideas have caught on from twentieth-century novels as extensively as 'Catch-22' from Joseph Heller's book of the same name, published in 1961, about a group of American fliers in the Second World War. 'It was a Catch-22 situation,' people will say, as if resorting to a quasi-proverbial expression like 'Heads you win, tails I lose' or 'Damned if you do, damned if you don't.' Heller (*b*.1923) appealed to a popular feeling that 'there's always a catch' – some underlying law which defeats people by its brutal, ubiquitous logic. As it happens, the saying was prophetic – anticipating the paranoia over conspiracy theories in the 1960s and the way the USA had 'painted itself into a corner' over Vietnam.

In the book, the idea is explored several times. Captain Yossarian, a US Air Force bombardier (bomb-aimer), does not wish to fly any more missions. He goes to see the group's MO, Doc Daneeka, about getting grounded on the grounds that he is crazy. Daneeka: 'There's a rule saying I have to ground anyone who's crazy.' Yossarian: 'Then why can't you ground me? I'm crazy . . .' Daneeka: 'Anyone who wants to get out of combat duty isn't really crazy.' This is the catch – Catch-22:

> Which specified that a concern for one's own safety in the face of dangers that were real and immediate was the process of a rational mind. Orr was crazy and could be grounded. All he had to do was ask; and as soon as he did, he would no longer be crazy and would have to fly more missions. Orr would be crazy to fly more missions and sane if he didn't, but if he was sane he had to fly them. If he flew them he was crazy and didn't have to; but if he didn't want to he was sane and had to. Yossarian was moved very deeply by the absolute simplicity of this clause of **Catch-22** and let out a respectful whistle.
>
> 'That's some catch, that Catch-22,' he observed.
> 'It's the best there is,' Doc Daneeka agreed.[34]

Down to the seas again

Is it 'I must down' or 'I must *go* down to the seas again' in the poem 'Sea Fever' by John Masefield (1878–1967)? There is no definite answer, except that **I must down to the seas again** without the 'go' appears to have been his original intention. An early draft of the poem has 'I must down' – indeed, it pursues a different course, beginning 'I must down to the roads again, to the vagrant life.' The finished manuscript of the poem is lost, however, though the repeated line was 'I must down' in the first published version of *Salt Water Ballads* in 1902. Heinemann Collected Editions of Masefield's poetry had 'down' in 1923, 1932 and 1938 but changed to 'go down' in 1946. *Selected Poems* in 1922 and 1938 both had 'go down'. No one knows how this divergence occurred – or why. However, the pull of Psalm 107 ('They that *go down to the sea* in ships, that do business in great waters') may have been a factor.

Elementary, my dear Watson!

The Sherlock Holmes catchphrase **Elementary, my dear Watson!** appears nowhere in the writings of Sir Arthur Conan Doyle (1859–1930) though the great detective does exclaim 'Elementary' to Dr Watson in *The Memoirs of Sherlock Holmes* ('The Crooked Man') (1894). Conan Doyle brought out his last Holmes book in 1927. His son Adrian (in collaboration with John Dickson Carr) was one of those who used the phrase in follow-up stories – as have adapters of the stories in film and broadcast versions. In the 1929 film *The Return of Sherlock Holmes* – the first with sound – the final lines of dialogue are:

Watson: Amazing, Holmes.
Holmes: Elementary, my dear Watson, elementary.

The female of the species

Rudyard Kipling (1865–1936) is 'one of those writers whom one quotes unconsciously,' wrote George Orwell (1942).[58] He went on: 'Kipling is the only English writer of our time who has added phrases to the language. The phrases and neologisms which we take over and use without remembering their origin do not always come from writers we admire . . .' Orwell then gave a list:

East is East, and West is West (1889)
The white man's burden (1899)
What do they know of England who only England know?
(1892/3)
The female of the species is more deadly than the male (1911)
Somewhere East of Suez (1892/3)
Paying the Dane-geld (1911)

One might add the lines from the much-quoted poem 'If' (1910):

If you can keep your head when all about you
Are losing theirs and blaming it on you . . .

And:

He travels fastest who travels alone (1888)
Flannelled fools at the wicket (1902)

Orwell then commented:

What the phrases I have listed above have in common is that they are all of them phrases which one utters semi-derisively . . . but which one is bound to make use of sooner or later . . . The fact is that Kipling, apart from his snack-bar wisdom and his gift for packing such cheap picturesqueness into a few words ('Palm and Pine' – 'East of Suez' – 'The Road to Mandalay'), is generally talking about things that are of urgent interest. It does not matter, from this point of view, that thinking people generally find themselves on the other side of the fence from him. 'White man's burden' instantly conjures up a real problem, even if one feels that it ought to be altered to 'Black man's burden' . . . Kipling deals in thoughts which are both vulgar and permanent.

Good fences make good neighbours

This idea is probably best known because of the poem *North of Boston* ('Mending Wall') by Robert Frost (1874–1963). Published in 1914, it includes the lines:

> My apple trees will never get across
> And eat the cones under his pines, I tell him.
> He only says, **Good fences make good neighbours**.

The thought is an old one. E. Rogers (1640) in a letter quoted in the Winthrop Papers wrote: 'A good fence helpeth to keepe peace between neighbours; but let us take heed that we make not a high stone wall, to keep us from meeting.'

However, as the poem makes clear, this is not Frost's point of view. It is the neighbour ('an old-stone savage armed') who says the line. Frost is pointing out that good fences do not necessarily make good neighbours at all: 'Before I built a wall I'd ask to know/ What I was walling in or walling out.'[9]

Frost suffered misquotation at the hands of President Kennedy (who much admired his work and had him read a poem at the 1961 Inauguration). As a rousing, uplifting end to speeches, Kennedy would frequently quote Frost's poem 'Stopping by Woods on a Snowy Evening' (1923):

> The woods are lovely, dark and deep.
> But **I have promises to keep**,
> And miles to go before I sleep,
> And miles to go before I sleep.

However, until Jacqueline Kennedy pointed it out to her husband, he would frequently combine this poem with another (by Emerson) and say: 'I'll hitch my wagon to a star/ But I have promises to keep . . .' Or he would work in the venue of his speech, as in 'Iowa is lovely, dark and deep . . .'

How odd of God

A frequently misattributed rhyme – perhaps because it was composed in an informal setting and not published originally in written form – is the one composed by the foreign correspondent W. N. Ewer (1885–1976):

**How odd
Of God
To choose
The Jews.**

In a letter to the *Observer* (13 March 1983), Alan Wykes, Honorary Secretary of the Savage Club, described the rhyme's origins: 'In the Savage Club, one of the guests was trying to make his mark with the Jewish pianist Benno Moisewitsch, who was not a man to be trifled with. "Is there," asked this hooray henry, "Any anti-semitism in the club?" To this Benno snarled back: "Only amongst the Jews." Trilby Ewer, on the fringe of this conversation, thereupon coined the quatrain, which has since passed into history.'

There has been more than one corollary or rejoinder. One, published in 1924, was by Cecil Browne:

But not so odd
As those who choose
A Jewish God
Yet spurn the Jews.

Another, quoted to me in the early 1960s, went:

Who said he did?
Moses. But he's a yid.

O O O O that Shakespeherian Rag

In *The Waste Land* – 1922, T. S. Eliot (1888–1965) provided notes to explain the numerous allusions. However, he neglected to mention that the lines:

O O O O that Shakespeherian Rag –
It's so elegant
So intelligent

had been taken from a popular song called 'That Shakespearian Rag' published in 1912 by the Edward Marks Music Corp. (in the USA) and written by Gene Buck, Herman Ruby and David Stamper. The chorus goes: 'That Shakespearian Rag, most intelligent, very elegant . . .'

Only connect

Of the epigraph on the title page of *Howard's End* (1910), the novel by E. M. Forster (1879–1970), Goronwy Rees was moved to write:[68] 'It could be said that those two words, so seductive in their simplicity, so misleading in their ambiguity, had more influence in shaping the emotional attitudes of the English governing class between the two world wars than any other single phrase in the English language.'

The words also occur in a passage in the book:

Only connect! That was the whole of her sermon. Only connect the prose and the passion, and both will be exalted, and human love will be seen at its height. Live in fragments no longer. Only connect, and the beast and the monk, robbed of the isolation that is life to either, will die.

Forster's message was that barriers of all kind must be dismantled if the harmony so lacking in modern life is to be found. The idea of connecting as part of a search for order demands self-awareness and personal responses. Man has to invest life with meaning by searching for wholeness and harmony at all levels of existence.

Forster came up with another seductive but ultimately more misleading idea when he stated in *Two Cheers for Democracy* ('What I believe') (1938): 'I hate the idea of causes, and **if I had to choose between betraying my country and betraying my friend, I hope I should have the guts to betray my country**.' This was quoted by the traitor Anthony Blunt when trying to persuade friends not to tell the British authorities what they knew about the 1951 defectors, Burgess and Maclean. Goronwy Rees replied to Blunt: 'Forster's antithesis was a false one. One's country [is] not some abstract conception which it might be relatively easy to sacrifice for the sake of an individual; it [is] itself made up of a dense network of individual and social relationships in which loyalty to one particular person formed only a single strand.'[68] Blunt, Burgess, and Maclean were of the between the wars generation at Cambridge, influenced by Forster's thinking.

They shall grow not old

Laurence Binyon (1869–1943) can be said to be one of the poets of the First World War though he did not fight in it. Shortly after it was over he published *The Four Years* which contained the poem 'For the Fallen' – but this had already appeared in *The Times* on 21 September 1914:

They shall grow not old, as we that are left grow old:
Age shall not weary them, nor the years condemn.
At the going down of the sun and in the morning
We will remember them.

Quoted at numerous Armistice Day and Remembrance Day services since, the opening phrase is frequently rendered wrongly as 'They shall not grow old', as also on a war memorial in Staines, Middlesex.

We must love one another or die

W. H. Auden became embarrassed by the line **We must love one another or die** in his poem 'September 1, 1939' ('the most dishonest poem I have ever written') because it was 'a damned lie' and because we must die in any case. When the editor of a 1955 anthology pleaded with Auden to include the entire text of the poem, Auden agreed provided that 'We must love one another *and* die' was substituted.[13]

CHURCHILL

He Mobilised the English Language

IN a long life spanning the years 1874 to 1965 Winston Churchill held most of the great offices of state and achieved the pinnacle of political power and glory as British Prime Minister during the Second World War. He served a further term as Prime Minister in peacetime from 1951–55. He won the Nobel Prize for Literature for his *History of the English-Speaking Peoples*. His public utterances were memorable. His humour is enshrined in numerous anecdotes.

Of the many remarkable sides to his character not least was his ability to write great speeches during the course of the Second World War when his energies were being sapped in every direction. On the other hand, perhaps he gained some reassurance and strength from calmly summarising progress and prospects in the form of crisp English prose. A torrent of words poured from him throughout the war especially in the form of written orders. As for his speeches, he wrote them all himself – usually dictating them to his secretary (as he had done when composing newspaper articles before the war). He would pace up and down the library at Chartwell as he spoke or he would find the movement of a motor car conducive to thought. Hence, his speeches were oratorical from the moment of conception. Quite how he managed to find the ten or twelve hours he sometimes needed for their composition is another matter.

One of Churchill's private secretaries in war and peace, J. R. Colville, described his method: 'The composition of a speech was not a task Churchill was prepared to skimp or hurry; nor, except on some convivial occasion, he was willing to speak impromptu. He might improvise briefly, but only to elaborate or clarify, and he stuck closely to the text he had prepared. Quick as was his wit and unfailing his gift for repartee, he was not a man to depart from the theme or indeed the very words that he had laboriously conceived in set-speech form. To the last he retained a sense of apprehension in addressing the House of Commons or, for that matter, any large assembly . . . he never, to my knowledge, spoke words that were not his own.'[42]

Here are some of the highlights from a distinguished speaking and writing career:

The status of Chinese workers in South Africa was mentioned in the King's speech to Parliament in 1906 as 'slavery'. Hence, an Opposition amendment of 22 February regretting: 'That your majesty's ministers should have brought the reputation of this country into contempt by describing the employment of Chinese indentured labour as slavery.'

Churchill, as Under-Secretary at the Colonial Office, replied by quoting what he had said in the previous election campaign:

The conditions of the Transvaal ordinance under which Chinese Labour is now being carried on do not, in my opinion, constitute a state of slavery. A labour contract into which men enter voluntarily for a limited and for a brief period, under which they are paid wages which they consider adequate, under which they are not bought or sold and from which they can obtain relief on payment of seventeen pounds ten shillings, the cost of their passage, may not be a healthy or proper contract, but it cannot in the opinion of His Majesty's Government be classified as slavery in the extreme acceptance of the word without some risk of **terminological inexactitude.**

This phrase has tended to be taken as a humorously long-winded way of saying 'lie', but the context shows that this is not the case. One of the first to misunderstand it, however, was Joseph Chamberlain. Of 'terminological inexactitude' he said: 'Eleven syllables, many of them Latin or Greek derivation, when one good English word, a Saxon word or a single syllable, would do!'

In Churchill's long speaking career, there was one thematic device he frequently resorted to for his perorations. It appears in many forms but may be summarised as **the broad, sunlit uplands** approach. An early example occurs at the end of a speech given at Enfield Lock on 19 September 1915 when Churchill's position was gloomy following the failure of the Gallipoli campaign: 'I cannot but express most sincerely my gratitude for all the exertions which are being made, and I earnestly trust you will not flag or slacken in these, so that by your efforts our country may emerge from this period of darkness and peril once more in the sunlight of a peaceful time.'

In his 'blood, toil, tears and sweat' speech in 1940 he hoped that: 'The life of the world may move forward into broad, sunlit uplands.' And in a filmed message prior to the 1951 General Election, he perorated: 'It is an uphill road we have to tread, but if we reject the cramping, narrowing path of socialist restrictions, we shall surely find a way – and a wise and tolerant government – to those broad uplands where plenty, peace and justice reign.'

On 28 January 1931, during a debate on the Trades Disputes Act, Churchill referred to recent efforts by the Prime Minister, Ramsay MacDonald, to conciliate Roman Catholic opinion regarding education reform (including the lowering of the school-leaving age to 15):

What is the Prime Minister going to do? I spoke the other day, after he had been defeated in an important division, about his wonderful skill in falling without hurting himself. He falls, but up he comes again, smiling, a little dishevelled but still smiling. But this is a juncture, a situation, which will try to the fullest the peculiar arts in which he excels. I remember when I was a child, being taken to the celebrated Barnum's Circus which contained an exhibition of freaks and monstrosities, but the exhibit on the programme which I most desired to see was the one described as **The Boneless Wonder**. My parents judged that the spectacle would be too revolting and demoralising for my youthful eyes, and I have waited fifty years to see the boneless wonder sitting on the Treasury bench.

Churchill succeeded Neville Chamberlain as Prime Minister in a dark hour: May 1940. His speech to the House of Commons on 13 May, inviting it to welcome the formation of a Government 'representing the united and flexible resolve of the nation to prosecute the war with Germany to a victorious conclusion', has become a classic. 'Of all the talents bestowed upon men, none is so

precious as the gift of oratory,' Churchill had written at Bangalore in
1897. With this speech – the first of an outstanding series delivered
in 1940 – he announced to the world that Britain would fight to the
death and that it had a leader. It was a short speech, matter-of-fact to
begin with and then rising to great heights. It ended:

To form an Administration of this scale and complexity is a serious
undertaking in itself, but it must be remembered that we are in the
preliminary stage of one of the greatest battles in history, that we
are in action at many other points in Norway and in Holland, that
we have to be prepared in the Mediterranean, that the air battle is
continuous and that many preparations, such as have been
indicated by my hon. Friend below the gangway, have to be made
here at home. In this crisis I hope I may be pardoned if I do not
address the House at any length today. I hope that any of my
friends and colleagues, or former colleagues, who are affected by
the political reconstruction, will make allowance, all allowance, for
any lack of ceremony with which it has been necessary to act. I
would say to the House, as I said to those who have joined this
Government: **I have nothing to offer but blood, toil, tears and
sweat.**

We have before us an ordeal of the most grievous kind. We have
before us many, many long months of struggle and of suffering.
You ask, what is our policy? I can say: It is to wage war, by sea,
land and air, with all our might and with all the strength that God
can give us; to wage war against a monstrous tyranny, never
surpassed in the dark, lamentable catalogue of human crime. That
is our policy. **You ask, what is our aim? I can answer in one
word: victory, victory at all costs, victory in spite of all terror,
victory, however long and hard the road may be**; for without
victory, there is no survival. Let that be realised; no survival for
the British Empire, no survival for all that the British Empire has
stood for, no survival for the urge and impulse of the ages, that
mankind will move forward towards its goal. But I take up my
task with bouyancy and hope. I feel sure that our cause will not be
suffered to fail among men. At this time I feel entitled to claim the
aid of all, and I say, 'Come then, **let us go forward together** with
our united strength'.

The House was momentarily stunned and then gave Churchill an
ovation. He was moved and almost in tears as he left the chamber.
To his aide, Desmond Morton, he said: 'That got the sods, didn't it?'
There is an echo in 'blood, toil, tears and sweat' of earlier speeches

and writings. The combination makes an early appearance in John Donne's line from *An Anatomy of the World* (1611): "Tis in vain to do so or mollify it with thy tears or sweat or blood.' Byron follows with 'blood, sweat and tear-wrung millions' in 1823 and this more usual order of the words was later enshrined in the name of the 1970s American band. Churchill seemed to avoid this configuration, however. In 1931, he had written of the Tsarist armies: 'Their sweat, their tears, their blood bedewed the endless plain.'

Perhaps the closest forerunner of Churchill's 'backs to the wall' exhortation was Giuseppe Garibaldi's impromptu speech to his followers on 2 July 1849 before Rome fell to French troops. The speech was not taken down at the time, so this version is made up of various accounts. Seated upon his horse in the Piazza of St Peter's, he declared: 'Fortune, who betrays us today, will smile on us tomorrow. I am going out from Rome. Let those who wish to continue the war against the stranger, come with me. I offer neither pay, nor quarters, nor provisions; I offer hunger, thirst, forced marches, battles and death. [Fame, sete, marcie forzate, battaglie e morte.] Let him who loves his country with his heart, and not merely his lips, follow me.'

As precedents go, this is obviously quite a close one and it is more than probable that Churchill had read G. M. Trevelyan's series of books about Garibaldi, published at the turn of the century, in which the lines occur.

Having launched such a famous phrase, Churchill referred to it five more times during the course of the war.

Clemenceau had said to the French on 20 November 1917: 'Finally you ask what are my war aims? Gentlemen, they are very simple: Victory'. And on 8 March 1918: 'My formula is the same everywhere. Home Policy? I wage war. Foreign policy? I wage war. All the time I wage war.'

The phrase 'Let us go forward together' was extracted from this speech and used to accompany a picture of Churchill in bulldog pose on a morale-boosting poster. Again, this was a form of words he had used more than once before. The previous January in Manchester, he had said: 'Let us go forward together in all parts of the Empire, in all parts of the Island. There is not a week, nor a day, nor an hour to lose.' Long before – on 14 March 1914 in a speech on the Ulster situation – he had concluded: 'I can only say to you let us go forward together and put these grave matters to the proof.'

At the end of May 1940, some 338,000 Allied troops were evacuated from the Dunkirk area of northern France – a formidable achievement celebrated as a victory when in fact it was a retreat. On 4 June Churchill spoke to the House of Commons and tried to check the euphoria. He ended, as always, however, on a note of hope:

The British Empire and the French Republic, linked together in their cause and in their need, will defend to the death their native soil, aiding each other like good comrades and to the utmost of their strength. Even though large tracts of Europe and many old and famous States have fallen or may fall into the grip of the Gestapo and all the odious apparatus of Nazi rule, we shall not flag or fail. We shall go on to the end. We shall fight in France, we shall fight on the seas and oceans, we shall fight with growing confidence and growing strength in the air, we shall defend our Island, whatever the cost may be, **we shall fight on the beaches, we shall fight on the landing grounds, we shall fight in the fields and in the streets, we shall fight in the hills; we shall never surrender.** And even if, which I do not for a moment believe, this island or a large part of it, were subjugated and starving, then our Empire beyond the seas, armed and guarded by the British Fleet, would carry on the struggle, until, in God's good time, the New World, with all its power and might, steps forth to the rescue and the liberation of the Old.

But France did not fight on. After its collapse, Churchill delivered to the House of Commons – and then broadcast – a speech on 18 June 1940, designed to show that Britain would not follow her example. 'For all of us, at this time, whatever our sphere, our station, our occupation or our duties, it will be a help to remember the famous lines: "He nothing common did or mean,/ Upon that memorable scene" ' – lines he had already mumbled at the Abdication of Edward VIII. He concluded:

What General Weygand called the Battle of France is over. I expect that the Battle of Britain is about to begin. Upon this battle depends the survival of Christian civilisation. Upon it depends our own British life, and the long continuity of our institutions and our Empire. The whole fury and might of the enemy must very soon be turned on us. Hitler knows that he will have to break us in this Island or lose the war. If we can stand up to him, all Europe may be free and the life of the world may move forward into broad, sunlit uplands. But if we fail, then the whole world, including the United States, including all that we have known and cared for, will sink into the abyss of a new Dark Age made more sinister, and perhaps more protracted, by the lights of perverted science. Let us therefore brace ourselves to our duties, and so bear ourselves that, if the British Empire and its Commonwealth last for a thousand years, men will say, **This was their finest hour**.

This is Churchill's version of what he said. *Hansard* differs in one or two details: for example, 'duty' for 'duties', 'lasts' for 'last'.

Before the war Churchill had not been rated very highly as a radio speaker. His penchant for high-flown and rococo rhetoric had not fitted the more informal ways of broadcasting. There was also the problem of a minor speech impediment. But now, what he had to say and the way he said it matched the hour. A pattern developed of his repeating over the radio speeches he had first delivered in the House of Commons. At the time, to a few, they appeared over-purple and deserving to be parodied. George Orwell[58] had a sneaking regard for them and recorded this view of a later broadcast in his diary for 28 April 1941: 'Churchill's speech last night very good, as a speech. But impossible to dig any information out of it . . . The men impressed by it, in fact moved . . . Churchill's oratory is really good, in an old-fashioned way, though I don't like his delivery.' Alex Comfort, writing under a pseudonym in 1943, called them 'resurrection puddings'.

The Battle of Britain raged from July to September 1940, when Germany's plans to invade Britain were shelved indefinitely. As early as 20 August, when he addressed the House of Commons, Churchill apportioned the credit for this great victory to the fighter pilots of the Royal Air Force:

> The gratitude of every home in our island, in our Empire, and indeed throughout the world, except in the abodes of the guilty, goes out to the British airmen who, undaunted by odds, unwearied in their constant challenge and mortal danger, are turning the tide of the World War by their prowess and by their devotion. **Never in the field of human conflict was so much owed by so many to so few.**

Here we have an echo of Shakespeare's Henry V speaking to his men before the Battle of Agincourt and talking of: 'We few, we happy few, we band of brothers.' The bookish phrase 'in the field of human conflict' tended to be dropped when the speech was quoted. It is interesting that Harold Nicolson, noting the speech in his diary, slightly misquoted this passage: '[Winston] says, in referring to the

Rudyard Kipling: '. . . more deadly than the male.'

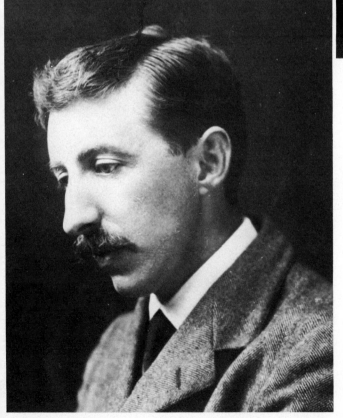

E. M. Forster (as a young man): 'Only connect.'

Winston S. Churchill: 'He mobilised the English language.'

From the *Evening Standard*, 1940.

"VERY WELL, ALONE"

Neville Chamberlain, *left*:
'Symbolic of the desire of our two
peoples never to go to war with
one another again.'

Adolf Hitler at a Nazi rally, 1934: 'Today Germany belongs to us
tomorrow the whole world.'

Lord Beaverbrook:
'The boys in the back-rooms.'

General Douglas MacArthur, *left*,
on arrival in Australia:
'I shall return.'

General Montgomery, 1942: 'Here we will stand and fight.'

RAF, "never in the history of human conflict has so much been owed by so many to so few".'

General (later Lord) Ismay recalled how the words had come to Churchill after a visit to the Operations Room of No. 11 Group, Fighter Command in mid-August:[40]

There had been heavy fighting throughout the afternoon; and at one moment every single squadron in the group was engaged; there was nothing in reserve, and the map table showed new waves of attackers crossing the coast. I felt sick with fear. As the evening closed in, the fighting died down, and we left by car for Chequers. Churchill's first words were: 'Don't speak to me; I have never been so moved.' After about five minutes he leaned forward and said, 'Never in the field of human conflict has so much been owed by so many to so few.' The words burned into my brain and I repeated them to my wife when I got home.

Churchill eventually included them in the speech which he dictated to his secretary, Mrs Kathleen Hill, from his bed in 10 Downing Street.

The 20 August speech ended with Churchill looking forward to future co-operation with the Americans:

The British Empire and the United States . . . will have to be somewhat mixed up together in some of their affairs for mutual and general benefit. For my own part, looking out upon the future, I do not view the process with any misgivings. I could not stop if it I wished; no one can stop it. **Like the Mississippi, it just keeps rolling along.** Let it roll. Let it roll on full flood, inexorable, irresistible, benignant, to broader lands and better days.

Here we have a reference to the song "Ole man River' (lyrics by Oscar Hammerstein) from the musical *Show Boat* (1927) – "Ole Man River, he just keeps rolling along.'

In France, the Resistance movement had a symbol – the Cross of Lorraine. Charles de Gaulle was told that Churchill had said: **the Cross of Lorraine is the heaviest cross I have had to bear.** He commented: 'If we consider that the other crosses Churchill had to bear were the German army, submarine warfare, the bombing of Britain and the threat of annihilation, then when he says that the heaviest of all these was de Gaulle, it is quite a tribute to a man alone, without an army, without a country, and with only a few followers' (Romain Gary, *Life*, December 1958). According to Remy,[74] the film producer Alexander Korda asked Churchill in 1948, 'Winston, did you really say that of all the crosses you ever had to bear, the heaviest was the Cross of Lorraine?' 'No,' Churchill replied, 'I didn't say it; but I'm sorry I didn't, because it was quite witty . . . and so true!'

Succeeded by the Labour leader, Clement Attlee, after the 1945 General Election, Churchill was obliged to attack the man who had been his deputy in the wartime coalition. A number of sharp phrases about Attlee were attributed to Churchill but he denied having described him as **a sheep in sheep's clothing**. D. W. Brogan[82] checked with Churchill who said he had used the phrase about Ramsay MacDonald, with rather more point. If so, he was echoing 'Beachcomber' (J. B. Morton) who may have originated it in his newspaper column in the 1930s.

After the war another joke that went the rounds was: **An empty taxi arrived at 10 Downing Street, and when the door was opened Attlee got out.** When Colville told Churchill that this was being attributed to him, 'after an awful pause' he commented gravely: 'Mr Attlee is an honourable and gallant gentleman, and a faithful colleague who served his country well at the time of her greatest need. I should be obliged if you would make it clear whenever an occasion arises that I would never make such a remark about him, and that I strongly disapprove of anybody who does.'

Remarks about two other Labour politicians of the same period were not denied. Of Sir Stafford Cripps, Churchill said: **There, but for the grace of God goes God**, adapting a remark made by John Bradford (who died in 1555) on seeing criminals going to their execution: 'There, but for the grace of God, goes John Bradford.'

Of the then young Labour MP Ian Mikardo, Churchill made the memorably double-edged remark: **He's not as nice as he looks.**

Few speeches have had the impact of the one Churchill delivered at Westminster College, Fulton, Missouri on 5 March 1946. This was in Harry S Truman's home state and the President introduced Churchill to the audience. By using the phrase 'Iron Curtain', he did not mark the start of the 'cold war', but reaction to the speech showed that America had abandoned any dream of co-operation with Stalin. Stalin himself denounced the speech as warmongering.

Though Churchill put the phrase 'Iron Curtain' into common parlance it was not original to him, nor was this the first occasion he had used it. It appeared in telegrams he sent to President Truman on

12 May 1945 ('An iron curtain is drawn down upon their front. We do not know what is going on behind') and 4 June ('I view with profound misgivings . . . the descent of an iron curtain between us and everything to the eastward'). In the debate on the King's Speech (16 August) when the new Labour Government had come to power, Churchill had said it was not impossible that 'tragedy on a prodigious scale is unfolding itself behind the iron curtain which at the moment divides Europe in twain.'

Before him there were any number of uses, all stemming from the iron 'safety' curtains introduced in theatres as a fire precaution in the eighteenth century. In the specific Soviet context, Ethel Snowden was using the phrase as early 1920 in her book *Through Bolshevik Russia*. Describing her arrival in Petrograd with a Labour Party delegation, she said: 'We were behind the "iron curtain" at last!' Joseph Goebbels, Hitler's propaganda chief, wrote in an article for the weekly *Das Reich* (dated 23 February 1945): 'Should the German people lay down its arms, the agreement between Roosevelt, Churchill and Stalin would allow the Soviets to occupy all Eastern and South-Eastern Europe together with the major part of the Reich. An iron curtain would at once descend on this territory . . .' These remarks were reprinted in British newspapers at the time.

Churchill said:

It is my duty . . . to place before you certain facts about the present position in Europe. **From Stettin in the Baltic to Trieste in the Adriatic, an iron curtain has descended across the Continent.** Behind that line lie all the capitals of the ancient states of Central and Eastern Europe. Warsaw, Berlin, Prague, Vienna, Budapest, Belgrade, Bucharest and Sofia, all these famous cities and the populations around them lie in what I must call the Soviet sphere, and all are subject in one form or another, not only to Soviet influence but to a very high and, in many cases, increasing measure of control from Moscow . . . The safety of the world, ladies and gentlemen, requires a new unity in Europe from which no nation should be permanently outcast.

In addition the speech introduced certain phrases like 'special relationship' and 'sinews of peace' which also passed into general use.

Churchill's memoirs of the Second World War were published in six volumes between 1948 and 1954. He took as the motto of the work some words that had occurred to him just after the First World War. Eddie Marsh, at one time Churchill's Private Secretary, recalled:

He produced one day a lapidary epigram on the spirit proper to a great nation in war and peace: **In war, resolution; in defeat, defiance; in victory, magnanimity; in peace, goodwill.** (I wish the tones in which he spoke this could have been 'recorded' – the first phrase a rattle of musketry, the second 'grating harsh thunder', the third a ray of the sun through storm-clouds; the last, pure benediction.)

In 1941, Churchill said the words had been devised (and rejected) as an inscription for a French War Memorial, in the form: 'In war fury, in defeat defiance . . .' Perhaps he had been inspired by one of the Latin quotations he knew – 'parcere subiectis et debellare superbos' ('spare the conquered and subdue the proud) – Virgil, *Aeneid*, vi, 854.

As with much of Churchill's wit, the following drollery was passed on by word of mouth. Lord George-Brown related it on my radio programme in 1978. But a written reference occurred in a 1957 letter.[33] When a colleague in the House of Commons tactfully told Churchill that several of his fly-buttons were undone, he said: 'No matter. **Dead birds don't fall out of nests**.'

On the occasion of Churchill's eightieth birthday (30 November 1954), both Houses of Parliament presented him with a portrait painted by Graham Sutherland. He did not like it and told Charles Doughty, secretary of the committee which organised the tribute: 'How do they paint one today? Sitting on a lavatory!' Later he said: 'Here sits an old man on his stool, pressing and pressing.' But he was persuaded to accept the portrait and did so, in a gracefully double-edged way, at a ceremony in Westminster Hall:

> This is the most memorable occasion of my life. I doubt whether any of the modern democracies abroad has shown such a degree of kindness and generosity to a party politician who has not yet retired and may at any time be involved in controversy . . . **the portrait is a remarkable example of modern art**. It certainly combines force and candour. These are qualities which no active member of either house can do without or should fear to meet.

Following Lady Churchill's death in 1977, it was revealed that such was her dislike for the portrait she had had it destroyed.

I have seen the following reproduced as Churchill's 'last words', but they were not. They were said on his seventy-fifth birthday: **I am ready to meet my Maker. Whether my Maker is ready for the ordeal of meeting me is another matter.** His actual last words were more prosaic. A man who used to sit with Churchill towards the end of his life once tried to assure me that the old man's last words were 'Bloody hot!' referring to some soup he had been given to eat. Mary Soames reported, however, that the last comprehensible words her father uttered were: **I'm so bored with it all.**

DENTOPEDOLOGY

Foot in Mouth

THE art of opening your mouth and putting your foot in it – 'dentopedology' – has been practised assiduously during the twentieth century. Politicians and others in the public eye have seized on the immense potential of the mass media for transmitting their goofs, gaffes, blunders and boo-boos to the largest possible audience:

The Revd William Spooner (1844–1930), Warden of New College, Oxford, strikes one as a nineteenth-century figure. Indeed, I suspect that most of his most notorious 'spoonerisms' (the OED has this coinage in existence by 1900) were committed before the period covered by this book ('kinquering kongs their titles take', 'the Lord is a shoving leopard', 'let us drink a toast to the queer old dean', and so on). In addition, many of the Revd Spooner's transposings of the beginnings of words are undoubtedly aprocryphal. Still, he had a wayward way with words and this certainly persisted until his death. James Laver, the fashion historian, once assured me he had heard from Spooner's own lips the phrase, **Through a dark glassly . . .** (this must have been in the 1920s or 1930s). Sir Julian Huxley recalled Spooner saying: 'It is no further from the north coast of Spitsbergen to the North Pole than it is **from Land's End to John of Gaunt**.' 'Poor soul – very sad; her late husband, you know, **a very**

sad death – eaten by missionaries – poor soul,' is also probably from the end of his life.

One is tempted to ask: if Dr Spooner had been an ornithologist, would he have called himself a word-botcher? The point is, of course, that he did not just botch words, he did so delightfully.

In the early 1930s, the American radio announcer Harry von Zell (1906–81) was due to introduce a broadcast by President Herbert Hoover. At the microphone, the words that actually came out of his mouth here: 'Ladies and gentleman. The President of the United States – **Hoobert Herver!**'

From 1928–49, 'Uncle Don' – Don Carney (1897–1954) was the host of a popular children's show on American radio. He spent a good part of his later life trying to deny that he had ever let slip one of the most famous clangers of all when, thinking he was off the air, he said: **I guess that'll hold the little bastards.**

The most famous British broadcasting boob came from Lieutenant-Commander Tommy Woodrooffe (1899–1978), a leading BBC radio commentator of the 1930s. On the night of 20 May 1937 he was due to give a fifteen minute description of the 'illumination' of the Fleet on the night of the Coronation Naval Review at Spithead. What he said, in a commentary that was faded out after less than four minutes, began like this:

At the present moment, **the** whole **Fleet's lit up.** When I say 'lit up', I mean lit up by fairy lamps. We've forgotten the whole Royal Review. We've forgotten the Royal Review. The whole thing is lit up by fairy lamps. It's fantastic. It isn't the Fleet at all. It's just . . . it's fairy land. The whole Fleet is in fairy land . . .

He concluded:

I was talking to you in the middle of this damn – in the middle of this Fleet. And what's happened is the Fleet's gone, disappeared and gone. We had a hundred, two hundred, warships all around us a second ago and now they've gone. At a signal by the morse code – at a signal by the Fleet flagship which I'm in now – they've gone . . . they've disappeared. There's nothing between us and heaven. There's nothing at all . . .

Eventually, an announcer said: 'The broadcast from Spithead is

111

now at an end. It is eleven minutes to eleven, and we will take you back to the broadcast from the Carlton Hotel Dance Band.'

That familiar BBC figure, A. Spokesman, commented later: 'We regret that the commentary was unsatisfactory and for that reason it was curtailed.' Naturally, many listeners concluded that Woodrooffe himself had been 'lit up' as the result of too much hospitality from his former shipmates on board HMS *Nelson*. But he denied this. 'I had a kind of nervous blackout. I had been working too hard and my mind just went blank.' He told the *News Chronicle*: 'I was so overcome by the occasion that I literally burst into tears . . . I found I could say no more.'

The phrase became so famous that it was used as the title of a musical at the London Hippodrome in 1938.

The BBC took a kindly view and the incident did not put paid to Woodrooffe's broadcasting career. In 1938–9 he was the sole commentator for the FA Cup Final, the Grand National and the Derby. Commentating on the Cup Final, he declared in the closing minutes: 'If there's a goal scored now I'll eat my hat.' There, was and he did. When war broke out he returned to the navy and did little broadcasting after 1939.

When a Pole arrived in the United States bearing an unpronounceable name, an immigration official renamed him 'Goldfish'. Eventually, he realised the trick that had been played on him and took the name 'Goldwyn'. But even as a successful Hollywood producer, Samuel Goldwyn (1882–1974) never quite managed to come to grips with the English language, as countless 'Goldwynisms' – apocryphal or not – attest.

But which did he really say? His biographer, Scott Berg, claims to be able to know. **Include me out** is genuine (indeed Goldwyn, speaking at Balliol College, Oxford, on 1 March 1945 acknowledged as much when he said: 'For years I have been known for saying "Include me out" but today I am giving it up for ever.') 'The trouble with this business is the dearth of bad pictures' and 'They're always biting the hand that lays the golden egg' also both have supporters. A too clever line like 'Anyone who goes to a psychiatrist needs his head examined' is bogus.

'We have all passed a lot of water since then' is said to be genuine – it came from a reminiscent discussion with Ezra Goodman. His remark about Louis B. Mayer's funeral – 'The reason so many people showed up was because they wanted to make sure he was dead' – is probably apocryphal, if only on the grounds that the funeral was poorly attended.

112

Hollywood writers vied to manufacture Goldwynisms and pass them off as genuine. George Oppenheimer won a competition to see who could first get one of these counterfeits in print with: 'It rolls of my back like a duck.'

Samuel Goldwyn Jr (interviewed by Michael Freedland in *TV Times* 13 November 1982) has commented on the 'twenty-eight' genuine sayings attributed to his father:

At first they were accidental, and he got caught up in them to the point, I think, where he occasionally made them up. There was a whole business about it when it became an image he wanted to do away with. He got very sensitive about it – he was *always* very sensitive about his use of English after running away from Poland at the age of eleven – when his sayings started to get quoted in the papers. A press agent, who had picked them up and done a little work on them, was told to start changing the image.

Goldwyn Jr agreed about **An oral contract is not worth the paper it's written on** but was doubtful about 'In two words – impossible': 'The real ones I can usually recognise because they have an edge to them. They were said in some kind of anger when the mind was working faster than the tongue could cope with.'

'Include me out!' apparently arose when Goldwyn and Jack L. Warner were having a disagreement over a labour dispute. Busby Berkeley who had made his first musical for Goldwyn was discovered moonlighting for Warner Brothers. Goldwyn said to Warner: 'How can we sit together and deal with this industry if you're going to do things like that to me? If this is the way you do it, gentlemen, include me out!'

The 1968 Democratic Convention in Chicago was disrupted by anti-Vietnam War riots. Mayor Richard J. Daley (1902–76) addressed the press: 'Gentlemen, get the thing straight once and for all. **The policeman isn't there to *create* disorder, the policeman is there to *preserve* disorder.**'

During the Three Day (working) Week imposed as a result of Britain's miners' strike in 1974, the Minister for Energy, Patrick Jenkin (*b*.1926), had more than one energy-saving idea for conserving the nation's fuel supplies. He was photographed using his electric razor by candlelight. In a broadcast, he was asked what advice he would give to householders:

Please could they switch off now, use the minimum of appliances, keep the lights off in any room that's not occupied, switch off electric heaters, keep one bar on if one bar will do – don't switch on two bars – and so on. [There are] so many things that people could do to reduce the consumption of electricity . . .**You don't even [need to] do your teeth with the light on. You can do it in the dark.**

BEFORE THE —WAR—

The Gathering Storm

THE roots of the Second World War lay partly in the determination of the Allies to extract every ounce of remorse from the Germans for their part in the First World War. It only takes a trip to the forest of Compiègne in northern France and the clearing where the Armistice was signed to understand some of the resentment which festered in the likes of Adolf Hitler. A grim message is carved, saying: **Here on 11 November 1918 succumbed the criminal pride of the German Reich, vanquished by the free peoples which it tried to enslave.** No wonder that Hitler himself went to Compiègne to enjoy the humiliation of the French leadership at the fall of France in 1940. Before the outbreak of the Second World War, however, hostilities began with a war of words:

Hitler came to power in January 1933. Next month, the Oxford Union Debating Society resolved by 275 votes to 153 **That this House will in no circumstances fight for its King and Country.** It has been suggested that this pacifist rather than disloyal motion, although adopted by an unrepresentative group of young people, encouraged Hitler to believe that his programme of conquests would go unchallenged by the British. There appears to be no evidence that Hitler ever referred to the Oxford Union debate, though Goebbels and his propaganda ministry certainly knew of it. Churchill wrote in

115

1948[16] that: 'In Germany, in Russia, in Italy, in Japan, the idea of a decadent, degenerate Britain took deep root and swayed many calculations.' Erich von Richthofen confirmed this view in the *Daily Telegraph* of 4 May 1965: 'I am an ex-officer of the old Wehrmacht and served on what you would call the German General Staff at the time of the Oxford resolution. I can assure you, from personal knowledge, that no other factor influenced Hitler more and decided him on his course than that "refusal to fight for King and Country", coming from what was assumed to be the intellectual élite of your country.' Sir John Colville, Churchill's Private Secretary during the war, recalled in a letter to *The Times* (12 February 1983): 'At Tubingen University in July 1933, I was contemptuously informed by a group of Nazi students that my contemporaries and I would never fight; and the Oxford debate was quoted in evidence.'

On the other hand, Hugh Greene, Berlin correspondent of the *Daily Telegraph* 1934–9, commented (1983): 'Obviously one did not have the opportunity of discussing the matter with Hitler personally, but one did talk from time to time with high Nazi officials and members of the German armed forces. I am sure that the subject was never mentioned. Why should Hitler concern himself with Oxford undergraduates when he could base his thinking on the attitude of British Ministers?'

Mussolini is known, however, to have referred to the debate several times. The choice of words in framing the motion was clearly influenced by the recruiting slogan of the First World War: 'Your King and Country Need You'.

The following year, during the weekend of 29 June/2 July 1934, there occurred 'Die Nacht der Langen Messer' – **The Night of the Long Knives** – a phrase that has passed into common use for any kind of surprise purge. This was when Hitler, aided by Himmler's black-shirted SS, liquidated the leadership of the brown-shirted SA. These undisciplined storm-troopers had helped Hitler gain power but were now getting in the way of his dealings with the German army. Some eighty-three were murdered on the pretext that they were plotting another revolution. The killings on the night of 29/30 June secured Hitler's position and that of the SS. 'It was no secret that this time the revolution would have to be bloody.' Hitler (1889–1945) explained to the Reichstag on 13 July. 'When we spoke of it, we called it "The Night of the Long Knives" . . . in every time and place, rebels have been killed . . . I ordered the leaders of the guilty shot. I also ordered the abscesses caused by our internal and external poisons cauterised until the living flesh was burned.' In using the phrase Hitler was quoting from one of the earliest Nazi marching songs.

In September 1934, a famous Nazi party slogan was unveiled for the first time at the Nuremberg Rally: **Ein Reich, Ein Völk, Ein Führer** ('One realm, One People, One Leader'). Later, in 1939, the Germans erected an enormous sign with these words upon it at Neufbrisach on the border with France. The French retaliated with an equally large sign proclaiming: 'Liberté, Egalité, Fraternité.'

The Nazi cry **Sieg Heil!** which is also very much associated with this period can be translated in a number of ways. The word 'sieg' means 'victory, conquest or triumph' so, taken with 'heil' ('hail!' as in 'Heil Hitler!'), the phrase means 'to victory!' On occasions, however, it may have been used as meaning no more than 'Hurrah!'

A shout which I believe to be of Nazi origin is still with us and, as a construction capable of innumerable variations, has passed into the language: **Today . . . . , Tomorrow the world!** The idea was contained in a slogan for the National Socialist Press: 'Heute Presse der Nationalsozialitsen, Morgen Presse der Nation' ('Today the press of the Nazis, tomorrow the press of the nation'). Dating from the early 1930s, this reached its ultimate form in: 'Heute gehort uns Deutschland – morgen die ganze Welt' ('Today Germany belongs to us – tomorrow the whole world'). By the outbreak of the Second World War, as John Osborne recalled, an English school magazine was declaring: 'Now soon it will be our turn to take a hand in the destinies of Empire. Today, scholars; tomorrow, the Empire.'

So common is the construction now that a New York graffito (reported in 1974) stated: 'Today Hollywood, tomorrow the world', and one from El Salvador (March 1982) ran: 'Ayer Nicaragua, hoy El Salvador, manana Guatemala!' ('Yesterday Nicaragua, today El Salvador, tomorrow Guatemala!') The *Guardian* (6 July 1982) carried an advertisement with the unwieldy headline: 'Self-Managing Socialism: Today, France – Tomorrow, the World?'

When Hitler appeared to be about to invade Czechoslovakia during late September 1938 in order to retrieve the territory of the German-speaking Sudetenland, Neville Chamberlain (1869–1940), the British Conservative Prime Minister flew to see him. On 26 September, speaking at the Berlin Sportpalast, Hitler outlined his position:

And now before us stands the last problem that must be solved and will be solved. **It is the last territorial claim which I have to make in Europe**, but it is the claim from which I will not recede

117

and which, God willing, I will make good . . .**With regard to the problem of Sudeten Germans, my patience is now at an end.**

Chamberlain said in a broadcast on 27 September: 'How horrible, fantastic, incredible it is that we should be digging trenches and trying on gas-masks here because of **a quarrel in a faraway country between people of whom we know nothing**.'

On 30 September he returned from a second visit to Hitler during which the Munich agreement was signed. Chamberlain hoped that his concessions – which included assigning the Sudetenland to Germany – would pave the way for peace. If Hitler honoured the agreement, well and good. If he broke it, then at least the world would be able to see that he was clearly guilty. And, to be fair to Chamberlain, such was the craving for peace in Europe that, whatever personal misgivings he may have had (and there is evidence that he experienced great discomfort at the role he had to play), he was swept along with the tide. At Heston airport he waved his famous piece of paper and said:

This morning I had another talk with the German Chancellor, Herr Hitler, and here is the paper which bears his name upon it as well as mine . . . 'We regard the agreement signed last night – and the Anglo-German Naval Agreement, as **symbolic of the desire of our two peoples never to go to war with one another again**'.

That night he spoke from a window at 10 Downing Street – 'Not of design but for the purpose of dispersing the huge multitude below' (according to his biographer Keith Feiling)[22] and said:

My good friends, this is the second time in our history that there has come back from Germany to Downing Street peace with honour. I believe it is **peace for our time**. Go home and get a nice quiet sleep.

Two days before, however, when someone had suggested the Disraeli phrase 'Peace with honour', Chamberlain had impatiently rejected it. A week later, Chamberlain was asking the House of Commons not to read too much into words 'used in a moment of some emotion, after a long and exhausting day, after I had driven through miles of excited and enthusiastic, cheering people.'

Chamberlain's phrase is often misquoted as 'Peace *in* our time' – as by Noel Coward in the title of his 1947 play set at the time of the Munich agreement. Perhaps Coward, and others, were influenced by the phrase from the *Book of Common Prayer*: 'Give Peace in our time, O Lord.'

The *Daily Express* declared at the top of its front page on 30 September 1938 that: **Britain will not be involved in a European war this year, or next year either.** Contrary to popular myth this was the only time the paper said as much in a headline though, occasionally, 'There will be no European war' appeared in leading articles. While the first half of the sentence turned out to be true, the second half 'or next year either' was inserted by the newpaper's proprietor, Lord Beaverbrook. He said: 'We must nail our colours *high* to the mast.' Something like the phrase 'Britain will not be involved in a European war' appeared eight times in the *Express* between September 1938 and August 1939.[90]

A copy of the paper bearing the message '*Daily Express* holds canvass of its reporters in Europe. And ten out of twelve say NO WAR THIS YEAR' was later shown with ironic effect in Noel Coward's film *In Which We Serve* (1942). It was seen bobbing up and down amid the wreckage of a British destroyer which had been torpedoed by the Germans. As a result, Beaverbrook launched a campaign to try and suppress the film.

On the night of 9/10 November 1938, the Nazis launched a pogrom against the Jews in retaliation for the murder of a German diplomat by a Jew in Paris. The euphemistic but still chilling phrase **Kristallnacht** ('Night of Broken Glass') was coined by Walther Funk, Hitler's Minister of Economics, to describe what happened when Nazi hooligans were let loose on the streets during this night of terror – 7,500 Jewish shops were looted, 101 synagogues were destroyed by fire and 76 demolished. In Nuremberg the synagogues were actually set on fire by the Fire Brigade.

When Germany invaded Poland on 1 September 1939, the British Government hoped initially that if Germany would agree to withdraw her troops, it would be possible to find a solution without going to war. On the evening of 2 September, Chamberlain appeared in the House of Commons and held out the prospect of a further Munich-style peace conference and did not announce any ultimatum. When the acting Labour Opposition leader, Arthur Greenwood, rose to respond, a Conservative MP shouted: 'Speak for England, Arthur!' For many years, it was generally accepted that the MP had been L. S. Amery (1873–1955) and, indeed, he wrote:[2] 'It was essential that someone should do what he had failed to do, or been unable to do . . . [and] that was to voice the feelings of the House and of the whole country. Arthur Greenwood rose . . . I dreaded a purely partisan speech, and called out to him across the floor of the House **Speak for England**.'

However, writing up an account of the session in his diary for 2 September, Harold Nicolson (whose usual habit was to make his record first thing the following morning) wrote: 'Bob Boothby cried out, "*You* speak for Britain." ' Boothby (*b*.1900) confirmed that he had said this when shown the diary passage in 1964. The explanation would seem to be that, after Amery spoke, his cry was taken up not only by Boothby but by others on the Tory benches. From the Labour benches came cries of 'What about Britain?' and 'Speak for the working classes!' Interestingly, nobody claims to have said the exact words as popularly remembered ('Speak for England, Arthur'). The intervention went unrecorded in *Hansard*. An ultimatum was delivered to the Germans at 9 am on Sunday 3 September. It expired at 11 am and fifteen minutes later, Chamberlain made a broadcast in a sad, broken voice:

I am speaking to you from the Cabinet Room at 10 Downing Street. This morning the British Ambassador in Berlin handed the German Government a final note stating that, unless we heard from them by eleven o'clock that they were prepared at once to withdraw their troops from Poland, a state of war would exist between us. **I have to tell you now that no such undertaking has been received, and that consequently this country is at war with Germany.**

You can imagine what a bitter blow it is to me that all my long struggle to win peace has failed.

Later the same day he told the House of Commons: 'This is a sad day for all of us, and to none is it sadder than to me. Everything that I have worked for, everything that I have hoped for, everything that I have believed in during my public life, has crashed into ruins.'

The Second World War had started.

1939–45

The Second World War

THEY did not call it 'The Second World War' straight-away for the simple reason that it was initially confined to Europe. Even so, a senior editor on *Time* mentioned the prospect of 'World War II' as early as June 1939. When the conflagration quite clearly *was* a world war, in 1942, President Roosevelt tried to find an alternative appellation. After rejecting 'Teutonic Plague' and 'Tyrants' War' he settled for 'The War of Survival'. But this did not catch on. Finally, in 1945, the American *Federal Register* announced that, with the approval of President Truman, the late unpleasantness was to be known as 'World War II'.

At first, back in 1939, it did not seem like any kind of war. Nothing happened. Chamberlain talked about 'The Twilight War'. On 22 December 1939, Edouard Daladier (1884–1970), the French Prime Minister, remarked: 'C'est une drôle de guerre' – which was translated at the time as 'It is a **phoney war**.' (The American spelling is 'phony'.) On 19 January 1940, the *News Chronicle* had a headline: 'This is Not a Phoney War: Paris Envoy.' And Paul Reynaud, the next French Prime Minister, used the phrase in a radio speech on 3 April 1940:

'Il faut en finir' – tel fut, dès le début, le refrain qu'on entendit. Et cela signifie qu'il aura pas de 'phoney peace' après une guerre qui

121

n'est nullement une 'phoney war'. ('It must be finished', that is the constant theme heard since the beginning. And that means that there will not be any 'phoney peace' after a war which is by no means a 'phoney war'.)

Speaking at the Conservative Central Council on 5 April, Neville Chamberlain drew attention to the apparent lack of German activity but unhappily drew the wrong conclusion:

Whatever may be the reason – whether it was that Hitler thought he might get away with what he had got without fighting for it, or whether it was that after all the preparations were not sufficiently complete – however, one thing is certain – **he missed the bus.**

The German attacks on Norway and Denmark in the spring of 1940 brought this period to a close. Even so, the belief current in a number of wars that it would be **All over by Christmas** was still prevalent. 'The war will be over by Christmas' was a phrase popular in 1861, during the American Civil War. It arose again in the First World War. In 1944, George Orwell recalled a conversation he had had with a youth in the Café Royal 'on the night in 1940 when the big ack-ack barrage was fired over London for the first time.' Said the youth: 'I tell you, it'll all be over by Christmas. There's obviously going to be a compromise peace.' Needless to say, none of these wars *was* over by Christmas.

On the night of Friday 16 February 1940, 299 British seamen were freed from captivity aboard the German ship *Altmark* as it lay in a Norwegian fjord. The destroyer *Cossack*, under the command of Captain Philip Vian, had managed to locate the German supply ship and a boarding party discovered that British prisoners were locked in its hold. As Vian described it, Lieut. Bradwell Turner – the leader of the boarding party – called out: 'Any British down there?' 'Yes, we're all British,' came the reply. 'Come on up then,' he said '**The Navy's here.**' The identity of the speaker of the phrase is in doubt, however. Correspondence in the *Sunday Telegraph* (February/March 1980) revealed that Turner denied he had said it, that Leading Seaman James Harper was another candidate, and that Lieut. Johnny Parker was the most likely person to have said it (he had certainly claimed that he did).

The Times on 19 February 1940 gave a version from the lips of one of those who had been freed and who had actually heard the exchange: 'John Quigley of London said that the first they knew of their rescue was when they heard a shout of "Any Englishmen here?" They shouted "Yes" and immediately came the cheering words, "Well, the Navy is here." Quigley said: – "We were all hoarse with cheering when we heard those words." '

Despite this coup, Norway was lost to the Germans – indeed, the whole of Scandinavia was – and criticism was growing over the British Government's conduct of the war so far. A War Cabinet had yet to be formed by Prime Minister Chamberlain and by May 1940 it was obvious that things were getting very bad indeed. In a dramatic speech to the House of Commons on 7 May, L. S. Amery, the Conservative back-bencher, said:

Somehow or other we must get into the Government men who can match our enemies in fighting spirit, in daring, in resolution and in thirst for victory. Some 300 years ago, when this House found that its troops were being beaten again and again by the dash and daring of the Cavaliers, by Prince Rupert's Cavalry, Oliver Cromwell spoke to John Hampden. In one of his speeches he recounted what he said. It was this: 'I said to him, "Your troops are most of them old, decayed serving men and tapsters and such kind of fellows" . . . You must get men of a spirit that are likely to go as far as *they* will go, or you will be beaten still' . . . We are fighting today for our life, for our liberty, for our all; we cannot go on being led as we are.

In his autobiography,[2] Amery recalled that when he had looked up the passage about Cromwell's comment on the old Parliamentary Army there had flashed across his mind Cromwell's other remark when he had dismissed the Rump of the Long Parliament in 1653. 'But I could only dare to go as far as I carried the House with me . . . I was not out for a dramatic finish, but for a practical purpose; to bring down the Government if I could . . . Now I felt myself swept forward by the surge of feeling which my speech had worked up on the benches round me.' And so Amery ventured:

I have quoted certain words of Oliver Cromwell. I will quote certain other words. I do it with great reluctance, because I am speaking of those who are old friends and associates of mine, but they are words which, I think, are applicable to the present situation. This is what Cromwell said to the Long Parliament when he thought it was no longer fit to conduct the affairs of the nation: 'You have sat too long here for any good you have been doing. Depart, I say, and let us have done with you. **In the name of God, go!**'

Chamberlain's Government did indeed go. Churchill became Prime Minister and formed a National Government on 10 May.

After the Fall of France, a cartoon caption in the London *Evening Standard* (18 June 1940) reflected the mood of the British nation. Drawn by David Low (1891–1963), it showed a British soldier confronting a hostile sea and a sky full of bombers. His words were: **Very well, alone.**

The incompetence of the former Chamberlain Government was not forgotten amid many dramatic happenings. In July 1940, under the pseudonym 'Cato', three journalists – Michael Foot, Frank Owen and Peter Howard – wrote a political tract with the title **Guilty Men** condemning the appeasers who had failed to prepare Britain for the fight. It caused a sensation and sold in hundreds of thousands. The taunt of 'guilty men' continued to be used by the Labour Party at the 1945 General Election and became a cliché of journalistic exposés – as in 'We name the guilty men . . .'

Meanwhile, the British public was being prepared for hostilities by a number of advertising campaigns designed to raise morale and warn against possible breaches of security. **Britain Can Take It** was one of the first slogans to be used and also one of the first to be abandoned (in December 1940). As Ian McLaine noted:[51] 'While the public appreciated due recognition of their resolute qualities, they resented too great an emphasis on the stereotyped image of the Britisher in adversity as a wise-cracking Cockney. They were irritated by propaganda which represented their grim experience as a sort of particularly torrid Rugby match.' The idea behind this slogan clearly lingered with Churchill, however. On the day following V-E Day in 1945 he remarked that London during the war had been 'Like a great rhinoceros, a great hippopotamus, saying: "Let them do their worst. London can take it." London could take anything.'

Introduced in mid-1940, **Careless Talk Costs Lives** became the most enduring of the war's security slogans, especially when accompanied by Fougasse cartoons. One, for example, showed men gossiping together in a club while behind them Hitler's head peeped through a painting. Another showed two women talking in front of Hitler wallpaper.

On 22 May 1940, Herbert Morrison (1888–1965), the Minister of Supply, sought a voluntary labour force in a broadcast which ended with the words: **Go to it!** This was used as a wall slogan in vivid letters echoing the public mood after Dunkirk. Perhaps to some it contained an echo of the First World War saying **If you know a better 'ole, go to it** which was said by 'Ol' Bill' (the creation of Bruce Bairnsfather) up to his waist in mud on the Somme.

The idea behind **Walls Have Ears** – that inanimate objects might have observational powers – is of very long standing. 'Fields have eyes and woods have ears' can be traced to 1225 and also appears in Chaucer's *Knight's Tale*. In the sixteenth century walls were literally given 'ears' in the Louvre so that conversations could be eavesdropped upon and in 1727 Jonathan Swift wrote: 'Walls have tongues and hedges ears.' During the 1930s in the Soviet Union secret police activities gave rise to the saying: 'Even walls have ears, comrade.' The idea surfaced again in Czechoslovakia during the Soviet occupation of August 1968 with the graffito, 'Listen to your ears, ears have walls.' Referring to the British ice-cream manufacturer T. Wall & Sons, a 1979 graffito warned: 'Walls have ears – I know, I've just found one in my ice-cream.'

Another exhortation that became a part of the language was one coined in 1939 to discourage evacuated Civil Servants from going home for Christmas. **Is Your Journey Really Necessary?** later (from 1941) became a question addressed to all civilians. This voluntary appeal to limit use of the railways was chosen in preference to any form of travel rationing.

Informal black propaganda was also in existence during the first full year of the war. The song **Hitler Has Only Got One Ball** (to the tune of 'Colonel Bogey') was a major popular contribution to the war effort but, as with most such efforts, we are never likely to know who started it:

> Hitler
> Has only got one ball!
> Goering
> Has two, but very small!
> Himmler
> Has something similar,
> But poor old Goebbels
> Has no balls at all!

What occupied readers of the *New Statesman* in the Spring of 1973 was the historical basis for the claim that Hitler was unitesticular.[60] It was suggested that the Soviet autopsy on Hitler's body had

125

confirmed the theory – but how had anybody known about it in 1940? Perhaps it was no more than a generalised slight against the enemy leadership's virility which conveniently fitted the tune and had grown out of the 'Goebbels/no-balls' rhyme.

Michael Flanders pointed jokingly to similar slights of earlier date such as 'Kaiser Bill – he's only got one pill' and Dibdin's 1797 'Alas poor Frenchie Buonaparte/ Hath but one, on its own, apart!' Martin Page revealed some anonymous information he had been given concerning a Czech refugee who had referred in *1938* to the fact that Hitler had been wounded in the First World War – since when 'ihm felt einer – he lacks one.' Indeed, the rumour had been widespread in Central Europe during the 1930s. There had also been a nineteenth-century American ballad about a trade union leader which began: 'Arthur Hall/ Has only got one ball.'

Churchill appointed Canadian-born Max Aitken, Lord Beaverbrook (1879–1964), as Minister of Aircraft Production. He fell to the task with a will and made a great success of it. In a broadcast on 19 March 1941, he paid tribute to the Ministry's Research Department. This transcript taken direct from a recording differs from that usually given:

> Let me say that the credit belongs to **the boys in the back-rooms**. It isn't the man who sits in the limelight like me who should have the praise. It is not the men who sit in prominent places. It is the men in the back-rooms.

In North America, the phrase 'back-room boys' can be traced at least to the 1870s but Beaverbrook can be credited with the modern application to scientific and technical boffins. His inspiration was quite obviously the film *Destry Rides Again* (1939) in which Marlene Dietrich jumps on the bar of the Last Chance saloon and sings the song entitled 'The Boys in the Back Room'. Beaverbrook once said that, 'Marlene Dietrich singing "The Boys in the Backroom" is a greater work of art than the Mona Lisa.'

The resistance movements in occupied Europe were encouraged from London by broadcasts over the BBC. 'Colonel Britton' was the pseudonym adopted by Douglas Ritchie (1905–67) in the BBC's English Service to Europe. He told resistance workers in one broadcast during the summer of 1941:

> You wear no uniforms and your weapons differ from ours, but

they're not less deadly. The fact that you wear no uniforms is your strength. The Nazi official and the German soldier don't know you. But they fear you . . . **The night is your friend. The 'V' is your sign.**

The 'V' for 'Victory' sign had first been introduced by Victor de Laveleye, the BBC's Belgian programme organiser, who suggested to his listeners on 14 January 1941 that they chalk it up wherever they could. The success of this campaign, short-lived though it was on radio, was crowned when Churchill adopted the sign. These kinds of broadcast were also used for sending coded messages to resistance workers in France. 'Le lapin a bu un apéritif', 'Mademoiselle caresse le nez de son chien', and 'Jacqueline sait le latin' are examples of signals used to trigger off sabotage operations or to warn of parachute drops.

One of the most chilling phrases of the war was Hitler's euphemism for the way resistance to the German occupation of Europe was to be dealt with. 'Nacht und Nebel' – **Night and Fog** – was the title of a 1941 decree issued over the Fuehrer's signature. It described a simple process: anyone suspected of a crime against the occupying forces was to disappear into 'Night and Fog'. Such people were thrown into the concentration camp system, in most cases never to be heard of again.

Alain Resnais, the film director, used the even more haunting French translation of the phrase – 'Nuit et Brouillard' – for his 1955 cinema short depicting a concentration camp.

The most sinister euphemism of all was 'Endloesung' – **Final solution** – for Hitler's plan to exterminate the Jews of Europe. It was used by Nazi officials from the summer of 1941 onwards to disguise the enormity of what they planned. Gerald Reitlinger[73] said that the choice of phrase was probably, though not certainly, Hitler's own. Before then, it had been used in a non-specific way to cover other possibilities – like emigration, for example.

Back in 1938, Franz Stuckart, who drafted and promoted the anti-Jewish Nuremberg Laws, had talked of 'the Final Solution of the Jewish Problem', though not in a genocidal sense. Reinhard Heydrich, Head of the Reich Security Police received an order from Reichsmarshall Goering dated 31 July 1941 which spoke of both 'total' and 'final' solutions:

I herewith commission you to carry out all preparations with regard to the organisation, the material side, and financial viewpoints, for a total solution of the Jewish question in those territories of Europe which are under German influence . . . I further commission you to submit to me as soon as possible a draft showing the administrative, material and financial measures already taken for the execution of the intended final solution of the Jewish question.

By this time the extermination groups were already at work. At the Nuremberg trials, Goering tried to wriggle out of it by saying that he had not known what the words implied. It is estimated that 'the Final Solution' led to the deaths of between four and a half and six million Jews.

The cry of the militant mid-1960s Jewish Defence League – **Never Again** – can be the only proper reaction to this. ('Never again' had been a cry applied during and after the First World War. As Churchill said of the French, 'with one passionate spasm' they cried 'Never again.')

With the United States entering the war and several million American servicemen passing through Britain from early 1942, two catchphrases caught on. The sight of relatively prosperous G.I.'s caused little boys to pester them for gifts, hence the cry **Any gum, chum?** Observation of their habits gave rise to the saying that they were **Overpaid, overfed, oversexed and over here.** The origination of this phrase has been attributed without any real basis to the comedian Tommy Trinder. Perhaps he was the first person to use it on the stage or on radio. Vernon Noble commented (1983): 'I doubt whether he invented it – it was one of those mass-conceptions. It had a kind of bitter-sweet, almost envious, tang about it.' It also contains an echo of the American expression from the First World War – **Over There**. George M. Cohan wrote a song with that title on 6 April 1917 after reading a newspaper headline announcing America's entry into the war. 'Overpaid &c' was revived in Australia when American troops arrived on 'R and R' (rest and recreation) leave from the Vietnam War.

Mitsuo Fuchida was the leader of the Japanese attack on the US Pacific Fleet in Pearl Harbour (7 December 1941). On confirming that the fleet was indeed being taken by surprise at dawn, he uttered the codeword: **Tora-tora-tora** to signal that the rest of the Japanese plan could be put into operation. 'Tora' means 'tiger'.

Following the attack, one of the first American successes was the sinking of a Japanese submarine in the South Pacific on 28 January, 1942. US Navy pilot Donald Mason (*b*.1913) dropped a depth charge on a surfaced sub and then radioed the concise alliterative news: **Sighted sub, sank same.**

US General Douglas MacArthur (1880–1964) was forced to pull out of the Philippines by the Japanese and left Corregidor on 11 March 1942. On 20 March he made his commitment to return when he arrived by train at Adelaide. He had journeyed southwards right across Australia and was just about to set off eastwards for Melbourne.

At the station, a crowd awaited him and he had scrawled a few words on the back of an envelope for him to say:

> The President of the United States ordered me to break through the Japanese lines and proceed from Corregidor to Australia for the purpose, as I understand it, of organising the American offensive against Japan, a primary object of which is the relief of the Philippines. I came through and **I shall return**.

MacArthur had intended his first words to have the most impact – as a way of getting the war in the Pacific a higher priority. But it was his last three words which caught on. The Office of War Information tried to get him to amend them to '*We* shall return', seeing that there would be objections to a slogan which seemed to imply that he was all-important and his men mattered little. MacArthur refused. In fact, the phrase had first been suggested to a MacArthur aide in the form of 'We shall return' by a Filipino journalist, Carlos Romulo. 'America has let us down and won't be trusted,' Romulo had said. 'But the people still have confidence in MacArthur. If he says he is coming back, he will be believed.' The suggestion was passed to MacArthur who adapted it and adopted it. Although he had talked in these terms before leaving the Philippines, his main statement was delivered on Australian soil.

MacArthur later commented:

> 'I shall return' seemed a promise of magic to the Filipinos. It lit a flame that became a symbol which focused the nation's indomitable will and at whose shrine it finally attained victory and, once again, found freedom. It was scraped in the sands of the beaches, it was daubed on the walls of the *barrios*, it was stamped on the mail, it was whispered in the cloisters of the church. It became the battle cry of a great underground swell that no Japanese bayonet could still.

As William Manchester[50] wrote: 'That it had this great an impact is doubtful . . . but unquestionably it appealed to an unsophisticated oriental people. Throughout the war American submarines provided Filipino guerillas with cartons of buttons, gum, playing cards, and matchboxes bearing the message.'

On 20 October 1944, MacArthur *did* return. Landing at Leyte, he said to a background of rifle and gunfire: 'People of the Philippines, I have returned . . . By the grace of Almighty God, our forces stand again upon Philippine soil.'

One of the most effective exhortations of the war was given by General Sir Bernard Montgomery (1887–1976) at the time he took command of the Eighth Army on 13 August 1942. Two months before the Battle of El Alamein he electrified his officers with a private pep talk in which he said, among other things:

> **Here we will stand and fight; there will be no further withdrawal**. I have ordered that all plans and instructions dealing with further withdrawal are to be burnt at once. We will stand and fight here. If we can't stay here alive, then let us stay here dead . . . Meanwhile, we ourselves will start to plan a great offensive; it will be the beginning of a campaign which will hit Rommel and his army for six, right out of Africa . . . The great point to remember is that we are going to finish with this chap Rommel once and for all. It will be quite easy. There is no doubt about it. He is definitely a nuisance. Therefore we will hit him a crack and finish with him.

A recording of this speech which is sometimes heard does not date from 1942 but was made after the war was over. It was based on shorthand notes made at the time. Monty's inimitable style has been much caricatured but the speech is compelling. The ensuing Battle of El Alamein (23 October/4 November 1942) marked the turn of the tide against the German/Italian Axis powers in North Africa. Montgomery later took the title of Viscount Montgomery of Alamein.

Second Front Now was the demand chalked on walls during 1942–3 (and supported by the Beaverbrook press in Britain) for an invasion of the European mainland, particularly one in collaboration with the Soviet Union. The Allied military command opposed the idea, preferring to drive Axis troops out of North Africa and the Mediterranean first. Churchill's argument against a Second Front was that Britain's resources were fully stretched already. The

Russians wanted a Second Front to draw German forces away from their Eastern Front.

It was during the North African campaign of November 1942 that US paratroopers are said first to have shouted **Geronimo!** as they jumped out of planes. It then became customary to do so and turned into a popular exclamation akin to 'Eureka!' There were a number of American Indians in the paratroop units who coined and popularised the expression, recalling the actual Apache Indian Geronimo who died in 1909. It is said that when he was being pursued by the army over some steep hills near Fort Sill, Oklahoma, he made a horseback leap into water down an almost vertical cliff. As the troops did not dare follow him, he cried 'Geronimo!' as he leapt. Some of the paratroopers who were trained at Fort Bragg and Fort Campbell adopted this shout, not least because it reminded them to breath deeply during a jump. In 1939, there had been a film entitled *Geronimo*.

Japanese forces made do with the traditional cry **Banzai!** which literally means '(May you live) ten thousand years!' In the war and after it came to mean 'Ten thousand years to the Emperor' or to 'Japan' but still seems a curious thing for a suicide pilot to say. Less frequently to be heard was **Go to Hell, Babe Ruth – American, you die!** evoking the name of the great baseball player and first shouted by Japanese soldiers in the Pacific during 1942.

A propaganda war-cry **Germany calling, Germany calling!** was used by William Joyce (1906–46) to introduce his broadcasts to Britain. He was given the nickname 'Lord Haw-Haw' by Fleet Street journalists because of a sneering delivery which made his call-sign sound more like 'Jarmany calling'. Although Joyce was treated mostly as a joke by wartime Britain, he did give rise to the manufacture of unsettling rumours. Although no one seemed to have heard the particular broadcast in question, it got about that 'Lord Haw-Haw' had said the clock on Darlington Town Hall was two minutes slow. His omniscience was apparently confirmed by the fact that the clock *was* two minutes slow. Although American-born, Joyce had a British passport at the outbreak of war and, on this technicality, he was executed as a traitor in 1946.

Two popular songs from the Second World War took their titles from sayings that caught the public fancy. **Comin' in on a Wing and a Prayer** (1943) had reputedly been said by a pilot coming in to land with a badly damaged plane. **Praise the Lord and Pass the Ammunition** (1942) was an actual quotation from an American naval

131

chaplain during the Japanese attack on Pearl Harbour. As to the name of the chaplain, there has been some dispute. Lieut Howell M. Forgy (*b.* 1908) is one candidate. He was on board the US cruiser *New Orleans* on 7 December 1941 and encouraged those around him to keep up the barrage when under attack. Another name mentioned is that of Captain W. H. Maguire. At first Captain Maguire did not recall having used the words but a year later said he might have done.

Following the D-Day landings in June 1944 on the north coast of France, Allied forces began to press towards Germany. First, Paris was liberated. The Allied Forces reached the French capital ahead of German Panzer divisions who would have tried to destroy it. When Adolf Hitler inquired of the Oberkommando der Wehrmacht at Rastenberg on 25 August 1944, 'Brennt Paris?' – **Is Paris burning?** – he received no reply.

In December, the Germans launched a counter-offensive in what came to be known as the Battle of the Bulge. General Anthony 'Old Crock' McAuliffe (1898–1975) was acting commander of the American 101st Airborne Division and was ordered to defend the strategic town of Bastogne in the Ardennes forest. This was important because Bastogne stood at a Belgian crossroads through which the advancing German armies had to pass. When the Americans had been surrounded like 'the hole in a doughnut' for seven days, the Germans said they would accept a surrender. On 23 December, McAuliffe replied: **Nuts!** The Germans first of all interpreted this one word reply as meaning 'crazy' and took time to appreciate that they were being told to go to hell. Encouraged by McAuliffe's spirit, his men managed to hold the line and thus defeat the last major enemy offensive of the war.

After the war was over there came the reckoning. At Nuremberg, from 1945–6, trials were held of twenty-four former Nazi leaders and other major war criminals. The legal basis of these trials did not go unquestioned.

The Charter of the International Military Tribunal (later affirmed by a resolution of the United Nations Assembly) specifically excluded the traditional German defence of 'superior orders' – 'The fact that a person acted pursuant to the order of his government or a superior does not relieve him from responsibility under international law, provided a moral choice was in fact possible to him.' It was no excuse for the common thief to say, 'I stole because I was told to steal' or for the murderer to plead, 'I killed because I was asked to kill.' The prosecution made it clear that there was a point where a man must refuse to answer his leader if he was also to answer to his conscience.

Nevertheless, the plea was often advanced. Churchill reported (1952) a talk he had had with Stalin at the Teheran Conference (November 1943): 'I [told him] that I was not against the toilers in Germany, but only against the leaders . . . He said that there were many toilers in the German divisions who fought under orders. When he asked the German prisoners who came from the labouring classes . . . why they fought for Hitler they replied that they were carrying out orders. He shot such prisoners.'

At Nuremberg, Rudolf Hoess, the commandant of Auschwitz from 1940–3, said in an affidavit: 'I was ordered to establish extermination facilities at Auschwitz in June 1941 . . .' Dieter Wisliceny reported that his friend, Adolf Eichmann, in charge of the Gestapo's Jewish Office, 'was in every respect a painstaking bureaucrat. He at once recorded in the files every discussion he ever had with any of his superiors. He always told me that the most important thing was to be covered at all times by one's superiors. He shunned all personal responsibility and took care to shelter behind his superiors . . . and to inveigle them into accepting liability for all his actions.'

This approach was summed up in the catchphrase **I was only obeying orders**, often used grotesquely in parody of such buck-passing. Not that everyone seemed aware of this. From the *New York Times* (6 July 1983): 'Herbert Bechtold, a German-born officer in the [US] counter-intelligence agency who became [the "handler" of Klaus Barbie, the Nazi war criminal] was asked if he questioned the morality of hiring a man like Barbie by the United States. "I am not in a position to pass judgement on that," Mr Bechtold replied, "I was just following orders."'

CATCHPHRASES

A catchphrase, in the broad sense, is simply a phrase that has 'caught on' with the public at large. This may happen because the public likes the sound of the phrase, simply finds it amusing or can easily slip it into conversation. Advertisers want people to remember their phrases so that their products will be remembered when it comes to buying. Something of the same motivation lies behind show business catchphrases – they help recognition of the performer or show. Although there were catchphrases in music hall and vaudeville during the last century, this has really been the century of the show business catchphrase because radio and television have greatly increased the chances of people hearing one on a regular basis and taking it up.

Those that follow are just a few of the many catchphrases derived from show business that have had a brief vogue at some time in this century. A fuller treatment of the subject can be found in my *Book of Slogans and Catchphrases*.[69]

Anyone for tennis?

The perkily expressed inquiry **Anyone for tennis?** – from a character entering through French windows, carrying a tennis racquet – has become established as typical of the 'teacup' theatre of the 1920s and 30s (also the alternative forms 'Who's for tennis?' and 'Tennis, anyone?'). A clear example of it being used has proved elusive, however, although there are any number of near misses. The opening lines of part II of Strindberg's *Dance of Death* (1901) are: 'Why don't you come and play tennis?' A *very* near miss occurs in the first act of Shaw's *Misalliance* (1910) in which a character asks: 'Anybody on for a game of tennis?' An informant assures me that the line was used in one of the shows presented in London by Edward Laurillard and George Grossmith – which must have been in the years 1914–21. Teddie in Somerset Maugham's *The Circle* (1921) always seems on the verge of saying it, but only manages; 'I say, what about this tennis?' Myra in Noel Coward's *Hay Fever* (1925) says: 'What a pity it's raining, we might have had some tennis.' Another informant assured me I could find it in Terence Rattigan's *French Without Tears* (1936) – which sounded a very promising source – but the phrase does not occur in the printed text. Perhaps it was just one of those phrases which was never actually said in the form popularly remembered?

Unfortunately, a terrible wild-goose chase was launched by Jonah Ruddy and Jonathan Hill in their book *Bogey: The Man, The Actor, The Legend* (1965). Describing Humphrey Bogart's early career as a stage actor (*c.*1921) they said: 'In those early Broadway days he didn't play menace parts. "I always made my entrance carrying a tennis racquet, baseball bat, or golf club. I was the athletic type, with hair slicked back and wrapped in a blazer. The only line I didn't say was: 'Give me the ball, coach, I'll take it through.' Yes, sir, I was Joe College or Joe Country Club all the time."

'It was hard to imagine him as the originator of that famous theatrical line – "Tennis anyone?" but he was.'

It is clear from this extract that the authors were adding their own gloss to what Bogart had said. Bartlett (1968)[5] joined in and said it was 'his sole line in his first play'. But Bogart (who died in 1957) had already denied ever having said it.

Alan Melville told me (1983):

I know who *claimed* to have said it in a play first: Freddy Lonsdale. But he was such a delightful liar he probably invented the invention. Years ago, just after the war, down in the South of France, he maintained that he'd first put it in a play – when quizzed, he couldn't remember which one – and was quite miffed that it had gone into general circulation without due acknowledgement being made to him as the creator.

In the form 'Anyone for Tennis?' the phrase was used by J. B.

Priestley as the title of a 1968 television play and in 1981 converted into *Anyone for Denis?* by John Wells as the title of a farce guying the husband of Prime Minister Margaret Thatcher.

Are you sitting comfortably?

Are you sitting comfortably . . . then we'll begin was the customary way of beginning a story on BBC radio's *Listen with Mother* broadcasts for small children. The phrase was used right from the programme's inception in January 1950. Julia Lang, the original presenter, recalled in 1982: 'The first day it came out inadvertently. I just said it. The next day I didn't. Then there was a flood of letters from children saying, "I couldn't listen because I wasn't ready." ' (Sometimes she said: 'Then *I'll* begin'.) It remained a more or less essential part of the proceedings until the programme was threatened with closure in 1982.

Back to square one!

The expression **Back to square one!** – meaning to go 'back to the beginning' – gained currency from the 1930s onwards through its use by radio football commentators in the UK. *Radio Times* used to print a map of the football field divided into numbered squares, to which commentators would refer: 'Cresswell's going to make it – FIVE – There it goes, slap into the middle of the goal – SEVEN – Cann's header there – EIGHT – The ball comes out to Britton. Britton manoeuvres. The centre goes right in – BACK TO EIGHT – Comes on to Marshall – SIX . . .' – an extract from the BBC commentary on the 1933 Cup Final between Everton and Manchester City. The idea had largely been abandoned by 1940, but the phrase lives on.

Coming on like Gangbusters

An American radio series that ran from *c.*1945–57 used to begin with the sound of screeching tires, machine guns and police sirens, followed by the cry: 'Gangbusters! With the co-operation of leading law enforcement officials of the United States, *Gangbusters* presents facts in the relentless war of the police on the underworld, authentic case histories that show the never ending activity of the police in their work of protecting our citizens.' Hence the American slang expression **to come on like gangbusters**, meaning to perform in a striking manner.

Don't forget the diver

Of all the many, many catchphrases sired by BBC Radio's hit comedy programme *ITMA* (1939–49), the one with the most interesting origin was spoken by Horace Percival as The Diver. It was derived from memories that the star of the show, Tommy Handley, had of an actual man who used to dive off the pier at New Brighton. '**Don't forget the diver**, sir, don't forget the diver,' he would say, collecting money. 'Every penny makes the water warmer, sir – every penny makes the water warmer.'

The radio character first appeared in 1940 and no lift went down for the next few years without somebody using The Diver's main catchphrase or another one: 'I'm going down now, sir!'

Good evening Mr & Mrs North America

Walter Winchell (1897–1972) was an ex-vaudevillian who became a top American radio newscaster. **Good evening Mr and Mrs North America and all the ships at sea. Let's go to press!** was the introduction to his zippy fifteen-minute broadcast on Sunday nights which started in 1932. By 1948 it was the top-rated radio show in the US with an average audience of 20 million people and transferred to TV in the 1950s. Winchell also ran a syndicated newspaper gossip column and narrated the TV series, *The Untouchables*. Many of his stories were pure fabrication.

Hello, sailor

A difficult one to fathom, this. The phrase may always have been around but with varying degrees of homosexual and heterosexual emphasis (cf. the old naval saying: 'Ashore it's wine, women and song; aboard, it's rum, bum and concertina'.) Nevertheless, as a camp catchphrase it had quite a vogue in the early 1970s, promoted in various branches of the media.

The first appearance of the phrase that I have come across is in Spike Milligan's script for 'Tales of Men's Shirts' in the BBC radio series *The Goon Show* (31 December 1959). **Hello, sailor!** is spoken, for no very good reason, by Minnie Bannister. In April 1978, however, Milligan told me that he thought he started the revival in one of his *Q* TV shows. To fill up space, he just sat and said it a number of times. Dudley Moore also used it, and the cast of radio's *I'm Sorry I'll Read That Again* promoted it heavily, perhaps influenced by there being a number of newsworthy sailors about in the early 1970s, including Prince Philip, Prince Charles, and the Prime Minister, Edward Heath.

Here's Johnny!

Said with a drawn-out, rising inflection on the first word, this has been Ed McMahon's introduction to Johnny Carson on NBC's

Tonight show (from 1961): [*Drum roll*] 'And now . . . **here's Johnny!**' It was emulated during Simon Dee's brief reign as chat-show host in Britain during the 1960s. The studio audience joined in the rising inflection of the announcer's 'It's *Simon* Dee!' Jack Nicholson playing a psychopath chopped through a door with an axe and said 'Here's Johnny!' in the film *The Shining* (1981).

Hi-yo, Silver, away!

'Who *was* that masked man?'

'A fiery horse with the speed of light, a cloud of dust, and a hearty **Hi-yo, Silver!** The Lone Ranger! With his faithful Indian companion, Tonto, the daring and resourceful masked rider of the plains led the fight for law and order in the early western United States. Nowhere in the pages of history can one find a greater champion of justice. Return with us now to those thrilling days of yesteryear . . . From out of the past come the thundering hoofbeats of the great horse Silver. The Lone Ranger rides again!'

'Come on, Silver! Let's go, big fellow! Hi-yo, Silver, away!'

The above was more or less the introduction to the masked Lone Ranger and his horse, Silver, in the various American radio and cinema accounts of their exploits, accompanied, of course, by Rossini's 'William Tell' overture.

Groucho Marx used to say that George Seaton (the first Lone Ranger on radio from 1933) invented the call 'Hi-yo, Silver!' because he was unable to whistle for his horse. It does indeed seem probable that the phrase was coined by Seaton and not by Fran Striker, the chief scriptwriter in the early days.

The Lone Ranger's Indian friend, Tonto, wrestled meanwhile with such lines as: **Him bad man, kemo sabe!** ('Kemos sabe' – whichever way you spell it – is supposed to mean 'trusty scout' and was derived from the name of a boys' camp at Mullet Lake, Michigan, in 1911.)[80]

It's a bird! it's a plane! it's Superman!

The comic-strip hero Superman was the brainchild of a teenage science fiction addict, Jerry Siegel, in 1933. Five years later Superman finally appeared on the cover of No. 1 of *Action Comics*. In 1940 Superman took to the air on America's Mutual Network with Clayton 'Bud' Collyer as the journalist, Clark Kent, who can turn into the Man of Steel when he is in a tight spot: 'This looks like a job for . . . Superman! Now, off with these clothes! **Up, up and awa-a-a-ay!** After appearing in film cartoons, Superman finally hit the live-action big-time on the screen in 1948 with a fifteen-episode serial.

It was from the radio series, however, that the exciting phrases came:

Announcer: Kellogg's Pep . . . the super-delicious cereal . . . presents . . . *The Adventures of Superman!* Faster than a speeding bullet! (*Ricochet*) More powerful than a locomotive! (*Locomotive roar*) Able to leap tall buildings at a single bound! (*Rushing wind*) Look! Up in the sky!'
Voice 1: **It's a bird!**
Voice 2 (female): **It's a plane!**
Voice 3: **It's Superman!**
Announcer: Yes, it's Superman – a strange visitor from another planet, who came to earth with powers and abilities far beyond those of mortal men. Superman! – who can change the course of mighty rivers, bend steel with his bare hands, and who – disguised as Clark Kent, mild-mannered reporter for a great metropolitan newspaper – fights **a never-ending battle for truth, justice, and the American Way.**

My name's Friday

The TV series *Dragnet* was made in America between 1951–8 and revived in 1967–9. It was largely the creation of Jack Webb (1920–82) who produced, directed and starred. As Police Sergeant Joe Friday he had a deadpan style which was much parodied. The show first appeared on radio in 1949 and was said to draw its stories from actual cases dealt with by the Los Angeles police – hence the famous announcement: 'Ladies and gentlemen, the story you are about to hear is true. **Only the names have been changed to protect the innocent.**'

The signature tune was almost a catchphrase in itself – 'Dum-de-dum-dum'. Joe Friday had a staccato style of questioning: 'Just the facts, ma'am' or **All we want is the facts, ma'am'**. And to add to the list of memorable phrases, here is the opening narration from a typical TV episode:

Ladies and gentlemen, the story you are about to see is true, the names have been changed to protect the innocent . . . **This is the city**. Everything in it is one way or the other. There's no middle ground – narrow alleys, broad highways; mansions on the hill, shacks in the gulleys; people who work for a living and people who steal. These are the ones that cause me trouble. **I'm a cop**. It was Monday April 17th. We were working the day-watch on a forgery detail. My partner: Frank Smith. The boss is Captain Welch. **My name's Friday** . . .

See you later, Alligator

Note how a phrase develops: according to Flexner,[26] 'See you later', as a form of farewell, entered American speech in the 1870s. By the 1930s it had some 'jive' use as **See you later, alligator**. To this was added the response: **In a while, crocodile.**

This exchange became known to a wider public through the song 'See You Later, Alligator' sung by Bill Haley and his Comets in the film *Rock Around the Clock* (1956), which recorded the origins of 'rock n' roll' – a term promoted if not coined by the New York disc-jockey Alan Freed *c*.1951–4. Princess Margaret and her set became keen users of the expression. There was a sudden vogue for keeping pet alligators, giving rise to rumours in London and New York that when owners got bored with them they flushed the reptiles down the lavatory. They then inhabited the sewers, growing ever larger.

The next stage was for the front and back of the phrase to be dropped, leaving simply 'Lay-tuh' as a way of saying goodbye.

The $64 Question

'Ah, that's **the sixty-four dollar question**, isn't it?' people will exclaim, when surely they mean the 'sixty-four *thousand* dollar question?' Well, put it down to inflation. *Webster's Dictionary* says that $64 *was* the highest award in a CBS radio quiz called *Take It or Leave It* which ran from 1941–8 and in which the value of the prize doubled every time the contestant got a right answer. That was how the saying entered common parlance – meaning 'that is the question which would solve all our problems if only we knew the answer to it'. An example of the original use in the mid-1950s is contained in a *Daily Express* article about P. G. Wodehouse written by Rene McColl: ' "Wodehouse, Esq.," I observed, "Could I, to use the vernacular of this our host nation, pop the jolly old 64-dollar question? If you were back in Germany, a prisoner, and you had it all to do again – would you do it?" '

Subsequently, in the US TV version of the show (1955–7), the top prize did go up to $64,000 though, cunningly, when ITV imported the show for British viewers shortly afterwards, the title was simply *The 64,000 Question* or *Challenge*, making no mention of the pounds involved.

Sock it to me

This phrase provided *Rowan & Martin's Laugh-In* (US TV 1967–73) with a much-repeated gag. The English actress Judy Carne, who became known as The **Sock it to Me** Girl, would appear and chant the phrase until – ever unsuspecting – something dreadful would happen to her. She would be drenched with a bucket of water, hit on the head, go through trap doors, get blown up or even shot from a cannon.

The phrase 'to sock it to someone' meant 'to put something bluntly' (and was used as such by Mark Twain). Negro jazz musicians gave it a sexual meaning, as in 'I'd like to sock it to her.'

The precise way in which the old phrase came to be adopted by *Laugh-In* was described to me by Judy Carne in 1980:

George Schlatter, the producer, had had great success in America with a show starring Ernie Kovacs, in the 1950s. The wife on that show used to get a pie in the face every week and got this enormous sympathy mail. So George wanted a spot where an actress would have *horrendous* things done to her each week – a sort of 'Perils of Pauline' thing – and then find a catchphrase to fit it.

In the summer of 1967, Aretha Franklin had a hit record with 'Respect' which featured a chorus repeating 'Sock it to me' over and over very rapidly.

George came up with the idea of making it literal. I said, 'Well, it should be cockney'. He said, 'How far are you prepared to go?' And I said, 'I'll do anything for a laugh. If I'm safe I don't mind what you do to me.'

It all happened very, very fast . . . in about three weeks we were No. 1 with 50 million people watching. The sayings caught on exactly the same time as the show did . . . It had a dirty connotation and it was also very clean and was great for the kids. That's why I think that it took off the way that it did – because it appealed to everyone at one level or another.

Among guest artists on the show who uttered the line were John Wayne, Mae West, Jack Lemmon, Jimmy Durante, Marcel Marceau (even), and Richard Nixon. The latter, running for the Presidency, said it on the show broadcast 16 September 1968. He pronounced it perplexedly: 'Sock it to *me*?'

This week's deliberate mistake

As a way of covering up a mistake that was *not* deliberate, this expression arose from the BBC radio series *Monday Night at Seven* (later *Eight*) in *c*.1938. Ronnie Waldman had taken over as deviser of the 'Puzzle Corner' part of the programme which was presented by

141

Lionel Gamlin. 'Through my oversight a mistake crept into "Puzzle Corner" one night,' Waldman recalled in 1954, 'and when Broadcasting House was besieged by telephone callers putting us right, Harry Pepper [the producer] concluded that such "listener participation" was worth exploiting as a regular thing. "Let's always put in a mistake", he suggested.'

Waldman revived the idea when he himself presented Puzzle Corner' as a part of *Kaleidoscope* on BBC Television in the early 1950s and **This week's deliberate mistake** has continued to be used as a joke phrase covering ineptitude.

Will the real — — — , please stand up!

In the American TV game *To Tell the Truth*, devised by Goodson-Todman Productions and shown from 1956–66, a panel had to decide which of three contestants all claiming to be a certain person was telling the truth. After the panellists had interrogated the challenger (and the impostors) they had to declare which person they thought was the real one. MC Bud Collyer would then say: **Will the real — — —, please stand up!** and he or she did so.

Yeah-yeah-yeah

In August 1963 the Beatles released a single called 'She Loves You' which was in the UK charts for thirty-one weeks and was for fourteen years Britain's all-time best-selling 45 rpm record. The repeated phrase **Yeah-yeah-yeah** (a Liverpudlian version of the American corruption – since the 1920s – of 'yes') became a hallmark of the Beatles.

Some of the spadework in Britain had been done by the non-Liverpudlian singer Helen Shapiro who had a hit in September 1961 with 'Walking Back to Happiness' which included the refrain 'Whoop Bah Oh Yeah Yeah'.

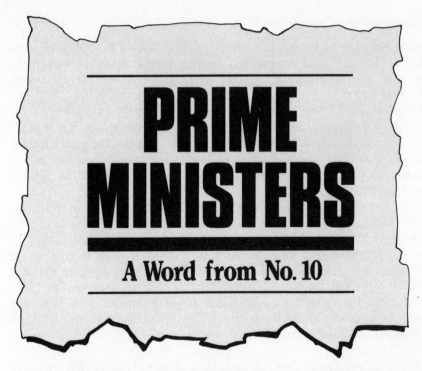

PRIME MINISTERS

A Word from No. 10

AT the time of the Suez crisis in 1956, Lady Eden, wife of the Prime Minister, declared: 'During the last few weeks **I have felt that the Suez Canal was flowing through my drawing room**.' This was a rare, quotable remark from the Downing Street residence of a notably unquotable Prime Minister. Malcolm Muggeridge said of Sir Anthony Eden that: 'He was not only a bore; he bored for England.' Earlier, in 1941, 'Cassandra' of the *Daily Mirror* had drawn upon a report in *Life* and told the story of Churchill returning a long-winded memorandum to Eden with the note: 'As far as I can see, **you have used every cliché except "God is love" and "Please adjust your dress before leaving"**.' Churchill took the unusual step of writing to the paper to complain about 'an absolutely untruthful story, which is of course extremely offensive both to me and Mr Eden.' But the point had been made.

Other British Prime Ministers were more successful in minting memorable phrases:

H. H. Asquith (1852–1928), Liberal Prime Minister (1908–16), had to deal with Opposition MPs pressing for a statement about the Parliament Act Procedure Bill on 4 April 1910. Pursued by a persistent inquirer, he gave this answer to a Supplementary Question: 'You had better **wait and see**.' In fact, this was the *fourth*

143

time Asquith had used the phrase. On 3 March he had replied to Lord Helmsey concerning the Government's intentions over the Budget and whether the House of Lords would be flooded with Liberal peers to ensure the passage of the Finance Bill: 'We had better wait and see.' So he was clearly deliberate in his use of the words. His intention was not to delay making an answer but to warn people off. Roy Jenkins commented:[43] 'It was a use for which he was to pay dearly in the last years of his premiership when the phrase came to be erected by his enemies as a symbol of his alleged inactivity.'

In consequence, Asquith acquired the nickname 'Old Wait and See' and a *Punch* cartoon appeared which showed a young officer on the bridge asking: 'Why is she pitching so much this morning?' To which the response was: 'Well, you see, sir, it is all a question of Weight and Sea.' During the First World War, French matches which often failed to ignite were known either as 'Asquiths' or 'Wait and sees'. Partridge[62] suggested that Asquith remembered 'Wait and see' as a catchphrase from the 1880s when he was in the legal chambers of Sir Henry James.

Before he succeeded Asquith as Liberal Prime Minister, David Lloyd George (1863–1945) was also involved in the controversy over the power of the House of Lords. On 26 June 1907, he questioned the Lords' role as 'watchdog' of the Constitution. The Conservative leader, A. J. Balfour, was using the party's majority in the upper chamber to block legislation by the Liberal government (in which Lloyd George was President of the Board of Trade):

> This is the leal and trusty mastiff which is to watch over our interests, but which runs away at the first snarl of the trade unions? A mastiff? It is the right hon. Gentleman's Poodle. It fetches and carries for him. It barks for him. It bites anybody that he sets it on to.

This passage is remembered in the phrase **Mr Balfour's poodle**.

As Prime Minister (1916–22), Lloyd George described Sir John Simon memorably: **He has sat so long upon the fence that the iron has entered into his soul.** 'The iron entered his soul' comes originally from Psalm 105:18 in the Psalter version.

Arthur Balfour (1848–1930), although he had been Conservative Prime Minister 1902–5, became Foreign Secretary in Lloyd George's wartime cabinet. Just before the British army in Palestine took

Jerusalem in 1917, Balfour sought to curry favour with Jews in the United States and central Europe by promising that Palestine should become a national home for the Jews and issued what has become known as the Balfour Declaration on 2 November 1917. This acted as a spur to Zionism and paved the way for the founding of the modern state of Israel in 1948 and the subsequent Middle East tensions. In a letter to Lord Rothschild, Balfour wrote: '**His Majesty's Government looks with favour upon the establishment in Palestine of a national home for the Jewish people . . .**' The ambiguous rider was: 'nothing shall be done which may prejudice the civil and religious rights of existing non-Jewish communities in Palestine.'

Stanley Baldwin (1867–1947) was between his second and third Conservative premierships and fighting for his political life when he attacked the Press Lords in a speech at Queen's Hall, London, during the Westminster St George by-election on 17 March 1931. The *Daily Mail* and the *Daily Express* had actively challenged Baldwin's leadership by supporting the Independent Conservative candidate on the issue of Empire Free Trade. Baldwin said:

The papers conducted by Lord Rothermere and Lord Beaverbrook are not newspapers in the ordinary acceptance of the term. They are engines of propaganda for the constantly changing policies, desires, personal wishes, personal likes and dislikes of two men . . . What the proprietorship of these papers is aiming at is power, and **power without responsibility – the prerogative of the harlot through the ages.**

Two eye-witness accounts of the startling effect his words had are worth recording. Harold Macmillan was at the meeting and sitting next to his father-in-law, the Duke of Devonshire, who took a sharp intake of breath and said: 'Good God, that's done it, he's lost us the tart's vote.' (Another version of this story is that a voice from the crowd cried: 'There goes the harlot's vote.') Lady Diana Cooper, wife of the winning Conservative candidate at the by-election, wrote: 'I saw the blasé reporters, scribbling semi-consciously, jump out of their skins to a man.'

After this, Baldwin's leadership was never challenged again. He wrote to his Aunt Edith: 'I thoroughly enjoyed hitting those two rascals and it has done a lot of good.' But there could be no reconciliation with Rothermere and Beaverbrook and the wounds festered thereafter. The words also caused a rift between Beaverbrook and Rudyard Kipling. Beaverbrook recognised that Baldwin had borrowed a phrase minted many years before by his cousin, Kipling. Kipling had used them in argument with Beaverbrook.

As Prime Minister again, Baldwin made a speech in the House of Commons on 10 December 1935 about the Abyssinian crisis in which he said:

> I shall be but a short time tonight. I have seldom spoken with greater regret, for my lips are not yet unsealed. Were these troubles over I would make a case, and I guarantee that no a man would go into the Lobby against us.

This became quoted as **My lips are sealed.**

Later, Baldwin made an astonishing admission to the House of Commons on 12 November 1936. Winston Churchill had reproached him for failing to keep his pledge that parity would be maintained against air forces within striking distance of British soil. Why had this happened? Baldwin replied:

> I put before the whole House my own views **with appalling frankness** . . . Supposing I had gone to the country and said that Germany was rearming, and that we must rearm, does anybody think that this pacific democracy would have rallied to that cry at that moment? I cannot think of anything that would have made the loss of the election from my point of view more certain.

Churchill commented later:[16] 'This was indeed appalling frankness. It carried naked truth about his motives into indecency. That a Prime Minister should avow that he had not done his duty in regard to national safety because he was afraid of losing the election was an incident without parallel in our Parliamentary history.' G. M. Young wrote: 'Never I suppose in our history has a statesman used a phrase so fatal to his own good name and at the same time, so wholly unnecessary, so incomprehensible.'

Keith Middlemas and John Barnes[6] took pains to assert that these judgements were made very much after the event and that the speech did not set off a horrified reaction at the time.

When Baldwin eventually stepped down, flushed with success from his handling of the Abdication crisis (which followed immediately after this speech), he made a statement to the Cabinet on 28 May 1937 which was later released to the press: 'Once I leave, I leave. **I am not going to speak to the man on the bridge and I am not going to spit on the deck.**'

Before he became Conservative Prime Minister (1957–63), Harold Macmillan (*b*.1894) developed his distinctive verbal technique. He used either patrician Edwardianisms or somewhat out-of-character, almost vaudevillian, catchphrases.

As Foreign Secretary to Anthony Eden, he attended a four-power summit conference at Geneva, where the chief topic for discussion was German reunification. Nothing much was achieved but the 'Geneva spirit' was optimistic and on his return to London he breezily told a press confererence on 24 July 1955: **There ain't gonna be no war.**

More typical was his airy reference to the resignation of the entire Treasury team (including the Chancellor of the Exchequer) from his Government in 1958. There had been a disagreement over budget estimates. In a statement at London airport before leaving for a Commonwealth tour on 7 January, he said: 'I thought the best thing to do was to settle up these **little local difficulties**, and then turn to the wider vision of the Commonwealth.'

On 30 January, in Canberra, he declared that **Jaw-jaw is better than war-war.** This was an echo of Churchill's 'To jaw-jaw is always better than to war-war,' spoken at a White House lunch in Washington on 26 June 1954.

The phrase that will be forever linked with the name of Harold Macmillan, however, was first used by him in a speech at Bedford on 20 July 1957. He took pains to use the phrase not boastfully but as a warning:

> Let's be frank about it. Most of our people have never had it so good. Go around the country, go to the industrial towns, go to the farms, and you'll see a state of prosperity such as we have never had in my lifetime – nor indeed ever in the history of this country. What is beginning to worry some of us is 'Is it too good to be true?' or perhaps I should say 'Is it too good to last?' For amidst all this prosperity, there is one problem that has troubled us, in one way or another, ever since the war. It is the problem of rising prices. Our constant concern today is: Can prices be steadied while at the same time we maintain full employment in an expanding economy? Can we control inflation?

Warning or not, the words still sounded like a boast. Macmillan repeated them in a House of Commons debate on 25 July: 'For the great mass of the people – there has never been such a good time or such a high standard of living as at the present day. I repeat what I said at Bedford, they have "never had it so good".' And he repeated the words yet again on 15 November.

Macmillan is said to have appropriated the phrase **You've never had it so good** from Lord Robens (a former Labour minister who had rejected socialism and who had used the phrase in conversation with the Prime Minister not long before). However, as 'You Never Had It So Good', it had been a slogan used by the Democrats in the 1952 US Presidential Election.

In his memoirs, Macmillan commented:[48] 'For some reason it was not until several years later that this phrase was taken out of its context and turned into a serious charge against me, of being too materialistic and showing too little of a spiritual approach to life . . . curiously enough these are the inevitable hazards to which all politicians are prone.'

Given the way 'You've Never Had It So Good' came to dog him, it would have been surprising if it had been used in any official campaign. As a slogan, it was rejected, in so many words, for the 1959 General Election by the Conservatives' publicity group, partly because it 'violated a basic advertising axiom that statements should be positive, not negative.' There was, however, an official poster which came very close with 'You're Having It Good, Have It Better'. The main Tory slogan was 'Life's Better under the Conservatives – Don't let Labour Ruin it.'

Exporting is fun is a more minor example of a Macmillan slogan that misfired, though in this case he never actually said it. The phrase was included in a 1960 address to businessmen but when he came to the passage he left out what was later to be considered a rather patronising remark. The press, however, printed what was in the advance text of the speech as though he had actually said it.

Harold Macmillan's other most remembered phrase came from a visit to southern Africa in 1960 (when one black African was seen to be carrying a banner saying: 'WE'VE NEVER HAD IT SO BAD.') Speaking to both Houses of the South African Parliament in Cape Town on 3 February, he gave his hosts a message they cannot have wanted to hear:

> The most striking of all the impressions I have formed since I left London a month ago is of the strength of this African national consciousness. In different places it may take different forms, but it is happening everywhere. **The wind of change is blowing through this continent.** Whether we like it or not, this growth of national consciousness is a political fact. We must all accept it as a fact, and our national policies must take account of it.

The speech had been drafted two months previously by Sir John Maud (British High Commissioner in South Africa), rewritten by Macmillan and Sir Norman Brook (Secretary to the Cabinet), and the phrase 'Wind of change' – though not, of course, original – came from the diplomat David Hunt. (In a similar windy metaphor, Baldwin had said in 1934: 'There is a wind of nationalism and freedom round the world, and blowing as strongly in Asia as elsewhere.')

Actually, Macmillan himself had used the phrase a month earlier at a State reception in Accra, Nigeria, on 9 January. Referring to the constitutional advance of old British colonies he had said: 'The wind of change is blowing right through Africa. This rapid emergence of the countries of Africa gives the continent a new importance in the world.' But no one paid any attention. What gave Macmillan's words their impact in South Africa was the context.

Later, Sir David Hunt noted:[39]

There was no reaction from the audience at the paragraph dealing with the 'Wind of Change'. I cannot say that I had expected any. As nobody had paid any attention to the phrase in Accra I thought I might as well use it again and had put it in with only a minor variation. But I had certainly never imagined that it would be seized on as the key phrase of the speech, nor intended it to be that . . . I suppose it may have had something to do with the fact that the phrase went very conveniently into a headline.

When Macmillan sought a title for one of his volumes of memoirs he plumped for the more common plural usage – '*winds* of change'.

Uncharacteristically, Harold Wilson (*b*.1916), Labour Prime Minister 1964–70, 1974–6, was unable to remember when he first uttered his dictum to the effect that: **A week is a long time in politics.** For someone who used to be able to name the columns of *Hansard* in which his speeches appeared, this seems a curious lapse. When I approached him about the matter in 1977, he also challenged the accepted interpretation of the words. 'It does not mean I'm living from day to day,' he said, but was intended as 'a prescription for long-term strategic thinking and planning, ignoring the day-to-day issues and pressures which may hit the headlines but which must not be allowed to get out of focus while longer-term policies are taking effect.'

Inquiries among political journalists led to the conclusion that in its present form the phrase was probably first uttered at a meeting between Wilson and the Parliamentary lobby in the wake of the Sterling crisis shortly after he first took office as Prime Minister in 1964. However, Robert Carvel, then of the London *Evening Standard*, recalled Wilson at a Labour Party conference in 1960 saying 'Forty-eight hours is a long time in politics.'

It was also in the first weeks of his premiership that Harold Wilson scored an 'own goal' in terms of appeals to the Dunkirk Spirit. In the House of Commons on 26 July 1961, he had said:

> **I myself have always deprecated** – perhaps rightly, perhaps wrongly – in crisis after crisis, **appeals to the Dunkirk spirit** as an answer to our problems because what is required in our economic situation is not a brief period of inspired improvisation, work and sacrifice, such as we had under the leadership of the Rt. Hon. Member for Woodford [Winston Churchill], but a very long, hard prolonged period of reorganisation and redirection. It is the long haul, not the inspired spirit, that we need.

Then in a hastily compiled speech – 'I was carried away' – to the Labour Party conference at Brighton on 12 December 1964, he said: 'I believe that **the spirit of Dunkirk will once again carry us through to success**.'

Both before and during his terms as Prime Minister, Harold Wilson seemed aware of the need to be quotable. He had a penchant for folksiness – as in **I'm an optimist, but I'm an optimist who takes his raincoat**, for example – and a nose for the memorable phrase.

Wilson's seemingly calculated attempts to play upon relatively humble origins received an early setback. As President of the Board of Trade, he stated in a speech at Birmingham in July 1948: 'The school I went to in the north was a school where **more than half the children in my class never had any boots** or shoes to their feet.' He also added – though this went unreported – 'They wore clogs, because they lasted longer than shoes of comparable price.' A former teacher, reacting to the abbreviated report, denied that any of Wilson's schoolmates had ever gone barefoot and soon the politician was being widely reported as having said that he himself had had to go barefoot to school. At the Conservative Party Conference in 1949, an MP called Ivor Bulmer-Thomas jibed: 'If ever he went to school without any boots it was because he was too big for them.' This remark has also been ascribed to Harold Macmillan without justification – an example of the way in which quotations from obscure sources get fathered upon more obvious ones. The incident was the first of many misunderstandings between Wilson and the press.

Contributing more successfully to Wilson's image was an interview given by his wife, Mary, to the *Sunday Times* when he became Labour leader in 1962. 'If Harold has a fault,' she said, 'it is that **he will drown everything with HP Sauce**.'

But at least he tried. On 1 October 1963, he told the Labour Party Conference at Scarborough: 'We are redefining and we are restating our socialism in terms of the scientific revolution . . . the Britain that is going to be forged in the white heat of this revolution will be no place for restrictive practices or outdated methods on either side of industry.' This is usually rendered as **The white heat of the technological revolution**.

During the 1964 General Election campaign he declared: 'What we are going to need is something like what President Kennedy had after years of stagnation – a programme of **a hundred days of dynamic action**.' In fact, Kennedy had specifically ruled out a 'Hundred Days' in the Rooseveltian sense, saying that his programmes could not be carried out even in a thousand days – hence the passage to this effect in his inaugural address.

On 4 November 1964, just after becoming Prime Minister, Wilson referred in the House of Commons to Peter Griffiths, a Conservative MP who had defeated the Foreign Secretary, Patrick Gordon Walker, in a by-election campaign with racialist overtones: 'Smethwick Conservatives can have the satisfaction of having topped the poll, of having sent a member who, until another election returns him to oblivion, will serve his time here as **a Parliamentary leper**.' Wilson commented later: 'My decision to use this phrase – not very fully thought out – was not, in fact, calculated for such a purpose; it was an expression of my anger about what had occurred.'

On 12 January 1966, the final communiqué of the Commonwealth Prime Ministers' Conference at Lagos employed a phrase from an unreported speech delivered by Wilson earlier the same day in which he made an unfortunate prediction: 'In this connection [the use of military force in Rhodesia] the Prime Ministers noted the statement by the British Prime Minister that on the expert advice available to him, the cumulative effects of the economic and financial sanctions might well bring the rebellion to an end within a matter of **weeks rather than months**.'

On 22 June 1966, he told the House of Commons during the sixth week of a national seamen's strike:

It is difficult for us to appreciate the pressures which are put on men I know to be realistic and responsible, not only in their executive capacity but in the highly organised strike committees in

151

the ports, by **this tightly knit group of politically motivated men**, who, as the last General Election showed, utterly failed to secure acceptance of their views by the British electorate, but who are now determined to exercise backstage pressures, forcing great hardship on the members of the union and their families, and endangering the security of the industry and the economic welfare of the nation.

Wilson later explained: 'I did not use the word "Communist", though no one in the House or in the press . . . had any doubts whom I had in mind.' Compare what his namesake Woodrow in the USA had said earlier about Senate isolationists who filibustered a bill to allow the arming of merchant vessels (4 March 1917): 'A little group of wilful men representing no opinion but their own, has rendered the great government of the United States helpless and contemptible.'

In his TV address following the devaluation of the pound (broadcast on 19 November 1967) Wilson said:

From now on the pound abroad is worth 14 per cent or so less in terms of other currencies. That doesn't mean, of course, that **the pound** here in Britain, **in your pocket** or purse or in your bank, has been devalued. What it does mean is that we shall now be able to sell more goods abroad on a competitive basis.

In 1971 Wilson justified himself thus:[97]

In my original draft, under the heading "What it means", I drew a distinction between what had happened to the pound internally, and externally . . . My first draft, written on the train, drew a distinction between the value – in bank, purse and pocket – of the immediate cash to be drawn, and the effect on prices . . . On returning to London I found a Treasury draft of my broadcast awaiting me . . . "Devaluation does *not* mean that the money in the hands of the British consumer, the British housewife at her shopping, is cut correspondingly (it said). It does not mean that the money in our pockets is worth 14 per cent less to us now than it was this morning." This was the only sentence of the Treasury draft I incorporated in the final version, replacing "money in our pocket" by the more alliterative "pound in the pocket". Though I was cautioned by a civil service adviser, I was reinforced by the words of one of my own staff whose maiden aunt had telephoned to express concern that her Post Office Savings Bank holdings had been slashed by three shillings in the pound.

152

Radio Times, April 21, 1939   Vol. 63   No. 812
Registered at the G.P.O. as a Newspaper

Price TWOPENCE

RADIO ✳ TIMES

JOURNAL OF THE BRITISH BROADCASTING CORPORATION

PROGRAMMES FOR APRIL 23–29

COMMENTATORS

TELEVISION CAMERAS

THE CUP FINAL
next Saturday

Follow the Commentaries
with this plan

The picture shows the rival captains—(left) S. Cullis, Wolverhampton Wanderers,
and (right) J. Guthrie, Portsmouth.

'Back to square one.'

The Lone Ranger (with Tonto, and suspect):
'Him bad man, kemo sabe!'

Jack Webb, *above*, in *Dragnet*: 'I'm
a cop . . . my name's Friday.'

Judy Carne, *right*: 'Sock it to me!'

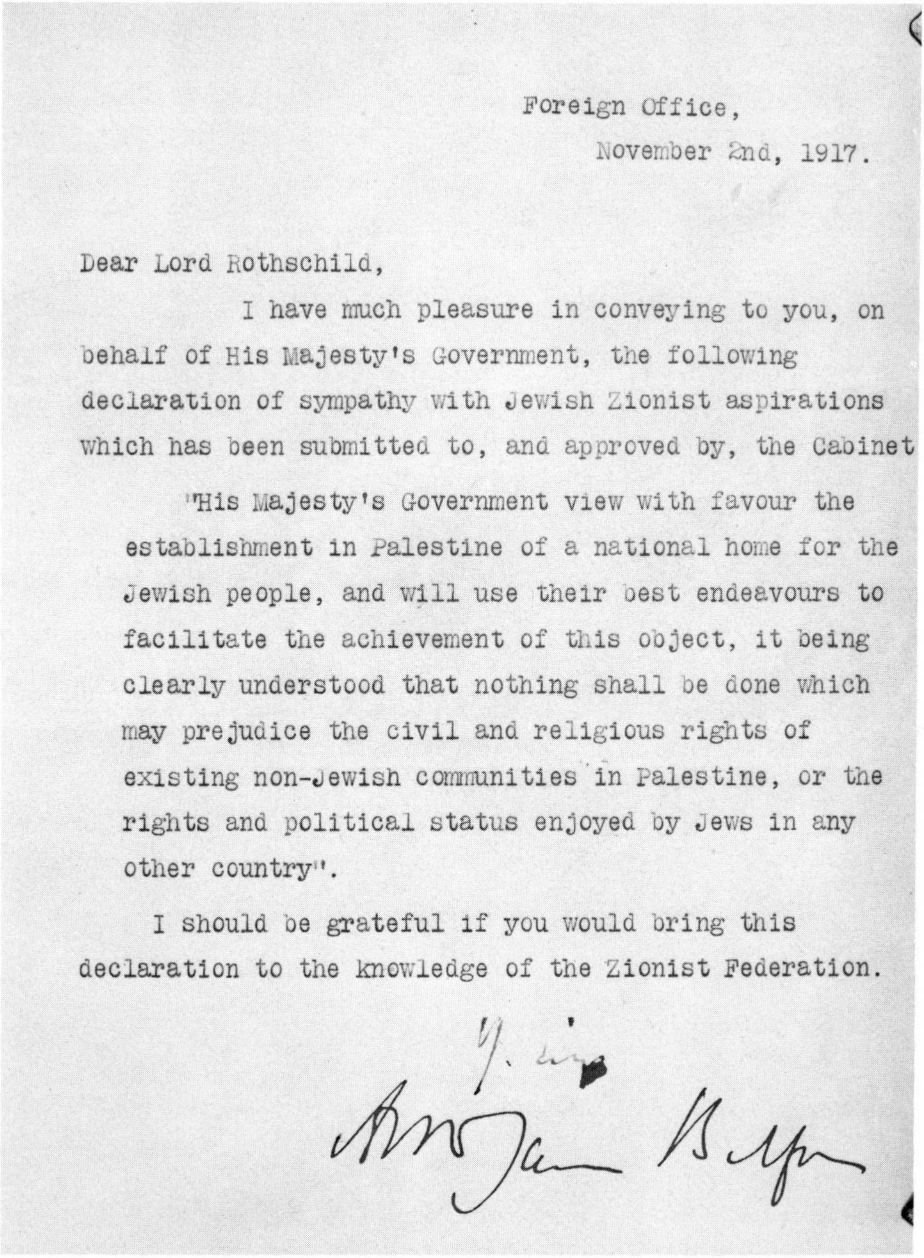

Foreign Office,

November 2nd, 1917.

Dear Lord Rothschild,

I have much pleasure in conveying to you, on behalf of His Majesty's Government, the following declaration of sympathy with Jewish Zionist aspirations which has been submitted to, and approved by, the Cabinet

"His Majesty's Government view with favour the establishment in Palestine of a national home for the Jewish people, and will use their best endeavours to facilitate the achievement of this object, it being clearly understood that nothing shall be done which may prejudice the civil and religious rights of existing non-Jewish communities in Palestine, or the rights and political status enjoyed by Jews in any other country".

I should be grateful if you would bring this declaration to the knowledge of the Zionist Federation.

Arthur James Balfour

The Balfour Declaration.

Harold Macmillan: 'Most of our people have never had it so good.'

Harold Wilson on TV, 1967: 'The pound here in Britain, in your pocket or purse . . .'

The following evening, the Opposition leader, Edward Heath, quoted Wilson's reference to the 'pound in your pocket' as a misleading pledge that prices would not rise as a result of devaluation. The cry was taken up by many others.

In the year after the broadcast, Edward Heath asked Wilson whether on reconsideration he would still have made the remark. 'As to the accuracy of what I said, the answer is, Yes,' replied Wilson. 'But recalling the warning of Rudyard Kipling – "If you can bear to hear the truth you've spoken,/ Twisted by knaves to make a trap for fools . . ." – I might have had second thoughts.'

Edward Heath (*b*.1916), Conservative Prime Minister 1970–74, acquired two hostages to fortune within the space of a month just before taking office. On 5 May 1970 he addressed the Franco-British Chamber of Commerce in Paris. Looking ahead to the forthcoming enlargement of the EEC through British, Irish and other member-ship, he said that this would not be in the interests of the Community: 'Except with the **full-hearted consent of the Parlia-ment and people** of the new member countries.' This statement – penned by Douglas Hurd, a Heath aide – was seized upon subsequently by those seeking a referendum on EEC entry.

The phrase which haunted Edward Heath most, however, was one that never actually passed his lips. A press release (No. G.E.228) made available by Conservative Central Office during the election campaign on 16 June 1970 contained a reference to possible tax cuts and a freeze on prices charged by nationalised industries: 'This would, **at a stroke**, reduce the rise in prices, increase productivity and reduce unemployment.'

In 1973, it was revealed that a former Tory Cabinet minister, Duncan Sandys, had been paid £130,000 in compensation for giving up his £50,000-a-year consultancy with the Lonrho company. The money was to be paid, quite legally, into an account in the Cayman Islands to avoid British tax. This kind of activity did not seem appropriate when the Government was promoting a counter-inflation policy. Replying to a question from Jo Grimond MP in the House of Commons on 15 May, Heath created a format phrase which was later applied to almost anything. He said: 'It is the unpleasant and **unacceptable face of capitalism**, but one should not suggest that the whole of British industry consists of practices of this kind.'

James Callaghan (*b*.1912), Labour Prime Minister 1976–9, was felled by a phrase he did not actually speak. Returning from a sunny summit meeting in Guadaloupe to Britain's 'winter of discontent' on

10 January 1979, he was asked by a journalist at a London airport press conference: 'What of the mounting chaos in the country at the moment?' (caused by various forms of industrial inaction). Callaghan replied: 'Please don't run down your country by talking about mounting chaos. If you look at it from the outside, you can see that you are taking a rather parochial view. I do not feel there is mounting chaos.' Next day, the *Sun* newspaper carried the headline: **Crisis? What crisis?**

Callaghan lost the May 1979 General Election. The editor of the *Sun* was given a knighthood by the incoming Prime Minister.

Margaret Thatcher (*b.*1925), Conservative Prime Minister 1979–, was more noted for her frequent recourse to quotation than for saying anything original herself. Even the sobriquet by which she was chiefly known came from another source. On 19 January 1976 she said in a speech: 'The Russians are bent on world dominance . . . the Russians put guns before butter.' A week later *The Times* reported that the Soviet Defence Ministry newspaper *Red Star* in an article signed by Captain Y. Gavrilov had accused this **Iron Lady** of seeking to revive the Cold War. The article wrongly suggested that she was known by this nickname in the UK at that time. On 31 January, speaking in her Finchley constituency, Mrs Thatcher made the title her own:

> Ladies and gentlemen, I stand before you tonight in my green chiffon evening gown, my face softly made up, my fair hair gently waved . . . the Iron lady of the Western World. Me? A cold war warrior? Well, yes – if that is how they wish to interpret my defence of values, and freedoms fundamental to our way of life.

Occasionally, the variant 'Iron Maiden' has been used (as by Marjorie Proops, *Daily Mirror*, 5 February 1975.)

It emerged very shortly after she became Prime Minister that a favourite expression of Mrs Thatcher's was **There is no alternative** (i.e. to her economic policies which included harsh measures such as cuts in public spending, increased unemployment, etc.). This was sometimes rendered as an acronym: 'TINA'.

MEDIA

The Clattering Train

THE early twentieth century witnessed the rise of the popular mass-circulation newspaper. In the 1920s came radio. Televison was establishing itself as the major medium of communication by mid-century. By the 1960s we were lumping them all together as 'the media'.

Max Aitken, Lord Beaverbrook, became a newspaper proprietor notorious for interfering with the running of his papers. 'I stand continually upon the watchtower in the daytime,' he would quote from Isaiah 21:8 – and in the night-time, too, one might add. His favourite inquiry as his mighty media machine rumbled on was: **Who is in charge of the clattering train?**

Ominously, this quotation is based on a misremembering of the poem:

> Who is in charge of the rattling train?
> The axles scream and the couplings strain
> And the pace is hot and the points are near
> And Sleep has deadened the driver's ear,
> And the signals flash through the night in vain
> For Death is in charge of the rattling train.

It is possible that he borrowed this expression from Churchill who quotes the poem (with 'rattling' as 'clattering' and 'scream' as 'creak') in the first volume of *The Second World War*.[16] Churchill said of the lines: 'I had learnt them from a volume of *Punch* cartoons which I used to pore over when I was eight or nine years old at school at Brighton.'

More messages from the media:

I seem to hear a child weeping

A prophetic cartoon appeared in the *Daily Herald* at the conclusion of the Versailles Peace Conference in 1919. Drawn by Will Dyson, it showed 'the Big Four' – President Wilson, Clemenceau, Orlando of Italy and Lloyd George – leaving the conference hall and hearing a child – signifying the next generation – bewailing the breakdown of their peace efforts. The headline is: 'Peace and Future Cannon Fodder'; the caption quotes 'The Tiger' (Clemenceau) as saying 'Curious! **I seem to hear a child weeping!**' Ironically, the child is marked '1940 Class'.

The brute force of monopoly

At the helm when the British Broadcasting Company (later Corporation) was set up in 1922 was a young Scotsman of decided views called John Reith (1889–1971). In his autobiography[72] he dealt with the prospect of competition in the early years of the BBC's life:

> If any competitive broadcasting was introduced it might compel some modification of the policy which had hitherto governed action. Or if the ether were surrendered to the power of money. Or if there were no intellectual or ethical responsibility. Or if some vested interest were in control. It was in fact the combination of public service motive, sense of moral obligation, assured finance and the **brute force of monopoly** which enabled the BBC to make of broadcasting what no other country in the world has made of it.

The BBC's monopoly in radio was not broken in the UK until 1973. Reith's own brooding personality probably harmed the BBC as much as it helped it. He once said the best form of government was 'despotism tempered by assassination'. When the BBC's coat of arms was chosen in 1927, a motto was suggested by one of the first five governors, Dr Montague Rendall: **Nation shall Speak Peace unto Nation.** This echoes a passage in Micah 4:3: Nation shall not lift up a sword against nation.' In 1932, however, it was decided that the BBC's mission was not primarily to broadcast to other nations but to provide a service for home consumption – and for the Empire.

Quaecunque ('whatsoever') was introduced as a fairly meaningless alternative – but it was supposed to lead people back to the grand Latin inscription (also composed by Rendall) in the entrance hall of Broadcasting House, London, and based on Philippians 4:8: 'Whatsoever things are beautiful and honest and of good report.' In 1948, 'Nation shall Speak Peace unto Nation' came back into use as the Corporation's main motto – appropriately, after the BBC's notable role promoting international understanding during the Second World War and in its external services.

The little old lady from Dubuque

When the *New Yorker* magazine was founded in 1925, its noted editor Harold Ross (1892–1951) declared in best metropolitan fashion: 'The *New Yorker* will not be edited for the old lady from Dubuque.' Later this line from the magazine's prospectus was rendered as **the little old lady from Dubuque**. The place is in Iowa. A man called 'Boots' Mulgrew who lived there used to contribute squibs to the Chicago *Tribune* signed 'Old Lady in Dubuque'. Ross, presumably, had heard of this line and consciously or otherwise developed it to describe the sort of person he was not creating the magazine for. (On the other hand, Malcolm Muggeridge once quoted a writer on the *Daily Express* who explained the huge readership of Beaverbrook newspapers in the UK by saying: 'I write for one little old reader.')

Ross read copy carefully and asked **Who he?** if he did not recognise a name (sometimes betraying his own ignorance). He said the only two names everyone knew were Houdini and Sherlock Holmes. (Compare the Duke of Wellington's reaction on hearing the names in a new administration: 'Who – who?')

Comment is free, but facts are sacred

C. P. Scott (1846–1932) was the influential editor of the *Manchester Guardian* for more than fifty-nine years – the longest editorship of a national newspaper anywhere in the world. In a signed editorial marking the paper's first hundred years on 5 May 1921, he wrote:

> The newspaper is of necessity something of a monopoly, and its first duty is to shun the temptations of monopoly. Its primary office is the gathering of news. At the peril of its soul it must see that the supply is not tainted. Neither in what it gives, nor in what it does not give, nor in the mode of presentation, must the unclouded face of truth suffer wrong. **Comment is free, but facts are sacred**.

This passage was seized upon fairly quickly by politicians and journalists who held Scott in great regard. A man of forthright ideas and integrity, he was said to have expressed surprise when it was suggested to him that some readers did not immediately turn to the leader page.

One picture is worth ten thousand words

This journalistic saying has about as much truth in it as its opposite – that one word is worth ten thousand pictures. Either proposition could be given a vestige of truth given the right circumstances. Turgenev in *Fathers and Sons* puts it rather less sweepingly: 'A picture shows me at a glance what it takes dozens of pages of a book to expound.'

The phrase is more interesting, however, as an example of reconstructed origins. The American Journal *Printers' Ink* for 10 March 1927 said: '**One picture is worth ten thousand words** . . . The same influence could not be created even with the same picture in any other advertising medium.' It ascribed this saying to a 'Chinese proverb'. Readers with long memories might have recalled that 'One look is worth a thousand words' was a saying the same journal had printed on 8 December 1921 and become suspicious. In fact, the 'proverb' was made up by one Frederick R. Barnard.

You are Mr Lobby Lud

A circulation-raising stunt for newspapers from 1927 onwards took the form of a challenge uttered by readers to a man they were told in advance would be in a certain area (usually a seaside resort) on a particular day. His description and photograph were given in the paper and 'You are so-and-so and I claim my five pounds' (or whatever the prize was) became the formula. The reader had, of course, to be carrying a copy of that day's paper. Vaguely knowing of the phrase, I was intrigued to meet Lord Ritchie-Calder in 1977. As a young journalist in the 1920s, he had not only discovered Agatha Christie when she went missing in 1926 but had also been 'Lobby Lud' in the days when readers of the *Daily News* could deliver the challenge: 'You are Lobby Lud and I claim my £10'.

However, I have since learned that it all began on 1 August 1927 in the *Westminster Gazette*. The name Lobby Lud came from the *Gazette's* telegraphic address – Lobby because of Westminster and Lud from Ludgate Circus. The correct challenge was: **You are Mr Lobby Lud – I claim the *Westminster Gazette* prize** (which initially was £50, though if it was unclaimed it increased weekly.) The first man to be 'Mr Lud' was William Chinn (who was still alive, aged 91, in 1983). Although a great success, the stunt did nothing for the *Gazette* – it closed the following year.

However, the idea was taken over by the *Daily News* and the *News Chronicle* and ran on for several years. As accuracy of challenge was all-important, there was clearly room for disappointment in the matter.

Wall Street lays an egg

The Wall Street crash of 1929 was celebrated in the showbiz paper *Variety* with the notable headline: **WALL STREET LAYS AN EGG**. Sime Silberman (1873–1933) is usually credited with coining most of the paper's more exuberant headlines. Another from about the same period went: **STICKS NIX HICKS PIX**, meaning that cinema-goers in rural areas were not attracted to films with bucolic themes. Later, when playwright Arthur Miller wed Marilyn Monroe, it was: **EGGHEAD WEDS HOURGLASS**.

Silberman founded *Variety* in 1905. Jack Conway is credited with creating the jargon of 'socko', 'boffo', and 'wow' which described goings-on in the showbiz world as if they were sporting events and provided the paper with its unique language.

In other papers this century there have been many noisy but few memorable headlines. Whether 'MACARTHUR FLIES BACK TO FRONT' and 'EIGHTH ARMY PUSH BOTTLES UP GERMANS' ever really appeared, I do not know. On the other hand, there have been so many peculiar lines that anything is possible. I have seen 'DR FUCHS OFF TO SOUTH ICE' with my own eyes.

However, the notoriously mousey headline **SMALL EARTH-QUAKE IN CHILE. NOT MANY DEAD** with which Claud Cockburn claimed to have won a competition for dullness among sub-editors on *The Times* during the 1930s has proved impossible to trace despite an exhaustive search. It may just have been a smoking-room story.

Our reporter made an excuse and left

With the rise of the mass-circulation newspapers came the rise of a two-faced mode of reporting which sought to depict vice and crime while covering itself with righteous condemnation and crusading zeal. The *People* which was founded in 1881 as a weekly (and became the *Sunday People* in 1971) was one of those muck-raking papers that developed a method of reporting sexual scandals which sometimes involved a reporter setting up a compromising situation – e.g. provoking prostitutes or pimps to reveal their game – and then making it clear that, of course, he had taken no part in what was on

159

offer. Having found out what he wanted, **our reporter made an excuse and left** – a classic exit line, probably from the 1920s onwards.) Another titillating cliché of the genre was to hint at some foul practice 'which we cannot describe in a family newspaper'.

The price of petrol has been increased by one penny

On 6 March 1942, the *Daily Mirror* published a cartoon by Philip Zec (1910–83) which reduced the Government to a frenzy. It showed a torpedoed sailor adrift on a raft in the sea. The caption had been suggested by the journalist 'Cassandra' (William Connor):**THE PRICE OF PETROL HAS BEEN INCREASED BY ONE PENNY – Official**.

This could be taken as a fairly reasonable suggestion that while seamen were risking their lives, it was inappropriate for people back home to moan about rising prices and for black marketeers to be making a profit. Zec's object was to urge the public not to waste precious petrol following the Government's authorisation of a penny increase in price. His original caption was 'Petrol is dearer now' but Cassandra said: 'You're a genius. But it needs a stronger caption. Bring in the penny rise. It'll dramatise the whole thing.'

Although readers responded enthusiastically to the cartoon, it was seen by Winston Churchill and the War Cabinet as yet another provocation. They had come under repeated criticism from the paper and now Churchill threatened to have the *Mirror* suppressed, believing that the cartoon suggested that sailors' lives had been put at risk to increase petrol companies' profits.[21]

Whose finger on the trigger?

25 October 1951 was General Election day in Britain and the *Daily Mirror* dramatised the choice between the incumbent Prime Minister, Clement Attlee, and Winston Churchill with a bold drawing of a pistol – labelled 'Big Issues of 1951' – and the headline 'WHOSE FINGER?' The rest of the page was given over to the following copy: 'Today your finger is on the trigger. See you defend peace with security and progress with fair shares. Vote for the Party you can really trust. The *Daily Mirror* believes that Party is Labour.' This front page was the culmination of a 'Whose finger?' campaign.

The *Mirror* had asked eight months earlier when Attlee had visited America to discuss the atom bomb: **'Whose finger** do you want **on the trigger** when the world situation is so delicate?' Then Churchill responded (6 October):

I am sure we do not want any fingers upon the trigger. Least of all do we want a fumbling finger . . . It will not be a British finger that will pull the trigger of a third world war. It may be a Russian finger or an American finger, or a United Nations Organisation finger, but it cannot be a British finger . . . the control and decision and the timing of that terrible event would not rest with us. Our influence in the world is not what it was in bygone days.

As it happens, the *Mirror* was unable to stir the electorate and the Conservatives came to power under Churchill. The Prime Minister then issued a writ for libel against the *Mirror* because he took the view that the slogan, usually rendered as 'Whose finger on the trigger?' implied that he was a warmonger. The case was settled out of court.[21]

Top people take *The Times*

In the mid-1950s, the London *Times* was shedding circulation, the end of post-war newsprint rationing was in sight, and an era of renewed competition in Fleet Street was about to begin. In 1954, the paper's agency, the London Press Exchange, commissioned a survey to discover people's attitudes towards 'the Thunderer'. They chiefly found it dull, but the management was not going to change anything, least of all allow contributors to be identified by name. The paper would have to be promoted for what it was. A pilot campaign in provincial newspapers included one ad showing a top hat and pair of gloves with the slogan 'Men who make opinion read *The Times*.'

It was not the LPE but an outsider who finally encapsulated that idea in a more memorable way. G. H. Saxon Mills was one of the old school of advertising copywriters. But he was out of a job when he bumped into Stanley Morison of *The Times*. As a favour, Mills was asked to produce a brochure for visitors to the newspaper. When finished, it contained a series of pictures of the sort of people who were supposed to read the paper – a barrister, a trade union official, and so on. Each was supported by the phrase: **Top People take *The Times*.**

This idea was adopted for the more public promotional campaign and first appeared in poster form during 1957, running into immediate criticism for its snobbery. But sales went up and however toe-curling it may have been, the slogan got the paper noticed and ran on into the early 1960s.

A licence to print money

Commercial television was not introduced to the UK until 1955. Initially, some of the companies lost a great deal of money, but soon

Sayings of the Century

things turned their way. Just after Scottish TV opened in August 1957, Roy Thomson (1894–1976), a Canadian newspaper-owner who headed the company, told neighbours in Edinburgh: 'You know, it's just like having **a licence to print** your own **money**.' The idea may have been current in America before Thomson used it, but – whatever the case – he kept on saying it and repeated it in an interview with *Time* magazine. Frequently quoted since, though less so when the truth of it began to diminish in the 1980s.

All human life is there

A briefly used, but memorable slogan for the *News of the World* (*c*.1958–9) was **All Human Life is There.** The only reference to this saying in the ODQ appears under Henry James. Even if we had never read his 'Madonna of the Future' (1879) – and we had not – we were told that it contained the line: 'Cats and monkeys, monkeys and cats – all human life is there.' What was the connection, if any, with the steamy British Sunday newspaper?

Copywriter Maurice Smelt told me the story: 'I simply lifted the words from the *Oxford Dictionary of Quotations*. I didn't bother to tell the client that they were from Henry James, suspecting that, after the "Henry James – Who he?" stage, he would come up with tiresome arguments about it being too high-hat for his readership. I did check whether we were clear on copyright, which we were by a year or two.'

Anyone here been raped and speaks English?

The absurdity of the war correspondent's job was encapsulated by a question heard during the war in the Congo (1960). Thousands of frightened Belgian civilians were waiting for a plane to take them to safety from the newly independent ex-Belgian colony when a BBC television reporter walked among them with his camera team and asked: **Has anyone here been raped and speaks English?** The incident was reported – and used as the title of a book (1978) – by Edward Behr who commented: 'The callous cry summed up for me the tragic, yet wildly surrealist nature of the country itself.'

A vast wasteland

John F. Kennedy appointed a lawyer, Newton Minow (*b*.1926), as chairman of the Federal Communications Commission. Minow told an audience of the National Association of Broadcasters in 1961 that if anyone watched American television from morn till night: 'I can assure you that you will observe **a vast wasteland**.'

The phrase stuck. Even with its literary echo of T. S. Eliot's *The*

162

Waste Land it was a more straightforward description of the medium than those used up to that point, including British critic Maurice Richardson's 'idiot('s) lantern' and 'chewing gum for the eyes' (American author and critic John Mason Brown).

MOI, GENERAL de GAULLE

CHARLES de Gaulle (1890–1970) wrote in his *Mémoires de Guerre*: 'Toute ma vie je me suis fait une certaine idée de la France.' Having a certain idea of France was what sustained him as wartime leader of the Free French, as head of provisional governments (1944–6) and as first President of the Fifth republic (1958–69).

At 6 pm on 18 June 1940 de Gaulle broadcast an appeal from London to Frenchmen betrayed by Petain's armistice with the Germans. He asked them to rally behind him in Britain and help form a Government in exile. It seems that very few French people actually heard this broadcast and, to de Gaulle's great annoyance, it was not recorded by the BBC, but it acquired symbolic importance:

I, General de Gaulle, now in London, call on all French officers and men who are at present on British soil, or may be in the future, with or without arms . . . to get in touch with me.

Here was a brigadier-general challenging the authority of the Marshal of France. By making such a call-to-arms, de Gaulle was taking a courageous step. This was the case even for a man whose high opinion of his abilities was to become legendary in the years to come.

164

His use of the first person singular has been seen as an early bid for the leadership of the Free French but at that moment, without any authority or backing, a personal appeal was all he could mount. Later, however, he did change to the even more regal style of 'We, General de Gaulle, leader of the Free French . . .' Oddly, his most memorable line did not occur in this broadcast but was incorporated in the proclamation dated '18 Juin 1940' and circulated in Britain at the end of that month: 'La France a perdu une bataille! Mais la France n'a pas perdu la guerre!' – **France has lost a battle, but France has not lost the war!**

Shortly after he returned home in triumph – but unable to secure his position politically – de Gaulle suffered the loss of his mentally retarded daughter, Anne. This was shortly before her twentieth birthday. Standing beside the grave, de Gaulle took his wife Yvonne by the hand and said the haunting words: 'Come. **Now she is like the others** . . .'

There are many versions of De Gaulle's aphorisms. **How can you govern a country which produces 246 different kinds of cheese?** is probably an accurate summing up of his view of the French people although the number of cheeses varies. 246 is Ernest Mignon's version in *Les Mots du General* (1962) while the *Oxford Dictionary of Quotations* (1979) has 'On ne peut rassembler les francais que sous le coup de la peur. On ne peut pas rassembler a froid un pays qui compte 265 specialité de fromages.' The date for this version is the 1951 election when de Gaulle's party, though largest, still did not have an overall majority. His remark to the effect that **I always thought I was Jeanne d'Arc and Buonaparte – how little one knows oneself** was apparently by way of reply to a speaker who had compared him with Robespierre (reported in *Figaro Littéraire* in 1958).

After awaiting the call for many years at Colombey-les-deux-Eglises, de Gaulle became President in 1958. He came to power amid the turmoil created by resistance from French colonialists to the idea of Algerian independence. De Gaulle eventually led his country in quite the opposite direction to the one expected of him but from the beginning he spoke with a forked tongue. On 4 June he flew to Algiers and told a rally **Je vous ai compris** – 'I have understood you' – which could have meant anything. He did, however, allow himself to shout the slogan **Vive l'Algérie française!** – 'Algeria is French' – which could have been taken to imply he supported the continuation of colonial rule. He played it down, however, by adding: 'After all, one says in current speech "French Canada", "Swiss Canada" . . .'

'Vive l'Algérie française' became the slogan of his right-wing opponents. The rhythm was tooted on car horns and the actual phrase was often delivered as part of the longer chant: 'Vive l'Algérie française, Vive la République, Vive la France!' **Vive de Gaulle!** was naturally used by his supporters, as it had been in the Second World War.

The word for which President de Gaulle was best known in Britain was **Non!** although he never made his rejections of her attempts to join the European Common Market so brief. On 14 January 1963, rather than informing the parties concerned direct, he dropped his veto bombshell at an elaborately staged press conference in Paris. He did not say 'no' in one word but questioned whether Britain was really up to EEC membership. Could his English friends transform themselves? That was the real question. 'It cannot be said that Britain is ready to do these things. Will she ever be? To that question only Britain can reply.'

Another example of de Gaulle's talent for irritation occurred on 25 July 1967 during a visit to Canada. He addressed a crowd from the balcony of Montreal town hall with the words 'Vive le Québec . . . **vive le Québec libre!**' ('Long live free Quebec!') – 'extempore remarks' aimed at supporting the separatist movement but which incurred the displeasure of the Federal Government. De Gaulle rapidly departed for home without visiting Ottawa as planned.

In private, de Gaulle had a colourful way of describing politicians. He called them 'pisse vinaigre' ('vinegar-pissers') or 'eunuchs of the Fourth Republic' or 'politichiens'. This last with its play on the French word for 'dog' leads us on to his word for the students who disrupted France during the May 1968 uprising. Returning from a visit to Romania, de Gaulle asked the Minister of Education: 'What about your students – still the chienlit?' Quite what this meant was much debated at the time. The polite dictionary definition of the word is a 'carnival masquerade' or 'ridiculous disguise' but if spelt 'chie-en-lit' it can mean 'bed-shitting' which seems more appropriate in the context. A day or two later on 19 May de Gaulle used the expression again at a Cabinet meeting while giving his view of the students' demands: **La réforme, oui; la chienlit, non** – 'Reform, yes; messing the bed, no.' It was his Prime Minister, Georges

Pompidou, who passed this remark on to the press. One of the many banners appearing in the streets at that time responded with a cartoon of the President and the charge 'La chienlit c'est lui!' This appeared outside the Renault factory at Billancourt where workers were staging a sit-in.

TITLES

Where the Kinquering Kongs Took Them From

I sometimes wonder whether writers in previous centuries existed chiefly to provide twentieth-century authors, playwrights and film-makers with titles for their works. A very large number of books, plays and films has a quotation for a title. It has become accepted practice and, to be sure, there can be a certain magic in titles – even if the origin is obscure or an allusion is likely to be lost on most people:

All Quiet on the Western Front The title of the novel by Eric Maria Remarque (1897–1970) has a complicated history. For a start, he did not call it that. Being German, his original title in 1929 was *Im Westen Nichts Neues* ('No News in the West'). When the novel was translated into English, a familiar phrase from the Allied side in the First World War was substituted. It had been used in military communiqués and newspaper reports and also taken up jocularly by men in the trenches.

Partridge[62] heard echoes in it of 'All quiet in the Shipka Pass' – cartoons of the 1877–8 Russo-Turkish War which he says had a vogue in 1915–16, though he never heard the allusion made himself. He rules out any connection with the American song title 'All Quiet along the Potomac' for no very good reason. This, in turn, came from a poem called 'The Picket Guard' by Ethel Lynn Beers (published 1861) – a sarcastic commentary on General Brinton McClellan's policy of delay at the start of the Civil War. The phrase had been used in reports from his Union headquarters and put in Northern newspaper headlines.

Call Me Madam Irving Berlin's musical was performed on Broadway in 1950, starring Ethel Merman as a woman ambassador appointed to represent the US in a tiny European state. It was inspired by the case of Pearl Mesta, the society hostess, whom Harry Truman appointed as ambassador to Luxembourg.

Why 'Call me Madam'? I suspect it arose from a misquotation. When Frances Perkins (1882–1965) was appointed Secretary of Labour by President Roosevelt in 1933, she became the first American woman to hold Cabinet rank. It was held that when she had been asked how she wished to be addressed in Cabinet she had replied, 'Call me Madam'. She denied this. Indeed, after the first Cabinet meeting reporters asked how they should address her. The Speaker-elect of the House of Representatives, Henry T. Rainey, answered for her: 'When the Secretary of Labour is a lady, she should be addressed with the same general formalities as the Secretary of Labour who is a gentleman. You call him "Mr Secretary." You will call her "Madam Secretary". You gentlemen know that when a lady is presiding over a meeting, she is referred to as "Madam Chairman" when you rise to address the chair.'[53]

Some of the newspapers put this ruling into Perkins's own mouth and that presumably is how the misquotation began. For years she had to put up with various other forms of address, of which 'Madam Perkins' she liked least. The misquotation occurs, for example, in *Ladies of Courage* by Eleanor Roosevelt and Lorena A. Hicock (1954): 'Some fool reporter wanted to know what to call her . . . "Call me Madam," she replied.'

The phrase lives on. Xaviera Hollander – the 'Happy Hooker' of the 1970s – was quoted as saying: 'You can call me mercenary, or call me madam, but as I always tell my customers – just call me anytime!'

Corridors of Power The novel with this title by C. P. Snow (1905–80) gave a phrase to the language which evoked an aspect of power peculiar to bureaucrats and civil servants – in that it is office-based power conducted in offices of the old kind (off corridors rather than open plan). He had used the idea before the 1964 novel. In *Homecomings* (1956) we read: 'The official world, the corridors of power, the dilemmas of conscience and egotism – she disliked them all.'

For a time, the title of Snow's 1959 Rede Lecture at Cambridge on the gap between science and literature and religion gave another much-used phrase to the language: *Two Cultures and the Scientific Revolution*. **The Two Cultures** became a catchphrase in discussions of the inability of the two camps to speak a common language or to understand each other at all.

The Fire Next Time   The epigraph in James Baldwin's 1963 book reads: 'God gave Noah the rainbow sign, / No more water, the fire next time.' In the novel this is described as 'that prophecy re-created from the Bible in a song by a slave'. As a warning of the use of fire in racial clashes it anticipates **Burn, baby, burn!** the black extremist slogan following the August 1965 riots in the Watts district of Los Angeles when thirty-four people were killed and entire blocks burned down.

For Whom the Bell Tolls   Ernest Hemingway had a special talent for choosing titles for his novels. This one he took from John Donne's famous passage beginning 'No man is an island'. His approach to the matter was described in a letter to Maxwell Perkins (21 April 1940):[4]

> I think it has the magic that a title has to have. Maybe it isn't too easy to say. But maybe the book will make it easy. Anyway I have had thirty some titles and they were all possible but this is the first one that has made the bell toll for me.
>
> Or do you suppose that people think only of tolls as long distance charges and of Bell as the Bell telephone system? If so it is out.
>
> The Tolling of the Bell. No. That's not right. If there is no modern connotation of telephone to throw it off, For Whom the Bell Tolls can be a good title I think.
>
> Anyway it is what I want to say. And so if it isn't right we will get it right. Meantime you have your provisional title for April 22.

Of Hemingway's own inventions, **The Sun Also Rises** is especially tantalising. It gave rise to the Hollywood nepotism joke about 'the son-in-law also rises'.

La Grande Illusion   The British pacifist, Sir Norman Angell (1872–1967), wrote a book about the futility of war entitled *Europe's Optical Illusion*, first published in 1909. A year later it was republished with the title *The Great Illusion*. The reason why the phrase has passed into common usage in French results from its use as the title of a film by Jean Renoir (1937) about French pilots captured by the Germans in the First World War. Angell was awarded the Nobel peace prize in 1933.

A Hard Day's Night Ringo Starr (*b*.1940) of the Beatles provided the group with the title of its first feature film in 1964. The title was not settled until filming was almost completed (one idea had been to call it 'Beatlemania'). Ringo was fond of saying 'It's been a hard day's night', though John Lennon had apparently used the phrase earlier in a poem.

In My Way Lord George-Brown chose an unusual way to refer to a well-known song when he took this title for his autobiography in 1971. He makes clear that he is referring to the song 'My Way' for which the English lyrics were written by Paul Anka in *c*.1969. The music is from a French composition 'Comme d'habitude' by Claude François and Jacques Revaux. Anka's version was finished: 'At three o'clock in the morning in New York. It was pouring with rain and it came to me. And I said "Wow, that is it, that's for Sinatra" . . . and then I cried.'

Frank Sinatra did indeed record the song with great success and it rapidly became a 'standard', sung by many other artists. The words became very special to many people, though a clear-eyed look at them reveals that they are at best not entirely literate. Their meaning is not entirely clear either. But this is the song's strength: people can (and have) read into it whatever they like – above all a feeling of the supremacy of the individual, that 'I' counts most of all. It gives them a feeling of justification – but with no real basis:

And now the end is near
And so I face the final curtain,
My friend, I'll say it clear,
I'll state my case of which I'm certain.
I've lived a life that's full, I've travelled each and ev'ry high-way
And more, much more than this, I did it my way.

Journey's End R. C. Sherriff's highly successful play from the 1930s about soldiers in the First World War might seem to have taken its title from Shakespeare's 'Journeys end is lovers meeting' or Dryden's 'The world's an inn and death the journey's end', but apparently not. In his autobiography *No Leading Lady* (1968)[85] he cryptically gave another source:

All that remained was to find a name for it. I never had flair for titles. With the plays for the Adventurers [an amateur group] it used to wait until somebody came up with a good one at rehearsal. I was on my own now, and it didn't come easily. I thought of calling it 'Suspense', but this didn't ring true because I couldn't honestly claim that it had any. 'Waiting' was a possibility, but it had the flavour of a restaurant or a railway station. The play didn't lend itself readily to an interesting title. One night I was reading a book in bed. I got to a chapter that closed with the words: 'It was late in the evening when we came at last to our Journey's End.' The last two words sprang out as the ones I was looking for. Next night I typed them on a front page for the play, and the thing was done.

The Long and the Short and the Tall   The play by Willis Hall (1959) took its title from a song of the Second World War, 'Bless 'Em All' (1940), or more likely its parody which contained many of the same lines:

> Sod 'em all. Sod 'em all,
> The long and the short and the tall,
> Sod all the sergeants and WO ones,
> Sod all the corporals and their bastard sons,
> For we're saying goodbye to them all,
> As back to their billets they crawl,
> You'll get no promotion
> This side of the ocean,
> So cheer up, my lads, sod 'em all.

Look, Stranger!   The BBC's use of W. H. Auden's phrase as the title of a TV series in 1976 revealed an interesting state of affairs. Auden's famous poem has two versions of its first line: 'Look, stranger, at this island now' and 'Look, stranger, on this island now'. 'At' is the original reading as it appears in the title poem of the collection *Look, Stranger!* published in 1936. But the American edition of 1937 was entitled *On this Island*. The text of the poem was changed to 'on' for the 1945 *Collected Poems*, published in America. Just to complicate matters, the poem's title was changed variously to 'Seascape' and 'Seaside'.

The reason for all this is that Faber and Faber (in the person of T. S. Eliot) applied the title *Look, Stranger!* to the collection that Auden wanted called 'Poems 1936' when he was inaccessible in Iceland. He said the Faber title sounded 'like the work of a vegetarian lady novelist' and made sure that it was subsequently dropped. In the process, the first line of the poem was altered.

Love in a Cold Climate   Evelyn Waugh wrote to Nancy Mitford on 10 October 1949 and said that the title of her novel had 'become a phrase. I mean when people want to be witty they say I've caught a cold in a cold climate and everyone understands.' The title was anticipated, however, by the poet Robert Southey in a letter to his brother Thomas on 28 April 1797: 'She made me half in love with a cold climate.'

Mean Streets   The title of this 1973 film was probably an allusion to Raymond Chandler who had written in *The Simple Art of Murder* (1950): 'Down these mean streets a man must go who is not himself mean; who is neither tarnished nor afraid' – describing the heroic qualities a detective should have in fiction.

Ernest Bramah had got there before him, however, with *Tales of Mean Streets* published about 1900, and Arthur Morrison with exactly the same title even earlier in 1891.

The Mousetrap   Agatha Christie's play which became the world's longest-running play following its first production in London (1952) was not casually titled. It is an allusion to *Hamlet* III.ii.247: 'What do you call the play?' . . . The Mousetrap . . . 'tis a knavish piece of work: but what of that.'

Oh, Calcutta!   Kenneth Tynan's sexually explicit and rather boring stage revue presented first on Broadway in 1969 took its title from a curious piece of word play. It is the equivalent of the French 'Oh, quel cul t'as', meaning – broadly speaking – 'Oh, what a lovely bum you have'. French 'cul' is derived from the Latin 'culus' or buttocks but, according to the context, may be applied to the female vagina or male anus. This may have come from the France of the Belle Epoque.

If nothing else, the show produced three memorable lines of criticism. An anonymous critic (in London) described it as 'Smithfield with songs' (alluding to the meat market); Sir Robert Helpmann, the dancer and choreographer (*b*.1909), commented: 'The trouble with nude dancing is that not everything stops when the music stops.' And Clive Barnes, drama critic of the *New York Times* (*b*.1927), revived a pattern for criticism of the 'gives so-and-so a bad name' kind when he wrote that it was: 'the sort of show that gives pornography a bad name.' (Walter Kerr – *b*.1913 – had written earlier: '*Hook and Ladder* is the sort of play that gives failure a bad name.')

The Razor's Edge   Somerset Maugham's 1945 novel took its title from the Katha-Upanishad: 'The sharp edge of a razor is difficult to pass over; thus the wise say the path to Salvation is hard.' Maugham, like Hemingway, took trouble to create curiosity with his titles. **Of Human Bondage** (1915) is the title of one of the books in Spinoza's *Ethics*. **The Moon and Sixpence** (1919) was taken from a review of *Of Human Bondage* in *The Times Literary Supplement* which said that the main character was: 'Like so many young men . . . so busy yearning for the moon that he never saw the sixpence at his feet.'[54]

The Road to Wigan Pier   George Orwell's title for his 1937 book about the North of England and the Depression alluded to an old music hall joke. A boat called 'The Wigan Packet' used to sail along the Leeds–Liverpool Canal daily (except Mondays) as far back as 1790. Although the journeys took many hours, passengers could go to Liverpool or Manchester. The joke about 'Wigan Pier' was started by George Formby Snr (1877–1921), billed in music hall as 'The Wigan Nightingale' (although in fact he was born in Ashton-under-Lyne). One tradition is that the joke started out of spite when he was booed off stage at the local theatre.

Room at the Top   John Braine's 1957 novel revived a saying to the effect that 'there is always room at the top'. This dates back at least to Daniel Webster, the American statesman (1782–1852), who when advised not to become a lawyer because the profession was overcrowded, replied: 'There is always room at the top.'

Softly, Softly   The BBC TV police drama series that grew out of the long-running *Z-Cars* in 1966 derived its title, in the first instance, from an unofficial motto of the Lancashire Constabulary Training School – 'Softly, softly, catchee monkey' (the Lancashire police had provided the inspiration for both series). This proverbial saying had been around since the early part of the century, though *Cassell's Book of Quotations* (1907) has the form: ' "Softly, softly," caught the monkey' – and gives a negro origin.

The Third Man   Carol Reed's 1949 film – from a script by Graham Greene and himself – was a thriller set among black-marketeers in post-war Vienna. The name must come from the cricketing term for the fielder on the off side near the boundary behind the batsman's wicket. However, it provided a ready-made tag following the 1951 defection to the Soviet Union of two British diplomats, Burgess and Maclean. It was apparent that they had been tipped off by a 'third man' and thus managed to scuttle away before their spying activities were revealed. From then on the hunt for the 'third man' continued. At last in 1963, Kim Philby followed them to Moscow and his identity was revealed. Not content with this, the hunt then began for a 'fourth man' who was later named as being Professor Anthony Blunt (in 1979). If there was a 'fifth man' or a 'sixth man', he has yet to be revealed, though speculation continues.

Where Were You When the Lights Went Out? A 1966 film celebrated the great New York power blackout of the previous year when the electricity supply failed and the birthrate was popularly supposed to have shot up nine months later. There may have been a music hall song with the title 'Where was Moses when the lights went out?', though this line seems to come from a popular rhyme (from early in the century?) that was completed with: 'Down in the cellar eating sauerkraut.'

Who's Afraid of Virginia Woolf The graffito 'Who's Afraid of Virginia Woolf?' – playing upon the Walt Disney song 'Who's Afraid of the Big Bad Wolf' – was used by Edward Albee as the title of a memorable play (first performed in 1962). Other titles derived from anonymous wall-scribblings included **Nostalgia isn't what it used to be** – a New York saying used by Simone Signoret for her autobiography (1978) – and **Stop the World I Want to Get Off**, the 1961 musical.

CINEMA

This is Where We Came In

IN the beginning was the image; the word came second.
The advent of sound to the cinema in 1929 was a unique
transformation in a medium of communication and yet only
occasionally have the words of a film had impact. The writer has
never had a dominant role to play; from early on he has tended to
become part of a committee process. Film scripts have rarely been
made available to the public, as play texts have been, and until the
coming of the video-cassette the only way to study dialogue was on
the basis of what you could remember. A few lines linger:

And so we say farewell . . .

The travelogues made by James A. Fitzpatrick (*b*.1902) were a
supporting feature of cinema programmes from 1925 onwards. With
the advent of sound, the commentaries to 'Fitzpatrick Traveltalks'
became noted for their parting words, summed up by the phrase **And
so we say farewell . . .** :

And it's from this paradise of the Canadian Rockies that we
reluctantly say farewell to Beautiful Banff . . .
And as the midnight sun lingers on the skyline of the city, we
most reluctantly say farewell to Stockholm, Venice of the
North . . .

176

With the picturesque impressions indelibly fixed in our memory, it is time to conclude our visit and reluctantly say farewell to Hong Kong, the hub of the Orient . . .

Frank Muir and Denis Norden's notable parody of the genre – 'Balham – Gateway to the South' – first written for radio *c*.1948 and later performed on disc by Peter Sellers (1958) accordingly contained the words: 'And so we say farewell to the historic borough . . .'

Another cliché of the travelogue was **The sun sinks slowly in the West . . .** Vernon Noble suggested to me (1983):

These commentaries were spoken by magic lantern lecturers or printed on film (to the accompaniment of romantic piano music) from the turn of the century. As likely an originator as any was Walter Jeffs, a Midlands journalist who took flickering travelogues, news films and comedies around the country. He joined the Thomas–Edison Animated Photo Company in 1901 and later toured his own cinematic show with great success: he died at the age of 80 in 1941.

Come up and see me some time

Mae West (1892–1980) had a notable stage hit on Broadway with her play *Diamond Lil* (first performed 9 April 1928). When she appeared in the 1933 film version entitled *She Done Him Wrong*, what she said to a very young Cary Grant (playing a coy undercover policeman) was:

You know I always did like a man in uniform. And that one fits you grand. Why don't you come up some time and see me? I'm home every evening.

As a catchphrase, the words have been rearranged to make them easier to say. That is how W. C. Fields says them *to* May West in the film *My Little Chickadee* (1939) and she herself took to saying them in the rearranged version: **Come up and see me some time.**

Come with me to the Casbah

A line forever associated with the film *Algiers* (1938) and its star, Charles Boyer, is **Come with me to the Casbah.** He is supposed to have said this to Hedy Lamarr. Boyer impersonators use it, the film was laughed at because of it, but nowhere is it said in the film. It was just a Hollywood legend that grew up. Boyer himself denied he has ever said it anywhere and thought it had all been started by a press agent.

The Cuckoo Clock

In Carol Reed's film *The Third Man* (1949), Orson Welles says to Joseph Cotten:

> In Italy, for 30 years under the Borgias, they had warfare, terror, murder and bloodshed, but they produced Michelangelo, Leonardo da Vinci and the Renaissance. In Switzerland, they had brotherly love; they had 500 years of democracy and peace – and **what did that produce? The cuckoo clock.**

It soon got around that Welles had added this speech to the basic script which was written by Graham Greene and Carol Reed. Indeed, it appears only as a footnote in the published script of the film. Then it was counter-suggested that the line was falsely being attributed to Welles, whereas it had actually been written by Greene. In 1977, Graham Greene confirmed to me that it *had* been written by Welles. During shooting of the film for reasons of timing the extra material had to be inserted.

Whether the idea was original to Welles is another matter. After all, he introduces the speech with: 'You know what the fellow said . . .'

Drop the gun, Looey!

Alistair Cooke writing in *Six Men*[19] remarked of Humphrey Bogart: 'He gave currency to another phrase with which the small fry of the English-speaking world brought the neighbourhood sneak to heel: **Drop the gun, Looey!**' Quite how Bogart did this, Cooke does not reveal. We have Bogart's word for it: 'I never said "Drop the gun, Louie" ' (quoted in Ezra Goodman, *Bogey: The Good–Bad Guy*).

It's just another of those lines that people would like to have heard spoken but which never were. At the end of *Casablanca* (1942) what Bogart says to Claude Rains (playing Captain Louis Renault) is: 'Not so fast, Louis.' Ironically, it is Renault who says: 'Put that gun down.'

5–4–3–2–1

A case of life following art: the backward countdown to a rocket launch was invented by the German film director Fritz Lang (1890–1976). He thought it would make things more suspenseful if the count was reversed – 5–4–3–2–1 – so in his 1928 film *By Rocket to the Moon* he established the routine for future real-life space shots.

Frankly, my dear . . .

The 1939 film *Gone With the Wind* was billed as **The Greatest Motion Picture Ever Made** and was certainly noted for an enormous amount of promotional hoop-la before it was completed.

It was based on the novel by Margaret Mitchell (1900–49) which took its title from Ernest Dowson's poem 'Non Sum Qualis Eram' (1896):

> I have forgot much, Cynara! Gone with the wind,
> Flung roses, roses, riotously with the throng,
> Dancing, to put thy pale lost lilies out of mind;
> But I was desolate and sick of an old passion,
> Yea, all the time, because the dance was long –
> I have been faithful to thee, Cynara! in my fashion.

The film makers clear in a prologue shown on the screen that what has 'gone with the wind' is the Old South – as a result of the American Civil War:

> There was a land of Cavaliers and Cotton Fields called the Old South. Here in this patrician world the Age of Chivalry took its last bows. Here was the last ever seen of the Knights and their Ladies Fair, of Master and Slave. Look for it only in books, for it is no more than a dream remembered, a Civilization gone with the wind . . .

The last scene of the picture, in which Scarlett O'Hara is finally abandoned by her husband Rhett Butler, although she believes she can get him back, contains the controversial moment when Rhett replies to her entreaty: 'Where shall I go? What shall I do?' with **Frankly, my dear, I don't give a damn.** This was only allowed on to the screen after months of negotiation with the Hays Office which controlled film censorship. In those days, the word 'damn' was forbidden usage in Hollywood under Section V.(1) of the Hays Code, even if it was what Margaret Mitchell had written in her novel. (She, however, had not thought of the 'frankly'.) Sidney Howard's original draft was changed to 'Frankly, my dear, I don't care.' The scene was shot with both versions of the line and the producer, David Selznick, argued at great length with the censors over which was to be used. He did this not least because he thought he would look like a fool if the famous line was excluded. He also wanted to show how faithful his film was to the original novel.

Selznick argued that the *Oxford English Dictionary* described 'damn' not as an oath but as a vulgarism, that many women's magazines used the word, and that preview audiences had expressed disappointment when the line was omitted. The censors suggested 'darn' instead. Selznick finally won the day – but because he was technically in breach of the Hays Code he was fined $5,000. The line still doesn't sound quite right: Gable had to put the emphasis, unnaturally, on 'give' rather than on 'damn'.

The last words of the film, spoken by Vivien Leigh, are: 'Tara! Home! I'll go home, and I'll think of some way to get him back. After all, **tomorrow is another day!**' The last sentence is as it appears in the Mitchell novel but the idea behind it has proverbial status. In Rastell's *Calisto & Melebea* (*c.*1527) there occurs the line: 'Well mother to morrow is a new day.'

If you want anything – just whistle

This catchphrase is not a direct quotation from a film. It is Lauren Bacall who says to Humphrey Bogart (and not, as is sometimes suggested, the other way round) in *To Have and Have Not* (1945):

> You know you don't have to act with me, Steve. You don't have to say anything, and **you don't have to do anything. Not a thing. Oh, maybe just whistle**. You know how to whistle, don't you, Steve? You just put your lips together and blow.

I'm as mad as hell

Peter Finch played a TV pundit-cum-evangelist in *Network* (1976) who exhorted his viewers thus:

> All I know is that first you've got to get mad. You've got to say, 'I'm a human being, goddammit! My life has value!' So I want you to get up now. I want all of you to get up out of your chairs. I want you to get up right now and go to the window, open it and stick your head out and yell, **I'm as mad as hell, and I'm not going to take this anymore!**

In 1978, Howard Jarvis, the social activist and author of California's Proposition 13 – the one that pegged taxes – campaigned with the slogan: 'I'm mad as hell and I'm not taking any more.' Fifty-seven per cent voted to reduce their property taxes. Jarvis entitled his book *I'm Mad as Hell* and credited Paddy Chayevsky, the screenwriter, with the coinage: 'For me, the words "I'm mad as hell" are more than a national saying, more than the title of this book; they express exactly how I feel and exactly how I felt about the woman who died at the County Building, as well as countless other victims of exorbitant taxes.'

It's all part of life's rich pageant

Peter Sellers as Inspector Clouseau has just fallen into a fountain in *A Shot in the Dark* (1964) when Elke Sommer commiserates with him: 'You'll catch your death of pneumonia.' Playing it phlegmatically as always, Clouseau replies: **It's all part of life's rich pageant.**

The origin of this happy phrase – sometimes 'pattern' or 'tapestry' is substituted for 'pageant' – was the subject of inquiry by Michael Watts of the *Sunday Express* in 1982. The earliest citation he came up with was from a record called 'The Game's Mistress', written and performed by Arthur Marshall (*b*.1910) in the 1930s. The monologue concludes: 'Never mind, dear – laugh it off, laugh it off. It's all part of life's rich pageant.'

It seemed like a good idea at the time

This useful everyday catchphrase has been traced by Leslie Halliwell[31] to a 1931 film called *The Last Flight*. This is the story of a group of American airmen who remain in Europe after the First World War. One of them is gored to death when he leaps into the arena during a bullfight. Journalists outside the hospital ask his friend why the man should have done such a thing. The friend (played by Richard Barthelmess) replies: 'Because **it seemed like a good idea at the time**.'

I want to be alone

Greta Garbo (*b*.1905) claimed that what she said was 'I want to be *let* alone' – i.e. she wanted privacy rather than solitude. Oddly, as Alexander Walker[94] observed:

Nowhere in anything she said, either in the lengthy interviews she gave in her early Hollywood days when she was perfectly approachable, or in the statements snatched on-the-run from the publicity-shy fugitive she later became, has it been possible to find the famous phrase, **I want to be alone**. What one can find, in abundance later on, is 'Why don't you let me alone?' and even 'I want to be left alone,' but neither is redolent of any more exotic order of being than a harassed celebrity. Yet the world prefers to believe the mythical and much more mysterious catchphrase utterance.

What complicates the issue is that Garbo herself used the lines

181

several times – in character. For example, in the 1929 silent film *The Single Standard* she gives the brush-off to a stranger and a subtitle declares: 'I am walking alone because I want to be alone'. And, as the ageing ballerina who loses her nerve and flees back to her suite in *Grand Hotel* (1932), she actually *says* it. Walker calls this 'an excellent example of art borrowing its effects from a myth that was reality for millions of people.'

The phrase was obviously well established by 1935 when Groucho Marx utters it in *A Night at the Opera*. Garbo herself says 'Go to bed, little father. We want to be alone' in *Ninotchka* (1939). So, it is not surprising that the myth has taken such a firm hold – particularly since Garbo became a virtual recluse for the second half of her life.

In 1983, at the death of Howard Dietz, the lyricist and MGM promotions executive, it was suggested that he had devised the saying as a publicity gimmick for Garbo.

Let's put on a show!

A staple line in the Mickey Rooney–Judy Garland movies of the late 1930s and early 1940s was something to the effect: 'Hey! I've got it! **Why don't we put on a show!**' The line took several forms. Another was **Let's do the show right here in the barn!** In *Babes in Arms* (1939) Rooney and Garland play the teenage children of retired vaudeville players who decide to put on a big show of their own, in the first of a series of films. They do not, however, actually say any of these lines, although they do express their determination to 'put on a show'. In whatever form, the line became a film cliché, now recalled only with amused affection.

Love means never having to say you're sorry

It was used in the film, in the book, and as a promotional tag for the film. It is a curiously empty line. In the last moments of the film *Love Story* (1970) Ryan O'Neal says it to Ray Milland, playing the father. He is quoting his student wife (Ali MacGraw) who has just died, in this three-Kleenex weepie. Eric Segal, who wrote the script, also produced a novelisation of the story in which the saying appears in the penultimate sentence as **Love means not ever having to say you're sorry.**

The insidious nature of the line is best demonstrated by the parodies that followed: a graffito (quoted 1974) said: 'A vasectomy means never having to say you're sorry'. The film *The Abominable Dr Phibes* (1971) was promoted with the slogan 'Love means not having to say you're ugly'.

A man's gotta do what a man's gotta do

Partridge[62] dated this as a catchphrase from *c*.1945. The only reference I have is to the Alan Ladd film *Shane* (1953) which was based on a Jack Shaeffer novel. Ladd does not say the line. He says: 'A man has to be what he is, Joey'. Another male character says: 'I couldn't do what I gotta do if . . .' and a woman notes: 'Shane did what he had to do.' Perhaps the phrase was used as a promotional slogan for the film.

A Martini, shaken not stirred

This example of would-be sophistication became a running joke in the immensely popular James Bond films of the 1960s and 70s. Without reading all Ian Fleming's Bond novels over again I can't swear for sure that the line was an invention of the screenwriters and not his.

However, the idea stems from the very first Bond novel, *Casino Royale*,[23] in which Bond orders a cocktail of his own devising. It consists of one dry Martini 'in a deep champagne goblet', three measures of Gordon's gin, one of vodka – 'made with grain instead of potatoes' – and half a measure of Kina Lillet. 'Shake it very well until it's ice-cold'. Bond justifies this fussiness a page or two later: 'I take a ridiculous pleasure in what I eat and drink. It comes partly from being a bachelor, but mostly from a habit of taking a lot of trouble over details. It's very pernickety and old-maidish really, but when I'm working I generally have to eat my meals alone and it makes them more interesting when one takes trouble.'

This characteristic was aped by the writers of the first Bond story to be filmed – *Dr No* (1962). A West Indian servant brings Bond a vodka and Martini and says: 'Martini like you said, sir, and not stirred'. *Dr No* also mentions the fad, though the words are not spoken by Bond. In the third film, *Goldfinger* (1964), Bond (played by Sean Connery) does get to say **A martini, shaken, not stirred** (he needs a drink after just escaping a laser death-ray) and there are references to it in *You Only Live Twice* (1967) and *On Her Majesty's Secret Service* (1969), among others.

The phrase was employed and played with in the numerous parodies of the Bond phenomenon on film, TV and radio, though – curiously enough – it is a piece of absolute nonsense. According to an expert, shaking a dry Martini 'turns it from something crystal-clear into a dreary frosted drink. It should be stirred quickly with ice in a jug'.

May the Force be with you

A delicious piece of hokum from *Star Wars* (1977) was the benediction: **May the Force be with you.** At one point Alec Guinness explains what it means: 'The Force is what gives the Jedi its power. It's an energy field created by all living things. It surrounds us, it penetrates us, it binds the galaxy together.'

The valediction turned up in Cornwall a short while after the film was released in Britain – as a police recruiting slogan.

Me Tarzan – you Jane

A box-office sensation of 1932 was the first sound Tarzan film – *Tarzan the Ape Man*. It spawned a long-running series and starred Johnny Weissmuller, an ex-US swimming champion, as Tarzan and Maureen O'Sullivan as Jane. At one point the ape man whisks Jane away to his tree-top abode and indulges in some elementary conversation with her: thumping his chest he says 'Tarzan!'; pointing at her he says 'Jane!' – so, in fact, he does not say the catchphrase commonly associated with him: **Me Tarzan, you Jane.** Interestingly, this great moment of movie dialogue was written by the British playwright and actor, Ivor Novello. In the original novel *Tarzan of the Apes* (1914) by Edgar Rice Burroughs the line does not occur – not least because, in the jungle, Tarzan and Jane are only able to communicate by writing notes to each other.

Play it again, Sam

As is widely known nowadays, nowhere in *Casablanca* (1942) does Humphrey Bogart – or anyone else – say the words **Play it again, Sam** to Dooley Wilson. He is the night club pianist and reluctant performer of the sentimental song 'As Time Goes By'. At one point Ingrid Bergman, as Ilsa, does have this exchange with him:

Ilsa: Play it once, Sam, for old time's sake.
Sam: Ah don't know what you mean, Miss Ilsa.
Ilsa: Play it, Sam. Play, 'As Time Goes By'.

Later on, Bogart as Rick, also tries to get Sam to play it:

Rick: Of all the gin joints in all the towns in all the world, she walks into mine! What's that you're playing?
Sam: Oh, just a little something of my own.
Rick: Well, stop it. You know what I want to hear.
Sam: No, I don't.
Rick: You played it for her, and you can play it for me.

Sam: Well, I don't think I can remember it.
Rick: If she can stand it, I can. Play it.

But, what the hell, if people think it should have been said, then why not! By the time of Woody Allen's film homage to Bogart – *Play It Again, Sam* – in 1972, the catchphrase was well established.

That's the way it crumbles, cookie-wise

Bartlett describes **That's the way the cookie crumbles** as an anonymous phrase from the 1950s. It was, however, given a memorable twist in Billy Wilder's film *The Apartment* (1960). The main characters make much play with the business jargon use of the suffix '-wise', as in 'promotion-wise' and 'gracious-living-wise'. Then Miss Kubelik (Shirley MacLaine) says to C. C. Baxter (Jack Lemmon): 'Why can't I ever fall in love with somebody nice like you?' Replies Baxter: 'Yeah, well, **that's the way it crumbles, cookie-wise.**'

We have ways of making you talk

The cliché threat of an evil inquisitor to his victim appears to come from 1930s Hollywood villains and was then applied to the Nazis from the Second World War onwards.

Leslie Halliwell[31] traced the earlier use to Douglas Dumbrille as the evil Mohammed Khan in *Lives of a Bengal Lancer* (1935). He says: 'We have ways of making *men* talk'.

A typical Nazi use can be found in the British film *Odette* (1950) in which the French resistance worker (Anna Neagle) is threatened with unmentioned nastiness by one of her captors. Says she, more than once: 'I have nothing to say.' Says he: **We have ways and means of making you talk.** After a little meaningful stoking of a fire, he urges her on with: 'We have ways and means of making a woman talk.'

Later, used in a caricature sense, the phrase saw further action in TV programmes like *Rowan and Martin's Laugh-In* (*c.*1968). Frank Muir presented a comedy series for London Weekend Television with the title *We Have Ways of Making You Laugh* (1968).

Would you be shocked if . . .

'Do you mind if I put on something more comfortable?' and 'Excuse me while I slip into something more comfortable?' are just two of the misquotations of a famous line that I have come across. What Jean Harlow as Helen actually says to Ben Lyon as Monte in *Hell's Angels* (1930) is: **Would you be shocked if I put on something more**

comfortable? It is, of course, by way of a proposition and she exchanges her fur wrap for a dressing gown.

You ain't heard nothin' yet!

Al Jolson (1888–1950) not only ad-libbed a line for the first full-length talking picture, *The Jazz Singer* (1927), he also provided a slogan for the coming age of the sound cinema. Michael Freedland described what happened:[28]

> The original idea was that *The Jazz Singer* would be a completely silent picture with just Jolson's songs and the occasional snatch of the background music . . . There were sub-titles for the picture . . . so no one was terribly concerned when Jolson started ad-libbing in front of the cameras . . . All was ready for Jolson to go into his first big featured number, 'Toot Toot Tootsie Goo'-bye'. But Alan Crosland, the director, had never worked with Jolson before. Just as he gave the signal for everything to roll, Al got into the spirit of the thing. 'Wait a minute, wait a minute,' he cried. **'You ain't heard nothin' yet**. Wait a minute I tell yer . . . you wanna hear "Toot Toot Tootsie"? All right, hold on.' . . . No screen playwright could ever have put those words in a script and got away with it. But the mikes were switched on, the film and Jolson were in motion and those sentences were preserved for posterity.

The recording makes it clear that Jolson did not add 'folks' at the end of his mighty line, as both Bartlett and the ODQ say he did.

You dirty rat!

James Cagney never said the words put in his mouth by countless impressionists – **You dirty rat!** In *Blonde Crazy* (1931) he did, however, call someone a 'dirty, double-crossing rat' – which, I suppose, amounts to the same thing.

You've got to come back a star!

A great film cliché but not when it was new-minted in *42nd Street* (1933). Warren Baxter as a theatrical producer says to Ruby Keeler as the chorus girl who takes over at short notice from an indisposed star: **You're going out a youngster – but you've got to come back a star!**

186

MARTIN LUTHER KING

I Have a Dream

THE largest protest rally in US history took place on 28 August 1963 when nearly 250,000 people joined the March on Washington – a Civil Rights demonstration that reached its climax near the Lincoln Memorial with a speech by the Rev. Dr Martin Luther King, Jr (1929–68). His sixteen-minute oration applied the repetitions and rhythms of a revivalist preacher to a clear challenge on the lack of negro progress since the Emancipation Proclamation of exactly one hundred years before.

King spoke initially from a text he had painstakingly concocted during the previous two days. It was more carefully prepared than any speech he had ever delivered. Without sleeping a wink the night before he had tried to compress his message into the eight minutes allotted him. Ed Clayton, a public relations agent in Atlanta and frequently a polisher of King's speeches, was telephoned for his opinions. Coretta King recalled her husband finishing it bone-weary and almost in collapse from exhaustion. After a while, during delivery, King gave way to his familiar technique of using almost ritualistic invocations of the Bible and American lore in a sob-laden voice. This deeply moving speech was great, not because it changed anything but because it was a masterly exposition of an unanswerable political message. It is reproduced here complete:

187

I am happy to join with you today in what will go down in history as the greatest demonstration for freedom in the history of our nation. Five score years ago, a great American in whose symbolic shadow we stand today signed the Emancipation Proclamation. This momentous decree came as the great beacon light of hope to millions of negro slaves who had been seared in the flames of withering injustice. It came as the joyous daybreak to end the long night of their captivity. But one hundred years later the negro still is not free. One hundred years later the life of the negro is still sadly crippled by the manacles of segregation and the chains of discrimination. One hundred years later the negro lives on a lonely island of poverty in the midst of a vast ocean of material prosperity. One hundred years later the negro is still languished in the corners of American society and finds himself an exile in his own land.

So we've come here today to dramatise the shameful condition. In a sense we've come to our nation's capital to cash a cheque. When the architects of our republic wrote the magnificent words of the Constitution and the Declaration of Independence, they were signing a promissory note to which every American was to fall heir. This note was a promise that all men – yes, black men as well as white men – would be guaranteed the unalienable rights of life, liberty and the pursuit of happiness. It is obvious today that America has defaulted on this promissory note in so far as her citizens of colour are concerned. Instead of honouring this sacred obligation, America has given the negro people a bad cheque – a cheque which has come back marked 'insufficient funds'. But we refuse to believe that the bank of justice is bankrupt; we refuse to believe that there are insufficient funds in the great vaults of opportunity of this nation. Se we've come to cash this cheque, a cheque that will give us upon demand the riches of freedom and the security of justice.

We are also come to this hallowed spot to remind America of the fierce urgency of now. This is no time to engage in the luxury of cooling off or to take the tranquillising drug of gradualism. Now is the time to rise from the dark and desolate valley of segregation to the sunlit pass of racial justice. Now is the time to lift our nation from the quicksands of racial injustice to the solid rock of brotherhood. Now is the time to make justice a reality for all of God's children. It would be fatal for the nation to overlook the urgency of the moment. This, the sweltering summer of the negro's legitimate discontent, will not pass until there is an invigorating autumn of freedom and equality. 1963 is not an end, but a beginning. Those who hope that the negro needed to blow off steam and will now be content will have a rude awakening if the nation returns to business as usual. There will be neither rest nor tranquillity in America until the negro is granted citizenship rights. The whirlwinds of revolt will continue to shake the foundations of our nation until the bright day of justice emerges.

There is something that I must say to my people who stand on the worn threshold which leads into the palace of justice: in the process of gaining our rightful place we must not be guilty of wrongful deeds. Let us not seek to satisfy our thirst for freedom by drinking from the cup of bitterness and hatred. We must forever conduct our struggle on the highest plain of dignity and discipline. We must not allow our recreative process to degenerate into physical violence. Again and again we must rise to the majestic heights of meeting physical force with soul force. The marvellous new militancy which has engulfed the negro community must not lead us to a distrust of all white people. For many of our white brothers, as evidenced by their presence here today, have come to realise that their destiny is tied up with our destiny.

We cannot turn back. There are those who are asking the devotees of civil rights 'When will you be satisfied?' We can never be satisfied as long as the negro is the victim of the unspeakable horrors of police brutality. We can never be satisfied as long as our bodies, heavy with the fatigue of travel cannot gain lodging in the motels of the highways and the hotels of the cities. We can never be satisfied as long as the negro's basic mobility is from a small ghetto to a larger one. We can never be satisfied as long as our children are stripped of their selfhood and robbed of their dignity by signs stating 'for whites only'. We cannot be satisfied as long as a negro in Mississippi cannot vote and a negro in New York believes he has nothing for which to vote. No, no, we are not satisfied and we will not be satisfied until justice rolls down like waters and righteousness like a mighty stream.

I am not unmindful that some of you have come here out of great trials and tribulations. Some of you have come fresh from narrow gaol cells. Some of you have come from areas where your quest for freedom left you battered by the storms of persecution and staggered by the winds of police brutality. You have been the veterans of creative suffering. Continue to work with the faith that unearned suffering is redemptive. Go back to Mississippi, go back to Alabama, go back to South Carolina and go back to Georgia. Go back to Louisiana, go back to the slums and ghettos of our northern cities, knowing that somehow this situation can and will be changed. Let us not wallow in the valley of despair, I say to you today, my friends.

So even though we face the difficulties of today and tomorrow, I still have a dream. It is a dream deeply rooted in the American dream. **I have a dream** that one day this nation will rise up and live out the true meaning of its creed – 'We hold these truths to be self-evident that all men are created equal.' I have a dream that one day on the red hills of Georgia sons of former slaves and the sons of former slave owners will be able to sit down together at the table of brotherhood. I have a dream that one day even the state of Mississippi – a state sweltering with the heat of injustice, sweltering with the heat of repression – will be transformed into an oasis of freedom and justice. I have a dream that my four little children will one day live in a nation where they will not be judged by the colour of their skin but by the content of their character. I have a dream today.

I have a dream that one day in Alabama, with its vicious racists, with its governor having his lips dripping with the words of interposition and nullification – one day right there in Alabama, little black boys and black girls will be able to join hands with little white boys and white girls as sisters and brothers. I have a dream today.

I have a dream that one day every valley shall be exalted, every hill and mountain shall be made low, the rough places will be made plain, and the crooked places will be made straight, and the glory of the Lord shall be revealed, and all flesh shall see it together. This is our hope. This is the faith that I go back to the South with. With this faith we will be able to transform the jangling discords of our nation into a beautiful symphony of brotherhood. With this faith we will be able to work together, to pray together, to struggle together, to go to jail together, to stand up for freedom together, knowing that we will be free one day. This will be the day when all of God's children will be able to sing with new meaning 'My country' tis of thee, sweet land of liberty, of thee I sing. Land where my fathers died, land of the pilgrim's pride, from every mountainside, let freedom ring.'

And if America is to be a great nation, this must become true. So, let freedom ring from the prodigious hilltops of New Hampshire! Let freedom ring from the mighty mountains of New York! Let freedom ring from the heightening Alleghenies of Pennsylvania! Let freedom ring from the snowcapped Rockies of Colorado! Let freedom ring from the curvaceous slopes of California!

But not only that: let freedom ring from Stone Mountain of Georgia! Let freedom ring from Lookout Mountain of Tennessee! Let freedom ring from every hill and mole hill of Mississippi! From every mountainside, let freedom ring!

And when this happens, when we allow freedom to ring, when we let it ring from every village and every hamlet, from every state and every city, we will be able to speed up that day when all of God's children, black men and white men, Jews and gentiles, Protestants and Catholics, will be able to join hands and sing in the words of the old negro spiritual: 'Free at last, free at last, thank God Almighty, we are free at last!'

The extent to which King was summoning up themes and phrases from his own speeches dating back to 1956 can be illustrated by this extract from a speech he had delivered in Detroit on 23 June 1963. Spoken with less assurance, this version can be seen as a kind of dress rehearsal for Washington:

I have a dream this afternoon that one day men will no longer burn down houses and the church of God simply because people want to be free. I have a dream this afternoon that there will be a day when we will no longer face the atrocities that Emma Teale had to face or Medgar Evers had to face, that all men can live with dignity. I have a dream this afternoon that my four little children will not come up in the same young days that I came up in, that they will be judged on the basis of the content of their character, not the colour of their skin. Yes, I have a dream this afternoon that one day in this land the words of Amos will become real and justice will roll down like waters and righteousness like a mighty stream.

I have a dream this evening [sic] that one day we will recognise the words of Jefferson that all men are created equal, that they are endowed by their Creator with some unalienable rights and among these life, liberty and the pursuit of happiness. I have a dream this afternoon – I have a dream that one day every valley shall be exalted and every hill and mountain shall be made low, the rough places will be made plain and the crooked places will be made straight. And the Glory of the Lord shall be revealed and all flesh shall see it together. I have a dream this afternoon that the brotherhood of man will become a reality in this day.

With this faith I will go out and carve a tunnel of hope through the mountain of despair. With this faith I will go out with you and transform dark yesterdays into bright tomorrows. With this faith

191

we will be able to achieve this new day, when all of God's children, black men and white men, Jews and gentiles, Protestants and Catholics, will be able to join hands and sing with the negroes in the spiritual of old: **Free at last, free at last, thank God Almighty, we are free at last!**

Martin Luther King was assassinated on 4 April 1968. Did he have a premonition of death? The night before he had referred in a Memphis speech to attempts on his life:

It really doesn't matter with me now. Because **I've been to the mountain top**. Like anybody I would like to live a long life. Longevity has its place. But I'm not concerned about that now. I just want to do God's will. And He's allowed me to go up to the mountain top. And I've looked over and I've *seen* the promised land. And I may not get there with you. But I want you to know tonight that we as a people *will* get to the promised land. So I'm happy tonight. I'm not worried about anything. I'm not fearing *any* man.

He was buried in South View Cemetery, Atlanta, Ga. On his grave was carved a slightly altered version of the words with which he had ended his 'I have a dream' speeches, and indeed, his last 'mountain top' speech:

FREE AT LAST, FREE AT LAST
THANK GOD ALMIGHTY
I'M FREE AT LAST.

The Tiger: "Curious! I seem to hear a child weeping!"

From the *Daily Herald*, 1919.

"The price of petrol has been increased by one penny"—Official

From the *Daily Mirror*, 1942.

THURS
OCT. 25
1951

Daily Mirror

1½d
No. 14,915

FORWARD
WITH THE
PEOPLE

Registered at G.P.O. as a Newspaper.

WHOSE FINGER?

BIG ISSUES OF 1951

Today YOUR finger is on the trigger

SEE YOU DEFEND

PEACE with SECURITY and PROGRESS with FAIR SHARES

VOTE FOR THE PARTY YOU CAN REALLY TRUST

The 'Daily Mirror' believes that Party is Labour

Front page of the *Daily Mirror*, 1951.

Advertisement for *The Times*, 1957.

General de Gaulle in London, 1940: 'France has lost a battle, but France has not lost the war.'

Orson Welles, *above*, (with Joseph Cotten) in *The Third Man*: 'What did that produce? The cuckoo clock.'

Sean Connery (with Joseph Wiseman) in *Dr No*: 'A martini, shaken, not stirred.'

Clark Gable (with Vivien Leigh) in *Gone With the Wind*: 'Frankly, my dear . . .'

Greta Garbo in *Grand Hotel*: 'I want to be alone.'

Wilson, Bogart and Bergman in *Casablanca*: 'Play it again, Sam.'

Al Jolson: 'You ain't heard nothin' yet

ADVERTISING

It Pays to Sloganise

THE twentieth century has been an age of slogans: they have leapt out at us from countless billboards, TV screens, T-shirts, bumper-stickers and buttons. They have been designed by advertisers to sell everything from deodorants to Democrats, from world wars to whisky. For a fuller treatment of this subject, see my *Book of Slogans and Catchphrases*.[69]

Here are some of the century's most notable advertising slogans – dealing with commercial products only (political slogans appear elsewhere) – together with some miscellaneous lines and phrases that have entered the language through advertising:

At 60 miles an hour . . .

The best-known promotional line there has ever been for an automobile was not devised by some copywriting genius but came from a car test of the 1958 Rolls-Royce Silver Cloud by the Technical Editor of *The Motor* magazine: **At 60 miles an hour the loudest noise in this new Rolls-Royce comes from the electric clock.** David Ogilvy, who had the idea of putting it into an advertisement, recalls presenting the headline to a senior Rolls-Royce executive in New York who shook his head sadly and said: 'We really ought to do something about that damned clock.'

Even the motoring journalist had not been entirely original. A

193

1907 review of the Silver Ghost in *The Autocar* read: 'At whatever speed the car is driven, the auditory nerves when driving are troubled by no fuller sound than emanates from the 8-day clock.'

The Big One

This boast, beloved of a certain type of advertiser – not least because of a fairly obvious *double entendre* – almost certainly dates back to 1907 when, in the USA, the Ringling Brothers Circus bought up the rival Barnum and Bailey circus. The two together were billed, understandably, as **The Big One**.

When the outfit closed in 1956, the *New York Post* had the headline: 'The Big One Is No More!' Wentworth & Flexner[26] also point out that a 'big one' is also a thousand dollar bill (from gambling use) and a nursery euphemism for a bowel movement.

Blondes have more fun

Shirley Polykoff's slogan for Lady Clairol, in use from 1957, was **Is it true . . . Blondes have more fun?** This was chosen from ten suggestions including 'Is it true that blondes are never lonesome?' and 'Is it true blondes marry millionaires?' Speculation about blondes, along these lines, goes back at least to the title of the novel by Anita Loos, *Gentlemen Prefer Blondes* (1925), to which she provided the sequel [but] *They Marry Brunettes*.

BO

'Body odour' was a new, worrying concept devised to sell Lifebuoy soap in the US from the early 1930s onwards. On radio they used to sing the jingle:

> Singing in the bathtub, singing for joy,
> Living a life of Lifebuoy –
> Can't help singing, 'cos I know
> That Lifebuoy really stops **B.O.**

The initials 'BO' were sung *basso profundo*, emphasising the horror of the offence. In the UK, TV ads showed pairs of male or female friends out on a spree, intending to attract partners. When one of the pair was seen to have a problem the other whispered helpfully: 'BO.'

Breakfast of Champions

A series of advertisements for Wheaties, the US breakfast cereal, which was running in 1950, featured this slogan together with sporting champions like Jackie Robinson: 'One of the greatest names

194

in baseball . . . this famous Dodger star is a Wheaties man: "A lot of us ball players go for milk, fruit and Wheaties," says Jackie . . . Had *your* Wheaties today?'

Kurt Vonnegut used the phrase **Breakfast of Champions** as the title of a novel in 1973.

Can *you* tell Stork from butter?

One of the earliest commercials on British TV (*c*.1956) showed housewives taking part in comparative taste tests between pieces of bread spread with real butter and Stork margarine. The challenge to their taste-buds was: **Can *you* tell Stork from butter?** The idea caused much amusement at the time and was often referred to in popular speech.

A Diamond is forever

In 1939, the South Africa-based De Beers Consolidated Mines launched a campaign to promote further the tradition of diamond engagement rings. The N. W. Ayer agency of Chicago (copywriter B. J. Kidd) came up with the line: **A diamond is forever**.

The line passed easily into the language, perhaps because the idea was an obvious one. Anita Loos in *Gentlemen Prefer Blondes* (1925) enshrined it in: 'Kissing your hand may make you feel very, very good but a diamond and safire bracelet lasts for ever.' Ian Fleming gave a variation of the phrase as the title of his 1956 James Bond novel *Diamonds are Forever*.

Technically speaking, however, they are not. It takes a high temperature, but, being of pure carbon, diamonds will burn.

Does she . . . or doesn't she?

This innuendo-laden phrase began life selling Clairol hair-colouring in 1955. The brain-child of Shirley Polykoff (who entitled her advertising memoirs *Does She . . . or Doesn't She?* in 1975),[64] the expression first arose at a party when a girl arrived with flaming red hair. Shirley Polykoff involuntarily uttered the line to her husband, George. As she tells it, however, her mother-in-law takes some of the credit for planting the words in her mind some twenty years previously. George told Shirley of his mother's first reaction on meeting her: 'She says you paint your hair. Well, do you?

When Ms Polykoff submitted **Does she . . . or doesn't she?** at the Foote Cone & Belding agency in New York (together with two ideas she wished to have rejected) she suggested it be followed by the phrase 'Only her mother knows for sure!' or 'So natural, only her mother knows for sure'. She felt she might have to change 'mother' to 'hairdresser' so as not to offend beauty salons (and **Only her hairdresser knows for sure** was eventually chosen).

First reaction was that the double meaning in the words would cause the line to be rejected. Indeed, *Life* magazine would not take the ad. But subsequent research at *Life* failed to turn up a single female staff member who admitted detecting any innuendo and the phrases were locked into the form they kept for the next eighteen years.

'J' underlines the double meaning in the slogan with this comment from *The Sensuous Woman* (1969): 'Our world has changed. It's no longer a question of "Does she or doesn't she?" We all know she wants to, is about to, or does.' A New York graffito, quoted in 1974, stated: 'Only *his* hairdresser knows for sure.'

Drinka Pinta Milka Day

The target was to get everyone drinking one pint of milk a day and the slogan was a piece of bath-tub inspiration that came from the client, namely Bertrand Whitehead, Executive Officer of the National Milk Publicity Council of England and Wales in 1958. The creative department of the Mather & Crowther agency took an instant dislike to **Drinka Pinta Milka Day** but Francis Ogilvy, the chairman, insisted on it being used despite their protests.

It was the kind of coinage to drive teachers and pedants mad but eventually 'a pinta' achieved a kind of respectability when it was accorded an entry in *Chambers' Twentieth Century Dictionary* and others.

Five o'clock shadow

This expression for the stubbly growth that some men acquire on their faces towards the end of the working day appeared in advertisements for Gem Razors and Blades in America before the Second World War. The slogan was: **Avoid 'Five O'Clock Shadow'**. A 1937 ad said: 'That unsightly beard growth which appears prematurely at about 5 pm looks bad.'

The most notable sufferer was Richard Nixon who may have lost the TV debates with John F. Kennedy in 1960 as a result. He recorded:[57] 'Kennedy arrived . . . looking tanned rested and fit. My television adviser, Ted Rogers, recommended that I use television make-up, but unwisely I refused, permitting only a little "beard stick" on my perpetual five o'clock shadow.'

Food shot from guns

Claude C. Hopkins (1867–1932), one of the great American

advertising gurus, created this odd selling line for Quaker Puffed
Wheat and Puffed Rice in the early 1900s. He wrote:

> I watched the process where the grains were shot from guns and I
> coined the phrase. The idea aroused ridicule. One of the greatest
> food advertisers in the country wrote an article about it. He said
> that of all the follies evolved in food advertising this certainly was
> the worst – the idea of appealing to women on **Food shot from
> guns** was the theory of an imbecile. But the theory proved
> attractive. It was such a curiosity-rouser that it proved itself the
> most successful campaign ever conducted in cereals.

Gone for a Burton

Folk memory suggest that **Gone for a Burton** was originally used in
the UK prior to the Second World War to promote a Bass beer
known in the trade as 'a Burton' (though, in fact, several ales are
brewed in Burton-upon-Trent). More positive proof is lacking. Early
in the war, the phrase was adopted as an idiom to describe what had
happened to a missing person, presumed dead, especially in the
RAF.

Another fanciful theory is that the phrase grew out of the fact that
RAF casualty records were kept in an office above or near a branch
of Burton Menswear in Blackpool.

Go to work on an egg

In 1957, Fay Weldon (*b*.1932), later known as a novelist and TV
playwright, was a copywriter on the British Egg Marketing Board
account at the Mather & Crowther agency. In 1981 she told me:

> I was certainly in charge of copy at the time **Go to work on an egg**
> was first used as a slogan as the main theme for an advertising
> campaign. The phrase itself had been in existence for some time
> and hung about in the middle of paragraphs and was sometimes
> promoted to base lines. Who invented it, it would be hard to say.
> It is perfectly possible, indeed probable that I put those particular
> six words together in that particular order but I would not swear to
> it.

Guinness is good for you

After 170 years without advertising, Arthur Guinness, Son &
Company, decided to call in the image-makers for their beer in 1929.
Oswald Greene at the S. H. Benson agency initiated some consumer
research (unusual in those days) into why people were drinking

Guinness. It transpired that people thought Guinness did them good, though the slogan based on this view was nearly rejected as being too ordinary and not clever enough.

Ask any British person to give an example of an advertising slogan and he is more than likely to say **Guinness is good for you**. It is etched on the national consciousness to such an extent that although the slogan was discontinued in *c.*1941 and has not been revived since 1963, people remember it as though they saw it yesterday.

Have a banana

Britain became 'banana-conscious' in the early years of the twentieth century following the appointment of Roger Ackerley as chief salesman of Elders & Fyffes, banana importers, in 1898. The phrase **Have a banana**, never a slogan as such, was popularly interpolated at the end of the first line of the song 'Let's All Go Down the Strand', published in 1904. It had not been put there by the composer but was so successful that later printings of the song always included it.

Other banana songs followed. In 1922, a further Elders & Fyffes campaign benefited from the composition **Yes, We Have No Bananas!** (a remark the composers took from a cartoon strip by Tad Dorgan and not, as they claimed, from a Greek fruit-store owner). Fyffes co-operated with the music publishers and distributed 10,000 'hands' of bananas to music-sellers with the inscription 'Yes! We have no bananas! On sale here'.

Heineken refreshes the parts

'I wrote the slogan,' said Terry Lovelock, 'during December 1974 at 3 am at the Hotel Marmounia in Marakesh. After eight weeks of incubation with the agency [Collett, Dickenson, Pearce], it was really a brainstorm. No other lines were written. The trip was to refresh the brain. Expensive, but it worked.'

The resulting line – **Heineken refreshes the parts other beers cannot reach** – became one of the most popular slogans ever heard in Britain. The merits of the lager were always demonstrated with amusing visuals – the 'droop-snoot' of Concorde raised by an infusion of the brew; a piano tuner's ears sharpened; a policeman's toes refreshed. There was also a strong topical element. When Chia-Chia, a panda from London Zoo, was sent off in 1981 to mate with Ling-Ling in Washington, a full-page press ad merely said 'Good Luck Chia-Chia from Heineken', the slogan being understood.

I love New York

In June 1977 the New York State Department of Commerce

launched a campaign to attract tourists. The first commercial showed
people enjoying themselves in outdoor activities – fishing, horseback
riding, camping, and so forth. Each one said something like: 'I'm
from New Hampshire, but I love New York,' 'I'm from Cape Cod,
but I love New York,' and ended with a man in a camping scene
saying: 'I'm from Brooklyn, but I loooove New York.'

Since then **I Love New York** has become one of the best-known
advertising slogans in the world and has been widely copied,
particularly with the word 'love' replaced by a heart-shape.

Charlie Moss at the Wells, Rich, Greene agency is credited with
having coined the phrase – though maybe he had heard the song
'How about you?' with lyrics by Ralph Freed which includes the line
'I like New York in June'.

I'm only here for the beer

In 1971, a visiting American copywriter, Ros Levenstein, contributed **I'm only here for the beer** to a British campaign for Double
Diamond beer. It passed into the language as an inconsequential
catchphrase but, from an advertising point of view, was not an ideal
slogan as it became detached from the particular brand of beer.

It beats . . . as it sweeps . . . as it cleans

Hoover carpet sweepers were invented by James Murray Spangler in
1908 but took their name from William H. Hoover who marketed
them. The machines' exclusive feature was 'triple action': the gentle
beating or tapping of the carpet to loosen dirt and grit, the strong
sucking, and the rotary brushing. The slogan **It beats . . . as it
sweeps . . . as it cleans**, coined by Gerald Page-Wood of Erwin
Wasey in Cleveland, Ohio, enshrined these points from 1919 and was
still in use in 1981.

I thought . . . until I discovered . . .

The common advertising notion of a way of life or belief being swept
away by some sudden revelation was given memorable form from
1970–5 in a series of slogans for Smirnoff vodka in the UK. The
variations included:

> **I thought** St Tropez was a spanish monk . . .
> Accountancy was my life . . .
> I was the mainstay of the public library . . .
> I thought the Kama Sutra was an Indian restaurant
> **. . . until I discovered Smirnoff.**

David Tree, an art director at the Young & Rubicam agency, recalled how he and John Bacon, the copywriter, had struggled for weeks to get the right idea. One day, after a fruitless session, he was leaving for lunch when he happened to glance at a magazine pin-up adorning the wall of their office. 'If we really get stuck,' he said, 'We can always say, "I was a boring housewife in Southgate until . . .".' (Southgate was where he was living at the time.)

Nice one, Cyril

The story of **Nice one, Cyril** is a classic instance of a phrase from advertising being taken up by the public, turned into a catchphrase, and then as suddenly dropped. Its origins were quite soon forgotten. The saying caught the imagination of British TV viewers in a 1972 advertisement for Wonderloaf. Two bakers were shown wearing T-shirts labelled 'Nottingham' and 'Liverpool' respectively. 'All our local bakers reckon they can taste a Wonderloaf and tell you who baked it,' a voice-over commentary explained. 'It was oven-baked at one of our local bakeries.' The following exchange then took place between the bakers:

Liverpool: Leeds? High Wycombe? It's one of Cyril's. Mmm. Good texture, nice colour, very fresh . . .

Nottingham: Cyril . . . I think it's one of Frank's down at Luton . . . it's definitely saying Newcastle to me . . .

The voice-over then intervened: 'The truth is, they can't say for sure. But we can say – '

Nottingham: Nice one, Cyril!

As a phrase, why did 'Nice one, Cyril' catch on? It had a sibilant ease, it was fun to say. More importantly it could be used in any number of situations, not least sexual ones. In 1973, the phrase was taken up by Tottenham Hotspur supporters of the footballer, Cyril Knowles. They even recorded a song about him which went:

Nice one, Cyril
Nice one, son.
Nice one, Cyril,
Let's have another one.

Comedian Cyril Fletcher used it as the title of his 1978 autobiography. The following year the word 'Cyril' was observed

200

added to the first kilometre sign outside a seaside resort in the South of France. Shortly afterwards, the phrase disappeared almost completely from use.

Nothing over sixpence

The first British Woolworth's opened in 1909 and was described as a 'threepence and sixpence' store, the equivalent of the 'five-and-ten' (cent) stores in America. Hence the phrase 'Nothing over sixpence' arose and lasted until the Second World War when prices could no longer be contained below this limit. A song dating from 1927 includes the lines:

To Woolworth's, Hobbs and Sutcliffe always go to get their bats,
Stan Baldwin gets his pipes there, and Winston get his hats;
And the Prince would never think of going elsewhere for his spats–
And there's **nothing over sixpence** in the stores!

Aneurin Bevan once said of a speech by Neville Chamberlain that it was 'like paying a visit to Woolworth's – everything in its place and nothing above sixpence.'

Put a tiger in your tank

The Esso Tiger had been around in the USA for a long time before 1964 when a cartoon version was introduced for the first time (a year later in the UK) to promote Esso petroleum. It became a national craze, with countless tiger tails adorning the petrol caps of the nation's cars. Subsequently the slogan **Put a tiger in your tank** went further afield: 'Mettez un tigre dans votre moteur' appeared in France; in Germany, 'Pack den Tiger in den tank'. In America, particularly, the slogan gave rise to numerous tiger derivatives: 'If you feel like a tiger is in your throat, reach for Guardets Lozenges . . .' A hamburger stand advertised: 'Put a tiger in your tummy.' Tiger Beer in the Japanese *Times* sloganned: 'Put a tiger in your tankard.' Standard Rochester Beer countered with: 'Put a tankard in your tiger.' The UK campaign ran for two years before it flagged.

Perhaps the slogan owed something to the Muddy Waters song '(I Want to Put a) Tiger in Your Tank' (by W. Dixon) which he was performing by 1960 and which gave double meanings to a number of motoring phrases.

Say it with flowers

Henry Penn of Boston, Mass., was chairman of the National Publicity Committee of the Society of American Florists in 1917. He was discussing the need for a slogan with Major Patrick O'Keefe (1872–1934), head of an agency. The Major suggested: 'Flowers are words that even a babe can understand' – a line he had found in a poetry book. Penn considered this too long. The Major, agreeing, rejoined: 'Why, you can **say it with flowers** in so many words.' Mr Penn's hand went bang! on the table. They had found their slogan.

Later came several songs with the title 'Say it with flowers'.

Stop me and buy one

Lionel and Charles Rodd were on the board of T. Wall & Sons, the British ice cream manufacturers, and are believed to have come up with **Stop me and buy one** in 1923. 8,500 salesmen with the slogan on their tricycles pedalled round Britain out of a national network of 136 depots. One salesman whose brakes failed as he descended a very steep hill introduced a slight variation as he hurtled to destruction: 'If you can stop me, you can have the lot.'

Tonic water by you-know-who

Out of the spy fever of the early 1960s came a memorable campaign for Schweppes tonic waters and mixers in the UK. It was thought up by Royston Taylor, copywriter, and Frank Devlin, art director, at Mather & Crowther. Taylor told me:

> In 1963, the James Bond films were just beginning. *Danger Man* was on TV. I came up with the idea of **Tonic water by you-know-who . . .** – the sort of thing you might say confidentially out of the side of your mouth in a bar. Frank Devlin suggested **What is the secret of Schhhh . . . ?** which accorded with the old copywriter's dream of not showing or even naming the product if it could possibly be avoided. We compromised, just using the first three letters of the brand name and half a bottle. The comedians soon picked it up. It 'made' William Franklyn, who used to appear in various comic spy situations.

When you got it, flaunt it

Braniff used the headline **When you got it, flaunt it** over airline ads *c.*1969 featuring celebrities like Sonny Liston, Andy Warhol and Joe Namath. Perhaps the line was acquired from the 1967 Mel Brooks movie *The Producers* where it appears as: 'That's it, baby! When you got it, flaunt it!'

Which twin has the Toni?

A headline that asks a question, a slogan that contains the brand name, and an idea that was dotty enough to be much copied. In the early 1950s Toni home perms featured pairs of identical twins (real ones) who also toured doing promotional work for the product. One had a Toni home perm, the other a more expensive perm – a footnote explained which was which in answer to the question **Which twin has the Toni?**

During the 1970 UK General Election, the Liberal Party produced a poster showing pictures of Harold Wilson and Edward Heath and the slogan 'Which twin is the Tory?'

You're never alone with a Strand

You're never alone with a Strand was the slogan of a – by now – classic British ad which caught the public imagination and yet failed to sell the product – a brand of cigarettes from W. D. & H. O. Wills. Devised in 1960 by John May of S. H. Benson, the campaign was to launch a new, cheap, filter cigarette called Strand. May decided to appeal to the youth market by associating the product not with sex or social ease but with 'the loneliness and rejection of youth'. 'The young Sinatra was the prototype of the man I had in mind,' says May. 'Loneliness had made him a millionaire. I didn't see why it shouldn't sell us some cigarettes.'

And so a Sinatra-clone was found in the 28-year-old actor, Terence Brook, who was also said to bear a resemblance to James Dean. He was shown mooching about lonely locations in raincoat and hat. In no time at all he had his own fan-club and the music from the TV ad – 'The Lonely Man Theme' – became a hit in its own right.

But the ads did not work. Viewers revised the slogan in their own minds to mean: 'If you buy Strand, then you'll be alone.' However much the young may have wanted to identify with the figure, they did not want to buy him or his aura. Or perhaps it was just not a very good cigarette. Nevertheless, it has not been forgotten.

You too can have a body like mine

'Charles Atlas' was born Angelo Siciliano in Italy in 1894. In America, he won the title of 'The World's Most Perfectly Developed Man' in a contest sponsored by Bernarr Macfadden and his *Physical Culture* magazine in 1922. He started giving mail order body-building lessons. A famous promotional strip cartoon showed 'How Joe's body brought him FAME instead of SHAME' – 'Hey! Quit kicking that sand in our face,' Joe says to a bully on the beach. Then he takes a Charles Atlas course – **You too can have a body like**

203

mine – and ends up with a girl by his side who says: 'Oh, Joe! You are a real man after all!'

Like Joe, Atlas had himself been 'a skinny, timid weakling of only seven stone' (hence the expression **I was a seven stone weakling**. 'I didn't know what real health and strength were. I was afraid to fight – ashamed to be seen in a bathing costume.' But after watching a lion rippling its muscles at the zoo, he developed a method of pitting one muscle against another which he later called 'Dynamic tension'. He died in 1972.

MAO TSE-TUNG

His Little Red Book

A feature of the Cultural Revolution which raged in China from 1966–9 was the little red book of *Quotations from Chairman Mao Tse-tung*. It contained the Great Helmsman's 'thoughts' and was quoted from and brandished while the Revolution tried to change the power structure and the motivation of the Chinese people. Back in 1960, Lin Piao, Minister of Defence, had produced a set of sayings which Mao revised. Next Lin started printing quotations from Mao in the *Liberation Army Daily*. In 1964 a pocket edition was produced for soldiers to carry about with them in their packs and this formed the basis of the first regular edition of the *Quotations*[52] published on 1 August 1965. While not pithy or particularly well expressed, even in translation, the quotations echoed themes that Mao had promoted over a much longer period.

As far as one can tell, Mao Tse-tung (1893–1976) thought his own 'thoughts' and did not need to have his writings and speeches ghosted. After all, in his younger days he had been a prolific writer on public affairs and wrote poetry almost all his life. To him, therefore, can be ascribed many of the slogans and catchwords of Chinese communism:

'Every Communist must grasp the truth, **Political power grows out of the barrel of a gun**.' The *Quotations* includes this remark from a work dated 6 November 1938.

'Let a hundred flowers bloom' was the slogan of a short lived experiment allowing freedom of dissent and first mooted in May 1956. In a meeting with officials and party leaders, Mao invited intellectual criticism of the regime:

I hope that everybody will express his opinions openly. It's no crime to talk, and nobody will be punished for it. We must **let a hundred flowers bloom** and a hundred schools of thought contend and see which flowers are the best and which school of thought is best expressed, and we shall applaud the best blooms and the best thoughts.

The movement was launched on 27 February 1957 in a major speech to an audience of 1800 influential Chinese. It had the title 'On the Correct Handling of Contradictions Among the People', but Mao himself found that his proposal did not have the support of the whole party and the press. When the official text was published on 19 June in the *People's Daily*, the horticultural image was given a sinister and revealing twist: 'Only by letting poisonous weeds show themselves above ground can they be uprooted.'

The campaign ran from 1 May but so great was the amount of criticism stirred up that it was ended by 7 June and reprisals taken against some of those who had spoken out. These were attacked as bourgeois rightists. Leaders of student riots were executed. Understandably, therefore, the passage about 'flowers blooming' is not included in the *Quotations*.

In December 1958, Mao spoke to the Central Committee at Wuchang and made use of two of his favourite expressions. He asked whether imperialism and reaction were real or paper tigers. They were 'in the process of being changed from real into paper tigers'. He also talked about the necessity to 'avoid certain impractical ideas that emerged from the 1958 **Great Leap Forward**.' This last was a key phrase for the enforced industrialisation introduced between May and July 1958 which followed a less radical 'leap forward' in 1956. This time it did not work either and was abandoned by mid-1960.

Mao's use of 'paper tigers' goes back to 1946 at least. In that year he told an American interviewer: '**All reactionaries are paper tigers**. In appearance, the reactionaries are terrifying, but in reality they are not so powerful. From a long-term point of view, it is not the reactionaries but the people who are really powerful.' Taken from the *Selected Works* this is how it appears in the *Quotations*.

206

'People of the world, unite and defeat the US aggressors and all their **running dogs**!' ('Statement Supporting the People of the Congo Against US Aggression', 28 November 1964.) This – not the first time Mao had used the expression – provided a vivid weapon for use against the 'lackeys' of the US during the Vietnam War. Edgar Snow recorded the term in 1937.

BUSINESS

Do You Sincerely Want to be Rich?

THE business world has not been noted for its communication skills, except in the more specialised area of advertising. Still, one or two phrases do stand out, though not always from the most scrupulous operators:

Bernie Cornfeld (b.1928) set up Investors Overseas Services in the 1960s. It was a gigantic mutual fund complex which at its height turned super salesmen into millionaires overnight by selling investment plans to people who disliked tax and currency regulations. However, the salesman paid themselves so much commission that there was very little profit and IOS eventually collapsed. *Do You Sincerely Want To Be Rich?* was the title of a book about this phenomenon.[67] The question was incorporated for this reason:

> At ten in the morning on the third Monday of every month a dozen or more hopefuls would assemble at 119 Rue de Lausanne to start their course. Bert Cantor had the job of teaching them how to sell. Bernie Cornfeld's job was to make them *want* to sell. They were asked numerous rhetorical questions. 'Are you Wellington Winner? or are you Louie the Loser?' 'Do you want to be used by the capitalist system? Or do you want to use it?' It was a catechism in which the right answers were obvious.

The most important question was asked implicitly in many forms . . . it was: **Do you sincerely want to be rich?**

This was a brilliant reading by Cornfeld from Adler and the theory of goals. For most people the answer is no – they would like to be rich, or would not mind being rich, but they *sincerely want* something else. Cornfeld's question was calculated to sort out the attitudes of his recruits. For those who said, yes, they did sincerely want to be rich, there was a logical follow through. If that was what they wanted, they must do what Bernie wanted them to do. And then he would make them millionaires.

Cornfeld was imprisoned for a while in Switzerland but later cleared of fraud after a seven-year investigation.

When Charles Chaplin, Mary Pickford, Douglas Fairbanks and D. W. Griffith, as film actors and director, founded the United Artists company to exploit their own talents in 1919, one of their former employers – sometimes named as Richard Rowland of Metro – complained: **The lunatics have taken over the asylum**.

The remark is also ascribed to Laurence Stallings, while David Lloyd George said in 1933: 'The world is becoming like a lunatic asylum run by lunatics.'

A cartoon believed to have appeared in *Collier's* Magazine (though *Ballyhoo* in 1932 has also been suggested) showed two trains about to collide. An American signalman is looking out of his box and the caption is: 'Tch-tch – **what a way to run a railroad!**'

The Boston & Maine railroad took up this idea when it sought: 'A statement which would explain some of the problems of the railroad in times of inclement weather.' It took up the 'stock railroad phrase', derived from the cartoon, and incorporated it between each paragraph of the advertisement as: 'That's A H**l of a Way to Run a Railroad!' Added at the foot of the ad was the line: 'But the railroad always runs.'

Thus the phrase passed into the language as an exclamation concerning chaos, in the form 'What a way (*or* hell of a way) to run a railroad/railway.'

An echo of the usage occurs in the title of G. F. Fiennes's *I Tried to Run a Railway* (1967) – he had worked for British Rail – and the Conservative Party 1968 poster: 'Higher unemployment . . . Higher taxation . . . Higher prices . . . What a way to run a country!'

Professor C. Northcote Parkinson (*b.*1909) first propounded the notion that subsequently became known as 'Parkinson's Law' in the *Economist* (19 November 1955): 'It is a commonplace observation that **work expands so as to fill the time available for its completion**.' Although these then became the opening words of a book (*Parkinson's Law or the Pursuit of Progress*, 1957) the law to which he gave his name was actually concerned with the pyramidal structure of bureaucratic organisations. Hence the Law's corollaries that: 'A perfection of planned layout is achieved only by institutions on the verge of collapse' and 'Subordinates multiply at a fixed rate regardless of the amount of work produced.'

A pre-echo may be found in the eighteenth-century Lord Chesterfield's letters: 'The less one has to do, the less time one finds to do it in.'

Scarcely less true and pointed than Parkinson's Law is the Peter Principle. This states that: **In a hierarchy every employee tends to rise to his level of incompetence** and was promulgated by Dr Laurence J. Peter (*b*.1919) and Raymond Hull in *The Peter Principle – Why Things Always Go Wrong*, published in 1969. Latterly, Dr Peter has tended to add the words 'and stay there' to his Principle. A longer version is: 'In every hierarchy, whether it be government or business, each employee tends to rise to his level of incompetence; every post to be filled by an employee incompetent enough to execute its duties.'

1959–73

The Vietnam War

ONE of the reasons why the United States tried to protect South Vietnam from a Communist take-over by North Vietnam in the years *c*.1959–73 was the so-called **Domino Theory**. The idea was that if one country in a certain zone – say, South-East Asia – was allowed to fall to the Communists, other countries would quickly follow suit. The old metaphor of falling over 'Like a stack of dominoes' was first used in the Vietnam context by the political columnist Joseph Alsop. Then President Eisenhower said at a press conference in April 1954: 'You have broader considerations that might follow what you might call the "falling domino" principle. You have a row of dominoes set up. You knock over the first one, and what will happen to the last one is that it will go over very quickly. So you have the beginning of a disintegration that would have the most profound influences.'

To an extent the theory was proved true. When South Vietnam collapsed, Cambodia then fell to the Communist Khmer Rouge and Laos was taken over by the Communist-led Pathet Lao:

The Vietnam War produced almost no patriotic American slogans (except perhaps **Love it or leave it**, from 1969) reflecting mixed support for an unpopular and ultimately unsuccessful operation. **Hearts and minds**, meaning what had to be won, was a slogan of

211

sorts for the US government. Its origins went back to Theodore Roosevelt's day when Douglas MacArthur, as a young aide, asked him (in 1906) to what he attributed his popularity. The President replied: '[To my ability] to put into words what is in their hearts and minds but not in their mouths.'[82]

In 1954, Earl Warren ruled in the case of Brown *v.* Board of Education of Topeka: 'To separate [Negro children] from others of similar age and qualifications solely because of their race generates a feeling of inferiority as to their status in the community that may affect their hearts and minds in a way unlikely ever to be undone.'

The Blessing in the Holy Communion service of the 1662 *Book of Common Prayer* is: 'The peace of God, which passeth all understanding, keep your hearts and minds in the knowledge and love of God, and of his Son Jesus Christ our Lord.' This is drawn from The Epistle of Paul the Apostle to the Philippians 4:7.

One slogan (*c.*1966) of those opposed to the war was recalled by Richard Nixon in his *Memoirs:*[57] 'The hatefulness of the attacks on Johnson's Vietnam policy was symbolised by that awful mindless chant shouted by anti-war demonstrators, **Hey, hey, LBJ, how many kids did you kill today?** First it frustrated him, then it disillusioned him, and finally it destroyed him.'

On the day of his Inauguration in 1969, Nixon himself heard the chant:

Ho, ho, ho Chi Minh,
The NLF is going to win.

In 1970 he heard the California chant:

One-two-three-four
We don't want your fucking war.

The old expression **light at the end of the tunnel** was dusted down and invoked with regard to the Vietnam War. In 1967, New Year's Eve invitations at the American Embassy in Saigon bore the legend: 'Come and see the light at the end of the tunnel.' President Kennedy had employed the expression *à propos* something else at a press conference on 12 December 1962: 'We don't see the end of the tunnel, but I must say I don't think it is darker than it was a year ago, and in some ways lighter.'

Somewhere about this period an allied expression arose: 'If we see the light at the end of the tunnel, it's the light of the oncoming train.'

This has been attributed to various people (like Bert Lahr, the actor), but in that precise form appeared in Robert Lowell's poem 'Day by Day' (1977).

The remark that best seemed to symbolise the futility of the war came from an unnamed American officer firing on Ben Tre. During the Communist-led Tet offensive against thirty South Vietnamese provincial towns on 8 February 1968, he said: **To save the town, it became necessary to destroy it.**

General Curtis E. LeMay (*b*.1906) was chief of the US Air Force under Presidents Kennedy and Johnson. To him is attributed the sentiment regarding the North Vietnamese that: **We should bomb them into the Stone Age.** (McGeorge Bundy is said to have replied: 'Maybe they're already there.') Hence the chant **Bombs away with Curt LeMay** that arose *c*.1967 from the protest movement. President Kennedy once made this shrewd observation on the man: 'Once you decide to send the bombers, you want men like LeMay flying them. But you can't let them decide if they should go or not.'

PROTEST
We're Against It

THE voice of protest has been armed in the twentieth century with the weapons of the mass media. To the traditional slogans shouted by protesters or scribbled on placards have been added the lapel badge and T-shirt phrase, the spray-painted graffito and the professionally produced jingle. The message is as in previous centuries, however: We're against it.

Ban the bomb

One of the simplest and best-known alliterative slogans, current in the US from 1953 and marginally later in the UK, was **Ban the Bomb**. CND – the Campaign for Nuclear Disarmament – was not publicly launched in the UK until early 1958. (Richard Crossman referred to 'Scrap the Bomb' in a 1957 press article.)

Better red than dead

A slogan of the British nuclear disarmament movement. Bertrand Russell wrote in 1958: 'If no alternative remains except communist domination or the extinction of the human race, the former alternative is the less of two evils' – hence the slogan. This was encapsulated in the slogan: **Better red than dead**. The counter-cry 'Better dead than red' became almost equally well established.

(In the 1964 film *Love with the Proper Stranger* Steve McQueen

214

proposed to Natalie Wood with a picket sign stating: 'Better Wed Than Dead.')

Black Power

This all-purpose slogan encompasses just about anything people want it to mean – from simple pride in the black race to a threat of violence. The Harlem Congressman Adam Clayton Power Jr said in a baccalaureate address at Howard University in May 1966: 'To demand these God-given rights is to seek **black power** – what I call audacious power – the power to build black institutions of splendid achievement.' On 6 June, James Meredith, the first black to attempt integration of the University of Mississippi (in 1962), was shot and wounded during a civil rights march. Stokely Carmichael, heading the Student Non-violent Co-ordinating Committee, continued the march, during which his contingent first used the shout. Carmichael used the phrase in a speech at Greenwood, Mississippi, the same month. It was also adopted as a slogan by the Congress for Racial Equality. However, the notion was not new in the 1960s. Langston Hughes had written in *Simple Takes a Wife* (1953): 'Negro blood is so powerful – because just *one* drop of black blood makes a coloured man – *one* drop – you are a Negro! . . . Black is powerful.[5,24,82]

In 1967, Martin Luther King launched a poster campaign round the slogan **Black is beautiful** but Stokely Carmichael had used the phrase at a Memphis civil rights rally in 1966. It may have its origins in The Song of Solomon 1:5: 'I am black, but comely.'

Burn your bra

A feminist slogan from America *c.*1970 – encouraging women to destroy an item of apparel quite clearly designed either (a) by a male chauvinist and/or (b) to make you more of a sex-object – was **Burn your bra**. The analogy is with the burning of draft cards as a protest against the Vietnam War.

Free the – – –

This all-purpose protest format came into its own in the 1960s usually in conjunction with a place and number: hence, **Free the Chicago 7** (people charged with creating disorder during the Democratic Convention in 1966), 'Free the Wilmington 10', and so on. Dignifying protesters with a group name incorporating place and number began with the 'Hollywood 10' (protesters against McCarthyite investigations) in 1947.

The form has become a cliché of sloganeering now. (Compare the graffito: 'Free the Indianapolis 500'.)

Make love not war

A 'peacenik' and 'flower power' sentiment from the mid-1960s onwards was **Make Love, not War**. It was not just applied to Vietnam but was used to express the attitude of a whole generation of protest. (It was written up [in English] at the University of Nanterre during the French student revolution of 1968.)

Not a penny off the pay

British coal mines which had come under government control during the First World War were returned to private ownership in 1921 and district instead of national rates of pay were instituted, despite a strike of three months. Trade slumped and mine-owners proposed reducing wages and increasing hours of work. A. J. Cook (1885–1931), the miners' leader, coined the slogan: **Not a penny off the pay, not a minute on the day** (though the phrases are sometimes reversed.) A Royal Commission under Sir Herbert Samuel investigated the problem and reported in March 1926, but neither miners nor owners would accept the findings, and the Government refused to intervene. Transport and other unions supported the miners and threatened the Prime Minister, Stanley Baldwin, with a General Strike unless the Government negotiated a settlement. The strike began on 4 May when trains, trams and buses throughout the country came to a stop. Troops and volunteers kept vital services running. By 12 May, the strike had collapsed, but the miners stayed out for seven months, then went back to work, their efforts largely having been in vain. They paid a heavy price in both pay and working hours.

Out of the closets and into the streets

A slogan for the US homosexual rights organisation known as the Gay Liberation Front arose *c.*1969 in the form: **Out of the closets and into the streets**. Starting point is the terms 'closet homosexual' or 'closet queen' for one who hides his inclinations as in a closet (small room rather than lavatory).

Power to the people

Shouted with clenched fist raised this was a slogan of the Black Panther movement and publicised as such by its leader, Bobby Seale, in Oakland, California, in July 1969. Also used by other dissident groups, as illustrated by Eldridge Cleaver: 'We say "All **Power to the People**" – Black Power for Black People, White Power for White People, brown Power for brown People, red Power for red People, and X Power for any group we've left out.' It was this somewhat

Martin Luther King, Jr: 'I have a dream . . .'

Nurse Edith Cavell's monument, London.

Wall's ice cream advertising, *c* 1923.

Mao Tse-tung: 'Let a hundred flowers bloom.'

Campaigning for women's suffrage
before the First World War.

generalised view of 'People Power' that John Lennon appeared to promote in the 1971 song 'Power to the people (Right on!)'.

'All Power to the Soviets' was a cry of the Bolsheviks during the Russian Revolution.

Turn on, tune in, drop out

'Tune in to my values, reject those of your parents; turn on [drug] yourself; deal with your problems and those of society by running away from them' – this was the meaning of the hippie philosophy as encapsulated in a slogan by one of the movement's gurus, Dr Timothy Leary (*b.*1920). **Turn on, tune in, drop out** was used as the title of a lecture by Leary in 1967 and the theme was explored further in his book *The Politics of Ecstasy*. (A graffito variant of the 'LSD motto' was: 'Turn on, tune in, drop dead.')

Votes for women

If a slogan is to be judged purely by its effectiveness, **Votes for women** was a very good slogan. The words may not sparkle, but they achieved their end.

Both Emmeline and Christabel Pankhurst, founders of the Women's Social and Political Union, have described how this particular battle-cry emerged. In October 1905, a large meeting at the Free Trade Hall, Manchester, was due to be addressed by Sir Edward Grey, who was likely to attain ministerial office if the Liberals won the forthcoming general election. The WSPU was thus keen to challenge him in public on his party's attitude to women's suffrage in Britain.

> Good seats were secured for the Free Trade Hall meeting. The question was painted on a banner in large letters, in case it should not be made clear enough by vocal utterance. How should we word it? 'Will you give women suffrage?' – we rejected that form, for the word 'suffrage' suggested to some unlettered or jesting folk the idea of suffering. 'Let them suffer away!' – we had heard the taunt. We must find another wording and we did! It was so obvious and yet, strange to say, quite new. Our banners bore this terse device: WILL YOU GIVE VOTES FOR WOMEN?

The plan had been to let down a banner from the gallery as soon as Sir Edward Grey stood up to speak. Unfortunately, the WSPU failed to obtain the requisite number of tickets. It had to abandon the large banner and cut out the three words which would fit on a small placard. 'Thus quite accidentally came into existence the slogan of the suffrage movement around the world.'

217

Alas, Sir Edward Grey did not answer the question, and it took rather more than this slogan – hunger-strikes, suicide, the First World War – before women got the vote in 1918. (In America, the Nineteenth Amendment, extending female franchise on a national scale, was ratified in time for the 1920 elections.)

SPORT

Winning Isn't Everything

PERSISTENT attempts have been made in this century to make out that sport is not about winning. On the eve of the 1908 Olympic Games in London, the Bishop of Pennsylvania preached in St Paul's Cathedral: 'The important thing is not so much to have been victorious as to have taken part.' A few days later, Baron Pierre de Coubertin (1863–1937), the man who founded the modern Olympic movement, concurred. Speaking at a banquet for officials of the games on 24 July he said: 'L'important dans ces olympiades, c'est moins d'y gagner que d'y prendre part . . . L'important dans la vie ce n'est point le triomphe mais le combat' – '**The most important thing in the Olympic Games is not winning but taking part**, just as the most important thing in life is not the triumph but the struggle. The essential thing in life is not conquering but fighting well.' De Coubertin repeated these words on several occasions in various forms and they later appeared on the electronic scoreboards during the opening ceremony of the Olympics, even if they were ignored by many of the people taking part.

Not to be outdone, the American poet and sports journalist Grantland Rice (1880–1954) said it again in *Alumnus Football*:

For when the One Great Scorer comes
To write against your name,

219

He marks – not that you won or lost –
But how you played the game.

The opposite point of view was put memorably by Vince Lombardi (1913–70), coach and general manager of the Green Bay Packers pro-football team from 1959 onwards. He said: **Winning isn't everything, it's the only thing.** The team was bottom of the league in Wisconsin but as a result of Lombardi's authoritarian ways, it became the holder of the best winning record in the National Football League.

Lombardi may have been pipped at the post in his exhortation, however. One Bill Veeck is reported as having said earlier: 'I do not think that winning is the most important thing. I think winning is the only thing.' Lombardi's version first appeared in print as: 'Winning is not the most important thing, it's everything.' This compares with what he said in a 1962 interview: 'Winning isn't everything, but wanting to win is.' Clearly Lombardi was not afraid to repeat his most famous utterance, even if he tried to mint it freshly every time. Even so, John Wayne, playing a football coach, said it in the 1953 movie *Trouble Along the Way.*

A variation on the theme came from the football coach Knute Rockne (1888–1931) in the 1920s. To the Wisconsin basketball coach Walter Meanwell, he said; 'Show me a good and gracious loser and I'll show you a failure.' This is usually quoted as: **Show me a good loser and I'll show you a loser.**

During his time as manager of the Brooklyn Dodgers baseball team (1951–4), Leo Durocher (*b.*1906) came up with *his* version – which also took more than one form: **Nice guys finish last** or 'Nice guys don't finish first.'

The notorious Committee to Re-Elect the President, which landed Richard Nixon in the Watergate soup in 1972, had its own variation: 'Winning in politics isn't everything, it's the only thing.'

The boxer Jack Dempsey (1895–1983) lost his World Heavyweight title to Gene Tunney during a fight in Philadelphia on 23 September 1926. He recalled:[20]

> Once I got to the hotel, Estelle (his wife) managed to reach me by telephone, saying she'd be with me by morning and that she'd heard the news. I could hardly hear her because of the people crowding the phone.
>   'What happened, Ginsberg?' (That was her pet name for me.)
>   **'Honey, I** just **forgot to duck.'**

This line was recalled by ex-sports commentator Ronald Reagan when explaining to *his* wife what had happened during the attempt on his life in 1981. Dempsey also had a couple of mottoes – for the ring: **Kill the other guy before he kills you** and – for life: **Keep punching**.

Another notable reaction to sporting defeat came from the lips of Joe Jacobs (1896–1940), manager of the boxer Max Schmeling. Believing his man to have been cheated of the Heavyweight title in a fight against Jack Sharkey on 21 June 1932, Jacobs shouted his protest into a microphone: **We wuz robbed!**

On another occasion, in October 1935, Jacobs left his sick-bed to attend the World series for the one and only time, in Detroit. Having bet on the losers, he opined: **I should have stood in bed.**

Leo Rosten in *Hooray for Yiddish*[79] put his own gloss on this last quotation: 'The most celebrated instance of this usage was when Mike Jacobs [sic], the fight promoter, observing the small line at his ticket windows, moaned, "I should have stood in bed!" *Stood* is a calque for the Yiddish *geshtanen*, which can mean both "stood" and "remained". Mr Jacobs' use of "of" simply followed the speech pattern of his childhood.'

Roy Cazaly (1893–1963) was an Australian Rules footballer who played for the South Melbourne team from 1921 and formed a 'ruck' combination with 'Skeeter' Fleiter and Mark Tandy, i.e. they were players who worked together but did not have fixed positions. According to *The Australian Dictionary of Biography*:

Though only 5ft 11ins. and 12$\frac{1}{2}$ stone, Cazaly was a brilliant high-mark; he daily practised leaping for a ball suspended from the roof of a shed at his home. He could mark and turn in mid-air, land and in a few strides send forward a long accurate drop-kick or stab-pass. Fleiter's constant cry **Up there, Cazaly!** was taken up by the crowds. It entered the Australian idiom, was used by infantrymen in North Africa in Word War II and became part of folk-lore.

The phrase was also incorporated in a song.

The most vocal athlete of the century was Muhammad Ali, formerly Cassius Clay (*b*.1942), who first became World Heavyweight boxing champion in 1964. Ali admitted that he copied his '**I am the greatest** . . . I am the prettiest' routine from a wrestler called Gorgeous George he once saw in Las Vegas. 'I noticed they all paid

221

to get in – and I said, This is a good idea.' In a moment of unusual modesty, Ali added: 'I'm not really the greatest. I only say I'm the greatest because it sells tickets.'

His boxing motto – **Float like a butterfly, sting like a bee** – was devised by his aide, Drew 'Bundini' Brown.

His most famous line of doggerel – **'You don't want no pie in the sky when you die,**/ You want something here on the ground while you're still around' (*c.*1978) contains an obvious response to *The Preacher and the Slave* by Joe Hill (1879–1915): 'Work and pray, live on hay,/ You'll get pie in the sky when you die.'

POLITICS

The Art of the Possible

THE definition of politics as the **art of the possible** has often been attributed to the British Conservative politician R. A. Butler (1902–82) who used it as the title of his slender but elegant memoirs published in 1971. In the preface to the paperback edition he wrote that he had subsequently received many queries from 'up and down the country' (a favourite English political phrase) as to the origin of the title and faithfully recorded that the expression appears first to have been used in modern times by Bismarck in 1866. Butler also mentioned references by Cavour, Salvador de Madariaga, Pindar and Camus. To these might be added John Kenneth Galbraith's rebuttal: 'Politics is not the art of the possible. It consists in choosing between the disastrous and the unpalatable.'

Butler himself was sometimes known as 'the best Prime Minister we never had' – a title that probably grew out of an exchange recorded in December 1955. Not for the last time passed over for the Conservative leadership, Butler was confronted by a Press Association reporter just as he was about to board an aircraft at London Airport. Criticism was growing over the performance of Anthony Eden, the Prime Minister. The reporter asked: 'Mr Butler, would you say that this [Eden] is **the best Prime Minister we have?**' Butler assented to this 'well-meant but meaningless proposition . . . indeed it was fathered upon me. I do not think it did Anthony any good. It did not do me any good either.'[12]

Butler seems an appropriate choice to usher in some notable sayings from the lips of politicians who did not actually make it to No 10 Downing Street or the White House. Also included here are some political remarks from outside British and American politics:

Who? Whom?

Nikolai Lenin was the pseudonym of Vladimir Ilyich Ulyanov (1870–1924), the leader of the 1917 Russian Revolution and the man who set communists forever calling each other 'Comrade'.

Almost all the remarks associated with him are attributed rather than direct quotations. He is said, for example, to have divided people into two categories. In every political transaction there are winners and losers, those who do and those to whom it is done. Hence, the inquiry: '**Who, whom?** We or they?'

In a 1936 publication, Sidney and Beatrice Webb attributed to Lenin the axiom: 'It is true that **liberty is precious – so precious that it must be rationed**.'

In 1904 he called a book he wrote about 'the crisis in our party' – **One Step Forward, Two Steps Back** – a phrase that has entered general political use to describe occasional shows of liberalisation by repressive regimes. In the early 1970s on BBC radio I regularly used to interview a pundit on Portuguese affairs about the Caetano regime. Without fail he would bring in this phrase to describe what was going on in Portugal.

A good five cent cigar

During a tedious debate in the US Senate, over which he was presiding, Vice-President Thomas R. Marshall (1854–1925) turned to the chief clerk, John Crockett, and opined: **What this country needs is a good five cent cigar.** Marshall was Woodrow Wilson's 'Veep' and thus this famous remark was uttered in 1917. At that time 'Owls' cigars cost six cents and 'White Owls', seven cents.

I have seen the future and it works

Lincoln Steffens (1866–1936) was an American muck-raking journalist who paid a visit to the newly formed Soviet Union as part of the William C. Bullitt diplomatic mission of 1919. As did a number of the first visitors to the new Soviet system, he returned with an optimistic view. His phrase for it was: **I have seen the future and it works**.

However, in his *Autobiography* (1931) he phrases it a little differently: ' "So you've been over into Russia?" said Bernard Baruch, and I answered very literally, "I have been over into the future, and it works." '

Bullitt said Steffens had been rehearsing this formula before arriving in the USSR. Later, however, he tended to use the shorter, more colloquial form himself.

A smoke-filled room

Suite 408–409–410 (previously rooms 804–5) of the Blackstone Hotel in Chicago was the original 'smoke-filled room' in which Warren Harding was selected as the Republican Party's presidential candidate in June 1920. The image conjured up by this phrase is of cigar-smoking political 'bosses' coming to a decision after much horse-trading.

Although he denied saying it, the phrase seemed to have come out of a prediction by Harding's chief supporter, Harry Dougherty (1860–1941). He foresaw that the convention would not be able to decide between the two obvious candidates and that a group of senators 'bleary eyed for lack of sleep' would have to 'sit down about two o'clock in the morning around a table in **a smoke-filled room** in some hotel and decide the nomination.' This was precisely what happened and Harding duly came out on top.

A bust in the snoot

Anglophobia was a cause promoted by William Hale Thompson (1867–1944) during a four-year period in the political wilderness before he successfully ran for his third term as Mayor of Chicago in 1927. There are various versions of what 'Big Bill', a famous urban demagogue, threatened to do if King George V ever set foot in the city (and no one had ever suggested that he might). Either he would 'punch King George in the snoot' or **bust King George in the snoot**. The usual American slang expression is 'to poke him one in the snoot' but, either way, Thompson did not get the chance: the King of England stayed away and protected his proboscis.

This is a good example of how difficult it is to pin down a saying that is quite widely known but not properly recorded. William H. Stuart, writing in his Chicago 'diary', *The Twenty Incredible Years* (1935), noted:

> The writer never heard him say it. It does not occur in any written statement or speech ever given in the press by Thompson. Undoubtedly he did say it – many times – in discussing British propaganda in the public school histories. Yes, he probably told many audiences that the King should stop sticking his nose into American school histories and should be 'busted on the nose' if he didn't.

On the other hand, Lloyd Wendt and Herman Kogan quote the following speech extracts in their 1953 biography *Big Bill of Chicago* – though perhaps they are recreations: 'I wanta make the King of England keep his snoot out of America! That's what I want. I don't want the League of Nations! I don't want the World Court! America first, and last, and always! That's the issue of the campaign. That's what Big Bill wants . . . I have no private war with the King of England, but I want him to keep his nose out of our schools.' Wendt and Kogan also quote Thompson's comment: 'What I said was "King George has got to keep his snoot out of Chicago's schools" . . . I say that the American people must not let King George lead us into another foreign war.'

Whatever the case, Thompson was re-elected and pursued his campaign further by suspending a school board superintendent for introducing pro-British textbooks. In the subsequent trial, Thompson attracted nationwide ridicule. At the next election he was defeated.

Safety first

The idea of 'Safety First' grew out of rail and motor transportation at the turn of the century. In the 1890s, railway companies in Britain maintained that 'the Safety of the Passenger is our First Concern'. In 1916, the London General Bus Company formed a London Safety First Council.

The political application of the words began in 1922 when they became a Conservative slogan. In 1929 **Safety First** was the phrase under which, famously, Stanley Baldwin fought for re-election and lost. In addition, posters showed the 'wise and honest' fact of the Prime Minister, smoking a pipe. Tory Party Central Office thought that the times demanded such a reassuring approach but were proved wrong. The party chairman, J. C. C. Davidson, who accepted the idea from Benson's advertising agency, had to take the blame. Baldwin himself thought the slogan uninspiring and ridiculous. Soon afterwards, Davidson was replaced.

In 1934, the National Safety First Association was formed, concerned with road and industrial safety. (Incidentally, the caution **Stop – Look – Listen** is said to have come originally from notices first displayed at American railroad crossings in 1912, devised by Ralph R. Upton.)

Bolshevism run mad

An early political sensation on British radio was made in a broadcast during the second 1931 General Election. On 17 October Philip Snowden (1864–1937), who had been Chancellor of the Exchequer in the 1929 Labour Government and who now held the same post in the National Government, had this to say about the Labour Party's plans – similar to the ones he had himself devised in 1929:

> I hope you have read the Election programme of the Labour Party. It is the most fantastic and impracticable programme ever put before the electors . . . This is not Socialism. It is **Bolshevism run mad.**

He later commented: 'My effort was universally believed to have a great influence on the result of the Election. The Labour Party gave me the credit, or, as they put it, the discredit of being responsible for the tragic fate which overtook them.'

How many divisions has he got?

Following the signing of a Franco-Soviet pact, the French Prime Minister, Pierre Laval, paid a visit to Joseph Stalin (1879–1953) in Moscow on 13 May 1935. As Churchill recounted it,[16] Laval asked the Soviet leader: 'Can't you do something to encourage religion and the Catholics in Russia? It would help me so much with the Pope?' 'Oho!' replied Stalin, 'The Pope! **How many divisions has *he* got?**'

You shouldn't be in the circus

Jimmy Maxton (1855–1946) was an Independent Labour Party MP. At a Scottish Conference of the Party in 1931 a motion was moved that the ILP should disaffiliate from the Labour Party. Maxton made a brief statement to the effect that he was against such a move. In the debate he had been told that he could not be in two parties – or ride two horses – at the same time: 'My reply to that is . . . that if my friend cannot ride two horses – what's he doing in the bloody circus?'

This expression, in the form **If you can't ride two horses at once, you shouldn't be in the circus** went on to have limited further use as a proverbial saying, not only in the political field.

Better to die on your feet

In a radio speech from Paris calling on the women of Spain to help defend the Republic (3 September 1936), Dolores Ibarruri ('La Pasionaria') (*b*.1895) declared: **It is better to die on your feet than to live on your knees**. According to her autobiography (1966), she had used these words earlier, on 18 July, when broadcasting in Spain. On that occasion she had also said: 'No pasarán' ('They shall not pass'). Both expressions became slogans for the Republican side

227

in the Spanish Civil War (1936–9). 'They shall not pass' was Pétain's call-to-arms in the First World War; 'Better to die on your feet' was probably derived from Emiliano Zapata (*c.*1877–1919), the Mexican revolutionary, to whom is attributed: 'Men of the South! It is better to die on your feet than to live on your knees!' ('Mejor morir a pie que vivir en rodillas.')

Franklin D. Roosevelt also used the expression in his message accepting an honorary degree from Oxford University, 19 June 1941: 'We, too, are born to freedom, and believing in freedom, are willing to fight to maintain freedom. We, and all others who believe as we do, would rather die on our feet than live on our knees.'

When I hear the word 'Culture' . . .

Hermann Goering is often linked with the remark: **When I hear the word 'Culture' I reach for my revolver.** In fact, it comes from a play by an unsuccessful Nazi playwright, Hanns Johst (1890–1978), who was president of the Reich Chamber of Literature, a group of authors, translators and publishers which excluded those who refused to toe the party line. In 1933 he wrote *Schlageter*, a play about a martyr of the French occupation of the Ruhr after the First World War. The line 'Wenn ich Kultur hore . . . entsichere ich meinen Browning' is more accurately translated as 'I release the safety catch of' – or 'I cock' – 'my Browning' (automatic rifle), and is said by a storm-trooper.

A 1960s graffito in New York had a revised version; 'Whenever I hear the word gun, I reach for my culture.'

Guns or butter

Two German Nazis may be said to have fathered the **Guns or butter** slogan – Hermann Goering and Joseph Goebbels – though Rudolf Hess also has to be considered. Goebbels (1897–1945) said in a Berlin address on 17 January 1936: 'We can do without butter, but, despite all our love of peace, not without arms. One cannot shoot with butter, but with guns.'

Later that year, Goering (1893–1946) said in a broadcast: 'Guns will make us powerful; butter will only make us fat.'

When a nation is under pressure to choose between material comforts and some kind of war effort, the choice has to be made between 'guns *and* butter'. Some will urge 'guns *before* butter'. However, Airey Neave in his book *Nuremberg* stated of Rudolf Hess: 'It was he who urged the German people to make sacrifices and coined the phrase: "Guns before butter".' This shared use of the idea may show no more than that they all subscribed to Hitler's policy of aggression rather than that any one of them in particular coined the phrase.

We are the masters now

It might seem in poor taste for a Labour government minister to crow: **We are the masters now!** After all, it was into the mouth of an imperialist that George Orwell put these words in his novel *Burmese Days* (1934): 'No natives in this Club! It's by constantly giving way over small things like that that we've ruined the Empire . . . The only possible policy is to treat 'em like the dirt they are . . . We've got to hang together and say, "We are the masters, and you beggars . . . keep your place." '

So quite why Sir Hartly Shawcross (*b*.1902), the Attorney General in Britain's first post-war Labour Government, did say something like it bears some examination. For a start it was not said, as one might expect, on the day new Labour MPs swarmed into the House of Commons just after their sweeping election victory. It was said on 2 April 1946 – almost nine months later. Then again, what Shawcross said was 'We are the masters at the moment' – though understandably the more pungent variant has passed into the language. A look at Hansard reveals precisely why he chose this form of words. He was winding up for the Government in the third reading of the Trade Disputes and Trade Unions Bill and drew attention to what he saw as the Conservative Opposition's lack of support for a measure it had promised to introduce if it had won the election:

> [We made this an issue at the election] when he invited us to submit this matter to the verdict of the people . . . I realise that the right hon. Member for Woodford [Winston Churchill] is such a master of the English language that he has put himself very much in the position of Humpty-Dumpty in *Alice* . . . 'When I use a word,' said Humpty-Dumpty, 'it means just what I intend it to mean, and neither more nor less.' 'But,' said Alice, 'the question is whether you can make a word mean different things.' 'Not so,' said Humpty-Dumpty, 'the question is which is to be the master. That's all.'
>
> We are the masters at the moment, and not only at the moment, but for a very long time to come, and as hon. Members opposite are not prepared to implement the pledge which was given by their leader in regard to this matter at the General Election, we are going to implement it for them.

At the end of the debate, the votes cast were: Ayes 349; Noes 182. When the House met again after the 1950 General Election – at which the Conservatives narrowly missed ousting Labour – Churchill commented: 'I like the appearance of these benches better than what we had to look at during the last $4^1{}_2$ years. It is certainly refreshing to feel, at any rate, that this is a Parliament where half the nation will not be able to ride rough-shod over the other half . . . I do not see the Attorney-General in his place, but no one will be able to boast "We are the masters now." '

Lloyd George Knew My Father

Even before David Lloyd George's death in 1945 Welsh people away from home liked to claim some affinity with the Great Man. In time, this inclination was encapsulated in the singing of the words '**Lloyd George knew my father,** father knew Lloyd George', over and over, to the tune of 'Onward Christian Soldiers', which they neatly fit. In Welsh legal and Liberal circles the credit for this happy coinage has been given to Tommy Rhys Roberts QC (1910–75) whose father did indeed know Lloyd George. Arthur Rhys Roberts was a Newport solicitor who set up a London practice with Lloyd George in 1897. The partnership continued for many years, although on two occasions Lloyd George's political activities caused them to lose practically all their clients.

The junior Rhys Roberts was a gourmet, a wine-bibber and of enormous, almost Cyril Smith proportions. Martin Thomas QC, a prominent Welsh Liberal of the next generation, recalls:

It was, and is a tradition of the Welsh Circuit that there should be, following the after-dinner speeches, a full-blooded sing-song. For as long as anyone can remember, Rhys Roberts's set-piece was to sing the phrase to the tune of 'Onward Christian Soldiers' – it is widely believed that he started the practice . . . By the 'fifties, it had certainly entered the repertoire of Welsh Rugby Clubs. In the 'sixties, it became customary for Welsh Liberals to hold a Noson Lawen, or sing-song, on the Friday night of Liberal Assemblies. It became thoroughly adopted in the party. I recall it as being strikingly daring and new in the late 'sixties for Young Liberals to sing the so-called second verse, 'Lloyd George knew my mother'. William Douglas-Home's play *Lloyd George Knew My Father* was produced in London in 1972. One of the leading Welsh Silks recalls persuading Rhys Roberts to see it with him.

Fair shares for all

At a by-election in the Battersea North constituency in June 1946, the Labour candidate, Douglas Jay (*b*.1907) was asked by his agent to provide a brief rhyming slogan. He suggested: 'Fair Shares for All, is Labour's Call.' From this by-election **Fair Shares for All** spread round the country in the next few years. It reflected a belief that had grown up during the war that workers were not fighting on behalf of the bosses. Everybody had been in it together and, after victory, must share the spoils – such as they were – equally.

The Cold War

The financier, statesman and Presidential adviser Bernard Baruch (1870–1965) used the term 'Cold War' to describe the tense atmosphere which had grown up between East and West following the Second World War but which fell short of actual fighting (i.e. a 'hot' or 'shooting' war). In a speech before the South Carolina Legislature when he was being presented with his portrait on 16 April 1947, he said: 'Let us not be deceived – **we are today in the midst of a cold war**.' A year later he was able to note a worsening of the situation to the extent that he could tell the Senate War Investigating Committee: 'We are in the midst of a cold war which is getting warmer.' Generally speaking, the situation so-described was thought to linger until the 1960s. At least, that is when the term was no longer applied so convincingly.

Baruch said the expression had been suggested to him first in June 1946 by his speechwriter Herbert Bayard Swope, former editor of the New York *World*, who had used the phrase privately since about 1940.

The columnist Walter Lippmann gave the term wide currency and is sometimes mistakenly credited with coining it. Swope clearly coined it; Baruch gave it currency.

Vermin

The fiery Welsh Left-Winger Aneurin Bevan (1897–1960) was on the eve of his most substantial achievement – launching the post-war Labour Government's National Health Service – when on 4 July 1948 he spoke at a rally in Belle Vue, Manchester. He contrasted Labour's social programme with the days of his youth between the wars when the Means Test reigned, when he had had to live on the earnings of his sister, and when he had been told to emigrate:

That is why no amount of cajolery, and no attempts at ethical or social seduction, can eradicate from my heart a deep and burning

231

hatred for the Tory Party that inflicted those experiences on me. So far as I am concerned they are **lower than vermin**. They condemned millions of first-class people to semi-starvation.

As abuse goes, it was traditional stuff. In Swift, the King of Brobdingnag considers Gulliver's fellow countrymen to be 'the most pernicious race of little odious vermin that nature ever suffered to crawl upon the surface of the Earth.' Nevertheless, in 1948 it caused a storm. Outside Bevan's home someone daubed 'VERMIN VILLA – HOME OF A LOUD MOUTHED RAT' and the Tory press went to town. The *Sunday Times* commented: 'Nothing said at a political meeting for a long time has been more talked about or will be longer remembered'. The *Sunday Dispatch* headlined: 'THE MAN WHO HATES 8,093,858 PEOPLE' (the number who had voted for the Conservatives at the previous election). Prime Minister Attlee quietly warned Bevan: 'Please, be a bit more careful in your own interest.'

The Minister was not allowed to forget his remarks for a long while. As Michael Foot described in his biography of Bevan:[27] 'Adult members of Conservative associations founded Vermin Clubs, pinned vermin badges on their breasts, or invaded Bevan's meetings with the chant "vermin, vermin" . . . Harold Laski guessed that it was worth two million votes to the Tories. If the claim was true, the one casual word was responsible for deciding in advance the outcome of the 1950 election.'

During the *Tribune* group meeting held on 29 September 1954 at the Labour Party Conference in Scarborough, Bevan countered Attlee's plea for a non-emotional response to German rearmament by saying:

I know that the right kind of leader for the Labour Party is a **desiccated calculating machine** who must not in any way permit himself to be swayed by indignation. If he sees suffering, privation or injustice he must not allow it to move him, for that would be evidence of the lack of proper education or of absence of self-control. He must speak in calm and objective accents and talk about a dying child in the same way as he would about the pieces inside an internal combustion engine.

This characterisation came to be applied to Hugh Gaitskell who beat Bevan for the leadership of the Labour Party the following year. In 1959, however, Bevan told Robin Day in a TV interview: 'I never called him that. I was applying my words to the synthetic figure, but the press took it up and it's never possible to catch up a canard like that, as you know.' After the interview was over, he added; 'Of course I wasn't referring to Hugh Gaitskell. For one thing Hugh is not desiccated – he's highly emotional. And you could hardly call him a calculating machine – because he was three hundred millions out.'

'Never hold discussions with the monkey when the organ-grinder is in the room' – a remark sometimes attributed to Churchill replying to a query from the British Ambassador in Rome as to whether he should raise a point with Mussolini or his Foreign Minister is best known as used by Bevan. During a post-Suez debate in 1957, he made it plain he preferred to address the Prime Minister (Harold Macmillan) rather than the Foreign Secretary (Selwyn Lloyd) and declared: 'If we complain about the tune, **there is no reason to attack the monkey when the organ grinder is present.**'

Executing a U-turn on unilateral disarmament at the Labour Party Conference at Brighton on 3 October 1957, Bevan warned delegates:

> If you carry this resolution and follow out all its implications and do not run away from it **you will send a Foreign secretary**, whoever he may be, **naked into the conference chamber** . . . Able to preach sermons, of course; he could make good sermons. But actions of that sort is not necessarily the way in which you can take away the menace of the bomb from the world.

J. B. Priestley in a *New Statesman* article (November 1957) riposted: 'The sight of a naked minister might bring the conference to some sense of our human condition . . . Our bargaining power is slight; the force of our example might be great.'

Nye Bevan was chief among various recipients of an oft-remembered snub from Ernest Bevin (1881–1951), Foreign Secretary in the post-war Labour Government. When someone remarked that Nye was his own worst enemy, Bevin replied: **Not while I'm alive he ain't.** It is impossible to say who originally inspired this remark but Bevin applied it also to Herbert Morrison and Emmanuel Shinwell.

Are you now or have you ever been?

'McCarthyism' was the name given to the pursuit and public ostracism of Americans suspected of Communist sympathies at the time of the war with Korea in the early 1950s. Senator Joseph McCarthy (1908–57) was the instigator of the 'witch hunts' which led to the 'blacklisting' of people in various walks of life, notably the movie business. Those appearing at hearings of the House of Representatives Committee on UnAmerican Activities (1947–*c*.1957) were customarily challenged with the question: **Are you now or have you ever been a member of the Communist Party?** Counsel Richard Arens would sometimes take things a stage further and thunder: 'Are you now or have you ever been a member of a godless conspiracy controlled by a foreign power?' – one of those questions, as in Latin, which anticipates the answer 'no' . . .

McCarthy's most memorable line before he was finally discredited was when, having battered a witness into incoherence, he would stride away declaring: **It makes me sick, sick, sick way down inside.**

The most notable of the refusals to inform on anybody came from the writer, Lillian Hellman (1905–84). In her letter to the committee she stated:

> I am most willing to answer all questions about myself . . . [But] to hurt innocent people whom I knew many years ago in order to save myself is, to me, inhuman, indecent and dishonourable. **I cannot and will not cut my conscience to fit this year's fashions.**

She was blacklisted as a result.

Enosis!

The cry **Enosis!** is Greek for 'union' and became widely known from about 1952 onwards in relation to the proposed unification of Cyprus with mainland Greece. In fact, the word had been used from about 1930 by Greek Cypriots opposed to British rule.

When independence from British rule – but not union with Greece – was achieved in 1960, the cry lived on during internal squabbles and beyond the death of the movement's leader, General Grivas. The Turkish invasion of 1974 and the partitioning of the island indefinitely postponed any movement towards the goal.

What's good for General Motors

President Eisenhower wished to appoint Charles E. Wilson (1890–1961) as Secretary for Defense. At hearings of the Senate Committee on Armed Services in January 1953, the former President of General Motors was asked about any possible conflict of interest, as he had accepted several million dollars worth of General Motors shares. He is generally thought to have replied: **What's good for General Motors is good for the country.**

In fact, what he said when asked whether he would be able to make a decision against the interests of GM and his stock, was:

> Yes, sir, I could. I cannot conceive of one because for years I thought what was good for our country was good for General Motors, and vice versa. The difference did not exist.

Wilson was finally persuaded to get rid of his GM stock, but he never quite lived down his (misquoted) remarks.

Of the new type of H-bomb tested at Bikini he approvingly said that it gave: **a bigger bang for a buck** (1954).

The smack of firm government

Why the 'smack' of firm government? Presumably because, from childhood, smacking goes with discipline. But it is a good phrase and has been traced[11] to a *Daily Telegraph* editorial written by the deputy editor, Donald McLachlan, on 3 January 1956. An attack on the performance to that date of the Prime Minister, Sir Anthony Eden, included the wounding phrase: 'Most Conservatives, and almost certainly some of the wiser Trade Union Leaders, are waiting to feel **the smack of firm government**.'

We will bury you

Speaking to Western diplomats at a reception for the Polish leader Wladislaw Gomulka at the Polish Embassy in Moscow on 18 November 1956, Nikita S. Khruschev (1894–1971) warned:

> We say this not only for the socialist states who are more akin to us. We base ourselves on the idea that we must peacefully co-exist. About the capitalist states, it doesn't depend on you whether or not we exist. If you don't like us, don't accept our invitations, and don't ask us to come and see you. Whether you like it or not, history is on our side. **We will bury you**.' [*Applause from colleagues. Laughter from Mr Gomulka.*]

The last two sentences were not reported at the time by either *Pravda* or the *New York Times* but they were by *The Times* – perhaps because the previous night at a Kremlin reception the British Ambassador, Sir William Hayter, had walked out when Khruschev described Britain, France and Israel as 'fascists' and 'bandits' (over the Suez affair).

'We will bury you' can also be translated as 'We will be present at your funeral', i.e. outlive you, and Khruschev made several attempts in later years to make plain that he meant 'outstrip' or 'beat' in the

235

economic sense rather than anything more threateningly literal. But the remark was blown up out of proportion by Western commentators.

Earlier that year, on 25 February, Khruschev, as Communist Party Secretary, had spoken to a secret session of the Party Congress and denounced Joseph Stalin. Among the charges was one that Stalin had promoted a **cult of personality** on his own behalf and undermined the collective leadership of the party. In due course, Khruschev was accused of much the same thing.

The Soviet leader was noted for his use of Soviet peasant axioms and this proclivity was much parodied at the time. In 1955, he spoke of the unlikelihood of the Soviet Union rejecting communism: 'Those who wait for that must wait **until a shrimp learns to whistle.**'

Khruschev's best-remembered intervention was hardly verbal, however. During a speech by Harold Macmillan on disarmament at the United Nations General Assembly on 29 September 1960 (following the collapse of a summit conference due to the U-2 spy-plane incident), Khruschev twice interrupted. He shouted interjections and pounded the desk with both fists. After Khruschev shouted (in Russian) 'You accept my disarmament proposals and I'll accept any controls', Macmillan said drily: 'I'd like that translated if I may.'

Life's better with the Conservatives

Life's better with the Conservatives . . . don't let Labour ruin it was a Conservative slogan which helped the party to a further period in power following the 1959 General Election. There was much to justify the claim: material conditions had improved for most people; the balance of payments was in surplus; gold and dollar reserves were at a high level; wages were up; taxation had gone down. The words emerged from consultations between Central Office and the Colman, Prentis & Varley advertising agency. In his book *Influencing Voters*, Richard Rose said he knew of four people who claimed to have originated the slogan. Ronald Simms was the PR chief at Central Office from 1957–67. He is said to have come up with 'Life is Good with the Conservatives, don't let the Socialists spoil it.' Lord Hailsham wanted 'better' instead of 'good' and CPV changed 'spoil' to 'ruin'.

On the other hand, Maurice Smelt wrote to me (1981):

The slogan was so successful that many people have claimed it (that always happens): but it was just a perfectly routine thing I did one afternoon in 1959, as the copywriter on the Conservative account at CPV. The brief . . . was to say something like 'you've never had it so good', but with less cynicism and more bite. The first five words were the paraphrase: and the whole ten told what I still think was a truth for its time. It's the slogan I am proudest of.

Fight and Fight and Fight Again

When the Austrian armies threatened France, Danton exhorted his fellow countrymen to: 'Dare! and dare! and dare again!' Hugh Gaitskell (1906–63), Leader of the Labour Party, used a similar construction memorably at the Party Conference on 3 October 1960. When, against the wishes of the Party leadership, Conference looked like taking what he called the 'suicidal path' of unilateral disarmament 'which will leave our country defenceless and alone', Gaitskell stood up to make the most important speech of his life – for his leadership was at issue as well. As Philip Williams describes in his biography of Gaitskell,[96] neither the Leader nor his wife had slept the previous night. 'He had written the peroration at 4 am and – for the first time since his maiden speech in the House fifteen years before – told her most of what he intended to say. He told her, too, that probably he would lose, retire to the back benches, and carry on the struggle from there.' He said, in part:

> It is not in dispute that the vast majority of Labour Members of Parliament are utterly opposed to unilateralism and neutralism. So what do you expect them to do? To change their minds overnight? . . . Supposing all of us, like well-behaved sheep were to follow the policies – suddenly – of unilateralism and neutralism, what kind of impression will this make upon the British people? . . . Do you think that we can become overnight the pacifists, unilateralists and fellow travellers that other people are? . . . The result (of the vote) may deal this party a grave blow . . . but there are some of us, I think many of us, who will not accept that this blow need be mortal . . . **There are some of us**, Mr Chairman, **who will fight and fight and fight again to save the Party we love.** We will fight and fight and fight again to bring back sanity and honesty and dignity so that our party with its great past may retain its glory and its greatness.

Although the speech made many delegates who were free to do so change their votes, the Party Executive was still defeated. It was, however, as one journalist wrote: 'Gaitskell's finest hour. He turned what looked like an exultant triumph for his enemies into the hollowest of paper victories . . . It was the greatest personal achievement I have ever seen in politics.'

237

Let's get America moving again

A recurring theme in election slogans is that of promising to move forward after a period of inertia. John Kennedy had the slogan **Let's Get America Moving Again** (sometimes ' . . . This Country Moving Again') in 1960 – Walt Rostow is credited with suggesting it.

The Irish politician, Jack Lynch, ran in 1980 under the banner: 'Get our country moving again.'

It is a short step from these to Ronald Reagan's 'Let's Make America Great Again' in 1980. All of them are interchangeable slogans that could apply to any politician or party in any country.

When the going gets tough

On John F. Kennedy's election as US President in 1961, attention was focused on several axioms said to come from the Boston–Irish political jungle or, more precisely, from the President's father, Joseph P. Kennedy (1888–1969). At this distance, it would be impossible to say for sure whether this wealthy, ambitious business-man/ambassador/politician originated these expressions, but he certainly instilled them in his sons:

When the going gets tough, the tough get going.
Don't get mad, get even.
If you want to make money, go where the money is.
We don't want any losers around here. In this family we want winners. Don't come in second or third – that doesn't count – but win. [i.e. 'Kennedys always come first'.]
We don't want any crying in this house' [rendered by his children as 'Kennedys don't cry'.]
Only winners come to dinner.

We're eyeball to eyeball

In the missile crisis of October 1962, the United States took a tough line when the Soviet Union placed missiles on Cuban soil. After a tense few days, the Soviets withdrew. Secretary of State Dean Rusk (*b*.1909) was speaking to an ABC news correspondent, John Scali, on 24 October and said: 'Remember, when you report this, that, eyeball to eyeball, they blinked first.' Columnists Charles Bartlett and Stewart Alsop then helped to popularise this as **We're eyeball to eyeball and the other fellow just blinked.** (Sometimes 'I think' is inserted before 'the other fellow'.)[82]

'Eyeball to eyeball' is a black American servicemen's idiom. Safire quotes a reply given by the all-black 24th Infantry Regiment to an inquiry from General MacArthur's HQ in Korea (November

1950) – 'Do you have contact with the enemy?' – 'We is eyeball to eyeball.'

Great Britain has lost an Empire

Truman's former Secretary of State, Dean Acheson (1893–1971) spoke at the Military Academy, West Point, on 5 December 1962. The son of a British Army officer who went to Canada, the home truth was all the more painful when he pointed out:

Great Britain to begin with **has lost an Empire and not yet found a role.** The attempt to play a separate power role – that is, a role apart from Europe, a role based on a 'special relationship' with the United States, a role based on being the head of a 'Commonwealth' . . . this role is about to be played out . . . Her Majesty's Government is now attempting, wisely in my opinion, to re-enter Europe.

Lord Chandos, President of the Institute of Directors, protested hotly that such words coming from one of President Kennedy's advisers were 'a calculated insult'. Prime Minister Harold Macmillan quietly observed that in any case the general drift of world affairs was against Britain or any other country trying to play 'a separate power role'.

The gnomes of Zurich

'Gnome' is a sixteenth-century word, coined (appropriately) by a Swiss in a mining context, and derived from the Greek 'ge-nomos', used to describe a species of creature said to live in the depths of the earth and to guard buried treasure.

Gnomes of Zurich was a term used to disparage the tight-fisted methods of the speculators in the Swiss financial capital who questioned Britain's creditworthiness and forced austerity measures on the Labour Government of Prime Minister Harold Wilson when it came to power in 1964. Faced with an enormous balance of payments deficit on taking office plus the so-called 'haemorrhaging' of the pound sterling, the Secretary of State for Economic Affairs, George Brown, spoke out against the speculators who were making a killing at the pound's expense.

He popularised the term, but in fact he appears to have acquired it from Harold Wilson himself. Speaking long before, on economic problems aggravated by the Suez crisis, in a speech to the House of Commons on 12 November 1956, Wilson said: 'On 5 September when the TUC unanimously rejected wage restraint, it was the end of an era, and all the financiers, all the little gnomes in Zurich and other finance centres about whom we keep on hearing, had started to make their dispositions in regard to sterling.' (He was quite right to cover himself by saying 'and other finance centres' because the principal target in later years was the Bank for International Settlement which is in Basle.)

The East is red

A paean to Chairman Mao, sung frequently during the Chinese Cultural Revolution (1966–9) of which it became the theme song, was **The East is Red**. When the first Chinese space satellite was launched in April 1970, it circled the earth, broadcasting the message: 'Tung fang hung – Mao Tse-tung' ('The east is red – Mao Tse-tung'.) The words of the song are:

> The East turns red, day is breaking,
> Mao Tse-tung arises over Chinese soil.
> He works for the good of the people,
> Of the people he is the saviour.
>   Mao Tse-tung loves the people
> He leads us along the right path.
> He leads us forward
> To build the new China.
>   The Party is our sun
> Which shines down everywhere.
> Since the Party is with us
> The people are free.

Extremism in the defence of liberty

Senator Barry Goldwater (*b*.1909), in his speech accepting the Republican nomination for President on 16 July 1964, said: 'I would remind you that **extremism in the defence of liberty is no vice.** And let me remind you also that **moderation in the pursuit of justice is no virtue!**'

The extremist tag did him no good in the subsequent election. Lyndon Johnson beat Goldwater with a landslide and rejoined: 'Extremism in the pursuit of the Presidency is an unpardonable vice. Moderation in the affairs of the nation is the highest virtue.'

Perhaps Goldwater would have done better to quote Thomas Paine's *The Rights of Man* (1792) directly: 'A thing moderately good is not so good as it ought to be. Moderation in temper is always a virtue; but moderation in principle is always a vice.'

BOMFOG
When Governor Nelson Rockefeller (1908–79) was competing against Barry Goldwater for the Republican nomination in 1964, reporters latched on to a favourite saying of the candidate – **the brotherhood of man under the fatherhood of God** – and rendered it by the initials 'BOMFOG'. In fact, they had been beaten to it by Hy Sheffer, a stenotypist on the Governor's staff who had found the abbreviation convenient for the previous five or six years. The words come from a much quoted saying of John D. Rockefeller (1874–1960): 'These are the principles upon which alone a new world recognising the brotherhood of man and the fatherhood of God can be established . . .'

Later, 'BOMFOG' was used by feminists to indicate language use that demeans women by reflecting patrician attitudes.

Communism with a human face
The brief flowering of an independent mood in Czechoslovakia during the 'Prague Spring' of 1968 was described at the time as either 'Socialism . . .' or **Communism with a human face.** Attributed to the First Secretary of the Czech Communist Party, Alexander Dubcek (*b.*1921), the expression was based on a resolution, recorded in the newspaper *Rudé právo* (14 March 1968), which referred to foreign policy acquiring 'its own defined face'. It was later applied to a liberalisation in domestic affairs.

The experiment was quashed when the Soviet Union invaded the country in August 1968. Dubcek was later removed from power.

The River Tiber foaming with much blood
On Saturday 20 April 1968, Enoch Powell (*b.*1912), the Conservative Opposition Spokesman for Defence made a speech which – as Harold Wilson remarked – 'would justify the claim that once made, British politics would never be the same again.'

It was addressed to the Annual General Meeting of the West Midlands Area Conservative Political Centre at the Midlands Hotel, Birmingham, and was on the subject of immigration in Britain. Powell quoted the views of one of his white constituents: 'In this country in fifteen or twenty years the black man will have the whip-hand over the white man' and he claimed that the population would include $3^{1}2$ million Commonwealth immigrants within fifteen or twenty years and between 5 and 7 million by the year 2000. Powell's answer was to stop, or virtually to stop, further inflow of immigrants and to promote maximum outflow. The speech was concluded with these words:

241

As I look ahead, I am filled with foreboding. **Like the Roman, I seem to see 'the River Tiber foaming with much blood'**. That tragic and intractable phenomenon which we watch with horror on the other side of the Atlantic but which there is interwoven with the history and existence of the States itself, is coming upon us here by our own volition and our own neglect. Indeed, it has all but come. In numerical terms, it will be of American proportions long before the end of the century. Only resolute and urgent action will avert it even now. Whether there will be the public will to demand and obtain that action, I do not know. All I know is that to see, and not to speak, would be the great betrayal.

Later the next day, Edward Heath, the Conservative leader, dismissed Powell from the Shadow Cabinet. He considered the speech 'to have been racialist in tone and liable to exacerbate racial tensions'. Given by the best of his generation of political orators, Powell's speech certainly produced an astonishing reaction in the public, unleashing anti-immigrant feeling that had largely been pent up until this point. At one point, thousands of London dockers singing 'Bye, bye blackbird' arrived at the House of Commons to protest against Mr Powell's dismissal. He received 100,000 letters of support within a few days, became a rallying point for disaffected Conservatives, and spoke out on many other issues in the following years, though never again holding ministerial office.

Few political speeches have sparked so much controversy or, indeed, at a stroke so changed a man's career. Asked many months after it was delivered whether he did not regret the speech, Powell said that in retrospect he would have changed the reference to the Tiber. He should have quoted the remark in Latin, he said, to emphasise that he was only evoking a classical prophecy of doom and not actually predicting a bloodbath.

In place of strife

Britain's 1966–70 Labour Government attempted a measure of trade union reform. The Secretary of State for Employment, Barbara Castle, introduced an ill-fated industrial relations White Paper (i.e. document setting out proposed legislation) on 19 January 1969. It was called **In Place of Strife**. This title was suggested by Mrs Castle's husband, Ted (later Lord) Castle (1907–79), a journalist, and echoed that of a book about disarmament written by an earlier Labour minister, Aneurin Bevan – *In Place of Fear* (1952). The legislation was abandoned, but the phrase was not forgotten quite so quickly.

242

It wiggles and it's shapely

At the age of 23, Miss Ainsley Gotto was credited with being the power behind the throne of John Gorton, the Australian Prime Minister (1968–71). Air Minister Dudley Erwin accused her of being the secretary who lost him his job, as she ruled the Prime Minister with 'ruthless authority'. Said he, when asked the reason for his dismissal in 1969: **It wiggles, it's shapely, and its name is Ainsley Gotto.** Twelve years later, Miss Gotto – no longer involved in Australian politics – commented: 'That was another life . . . I never wiggled, I was never aware of wielding power, and the rest was nonsense – the folklore of reporting.'

Nattering nabobs of negativism

Richard Nixon's choice of Spiro T. Agnew (*b.*1918) as his Vice-Presidential running mate at the 1968 Republican convention came as a surprise to everyone. Questioned by Mike Wallace of ABC, Agnew said: 'I agree with you that the name of Spiro Agnew is not a household name. I certainly hope that it will become one within the next couple of months.'

Before his forced resignation in 1973, Agnew's most notable contribution was as scourge of the media for their treatment of the Nixon Administration's Vietnam policy. On 19 October 1969 he told a dinner in New Orleans: 'A spirit of national masochism prevails, encouraged by **an effete corps of impudent snobs** who characterise themselves as intellectuals.' Buttons appeared soon afterwards bearing the slogan 'Effete snobs for peace'. On 11 September 1970 in San Diego, Agnew returned to the theme with a fresh burst of the alliteration for which he was already known: 'In the United States today we have more than our share of the **nattering nabobs of negativism**. They have formed their own 4-H Club – the "hopeless, hysterical hypochondriacs of history".' This passage was written by William Safire, later author of a more distinguished work: *Safire's Political Dictionary.*[82]

I would walk over my grandmother

When Richard Nixon sought re-election as US President in 1972, he surrounded himself with an unsavoury crew including Charles W. Colson (*b.*1931), a special counsel and White House hatchet man. '**I would walk over my grandmother** if necessary **to get Nixon re-elected!**' was his declared point of view. Later he reaffirmed: 'I am totally unconcerned about anything other than getting the job done . . . Just so you understand me, let me point out that the statement . . . "I would walk over my grandmother if necessary" is absolutely accurate.'

Subsequently convicted for offences connected with Watergate and emerging as a 'born again' Christian, Colson turned to walking on the water instead. In 1976 he commented:[17] 'The Watergate break-in sent reporters digging into the newspaper morgues for old clippings . . . Most stories contained a rehash of all the old dirty-tricks charges and that I had once boasted I would run over my grandmother if necessary to elect Nixon. I tried to steer a few reporters back to the original (1971) *Wall Street Journal* article. "I never said it," I protested, but it made such colourful copy no one heard me.'

He then recounted how in August 1972 'a little genie with a pitchfork' prodded him into sending an order to his campaign staff which included the reaffirmation quoted above.

> Within twenty-four hours a copy was leaked to the *Washington Post* and printed in full, the whole bombastic memo . . . My mother failed to see the humour in the whole affair, convinced that I was disparaging the memory of my father's mother. I received a flood of angry mail from grandmothers . . . Even though both of my grandmothers had been dead for more than twenty-five years (I was very fond of both), two press conferences were called during the campaign by 'Charles Colson's grandmother' to announce her support for McGovern, one by an elderly black woman in Milwaukee who managed to draw a large crowd of newsmen before the joke was discovered.

Such are the penalties for tangling with figures of speech.

No more Mr Nice Guy

When Richard Nixon ran for re-election in 1972, his challenger was Senator George McGovern. Until McGovern was selected, another likely runner was Senator Ed Muskie of Maine who had a soft, likeable image – indeed, his campaign for the nomination collapsed when he publicly burst into tears over a newspaper slur against his wife. Trying to counter an image that was such a liability, his team coined the in-house phrase **No more Mr Nice Guy**. The phrase 'Mr Nice Guy' was later applied to the equally straight Gerald Ford. A joke dating from the mid-1950s has Hitler planning to make a come-back: 'But this time – no more Mr Nice Guy.'

Twist slowly, slowly in the wind

Richard Nixon's henchmen may have acted wrongly and, for much of the time, spoken sleazily. Occasionally, however, they minted political catchphrases that have lingered. John D. Ehrlichman (*b*.1925), Nixon's Assistant for Domestic Affairs until he was forced to resign over Watergate in 1973, came up with one saying that caught people's imagination. In a telephone conversation with John Dean (Counsel to the President) on 7/8 March 1973 he was speaking about Patrick Gray (Acting Director of the FBI). Gray's nomination to take over the FBI post permanently had been withdrawn by Nixon during Judiciary Committee hearings – though Gray had not been told of this. Ehrlichman said: 'I think we ought to let him hang there. **Let him twist slowly, slowly in the wind**.'

In about 1968, during the Nixon election campaign, Ehrlichman is credited with devising a yardstick for judging whether policies would go down with voters in 'middle America': **It'll play in Peoria.** He later told William Safire:[82] 'Onomatopoeia was the only reason for Peoria, I suppose. And it . . . exemplified a place, far removed from the media centres on the coasts where the national verdict is cast.' Peoria is in Illinois.

The inoperative statement

As the Nixon White House was drawn deeper into the Watergate quagmire, the Press secretary, Ronald Ziegler (*b*.1939), a former jungle guide at Disneyland, had a tough time fielding reporters' questions. On 17 April 1973, President Nixon appeared and made a snap statement, changing his position and allowing his aides to testify before the Senate Watergate committee. He did not stop to answer questions. This was left to the hapless Ziegler. Reporters pressed him to say what had brought about this change of position and whether it implied that previous statements from the White House – to the effect that nobody there had been involved in the scandal – had been wrong. Ziegler 'stonewalled' several times, insisting that the President's latest statement was the 'operative' one. Johnny Apple of the *New York Times* asked: 'Would it be fair for us to infer, since what the President said today is now considered the operative statement, to quote you, that the other statement is no longer operative, that it is now inoperative?'

Ziegler eventually came out with: **This is the operative statement. The others are inoperative.** As a euphemism for 'lie', this phrase had a brief vogue in the years to come.

The social contract

While it was in Opposition from 1970–4, the British Labour Party developed the idea of a social 'compact' between Government and trades unions. In return for certain 'social' measures, like price subsidies, the unions would moderate their wage demands. This would mean that unpopular voluntary or statutory incomes policies could be abandoned.

This use of the words differed from that of Rousseau, Hobbes and Locke, in that they were thinking in terms of a compact between a government and a whole people, rather than with just one section of it.

Use of the words in this specific way has been credited to Dennis (later Lord) Lyons, a public relations consultant who advised the Labour party in five General Elections. James Callaghan declared at the Labour Party Conference on 2 October 1972: 'We say that what Britain needs is a new **Social Contract**. That is what this document (*Labour's Programme, 1972*) is all about.' Anthony Wedgwood Benn had used the term in a 1970 Fabian pamphlet, *The New Politics*.

Village tyrant

During the dictatorship of Idi Amin, President of Uganda from 1971–9, one of the white settlers in the country, Denis Hills, wrote a book called *The White Pumpkin*.[37] Unwisely, he described Amin as a 'black Nero', **a village tyrant** and a 'tyrant ruling by fear'. In April 1975, while the book was still only in manuscript, Hills was arrested, found guilty of treason and sentenced to be shot by firing squad. Only after the Queen had written to Amin urging clemency and James Callaghan, the Foreign Secretary, had been forced to pay a visit to Uganda, was Hills saved. The offending four word phrase was deleted from the main body of the book as published in 1975 but was referred to in a postscript.

As a term of abuse, the phrase 'village tyrant' had had an earlier outing in 1946. When Dr Roland Cockshutt of the BMA was negotiating with Aneurin Bevan, the Minister of Health, over the setting up of the National Health Service, he described one of their encounters, thus: 'We might have been going to meet Adolf Hitler . . . [yet] he is no village tyrant, but a big man on a big errand.'

Not in a thousand years

Ian Smith (*b*.1919) was leader of the illegal regime in Rhodesia following UDI, the Unilateral Declaration of Independence, in 1965. This move was designed by the white population to prevent the UK imposing a settlement on its African colony which would involve rule by the black majority. The British position was expressed in the so-called Five Points hammered out by the Labour Government. These were summed up *c*.1966 in the acronym 'NIBMR', meaning 'No Independence Before Majority Rule' (sometimes expressed as **NIBMAR** – ' . . . Majority African Rule').

In a broadcast speech on 20 March 1976, Smith went on record, thus: 'Let me say again, I don't believe in black majority rule ever in Rhodesia. **Not in a thousand years**.' He may not have believed in it, but it became a fact in 1979.

Savaged by a dead sheep

Denis Healey (*b*.1917), a leading Labour Party politician in the UK has been noted for vivid phraseology. In 1978, as Chancellor of the Exchequer, he described being attacked by his opposite number in the Conservative Party – Sir Geoffrey Howe – as **like being savaged by a dead sheep**.

Earlier, in February 1976, he said Left-Wing opponents of his public expenditure cuts 'must be **out of their tiny Chinese minds**' and attracted inevitable complaints from the Chinese community in Britain.

His most memorable political pronouncement was delivered in a speech at the Labour Party Conference in October 1973: 'Labour's programme will cost money and the only way to raise that is through taxation . . . I warn you there are going to be **howls of anguish** from the 80,000 people who are rich enough to pay over seventy-five per cent [tax] on the last slice of their income.'

Well may he say 'God Save the Queen'

In an effort to resolve an impasse which had arisen in the running of the Australian Government in 1975, the Governor-General, Sir John Kerr, dismissed the Labour Prime Minister, Gough Whitlam, and dissolved Parliament pending a General Election.

On 11 November, the Governor-General's official secretary read an election proclamation from the steps of Parliament House in Canberra, ending with the words 'God Save the Queen'. Whitlam (*b*.1916) had been taken completely by surprise and made the following off-the-cuff remarks:

Well may he say 'God Save the Queen', because nothing will save the Governor-General. The proclamation which you have just heard read by the Governor-General's official secretary was countersigned 'Malcolm Fraser' who will undoubtedly go down in Australian history from Remembrance Day 1975 as 'Kerr's cur' . . . Maintain your rage and your enthusiasm through the campaign for the election now to be held and until polling day.

Constitutionally, it is quite likely that Sir John Kerr had acted improperly, but the Australian electorate did not return Whitlam's government at the ensuing election. Instead, the Liberals under 'Kerr's cur' took office.

How'm I doing?

Ed Koch (*b*.1924) was the Mayor of New York City from 1977. He helped balance the books after a period of bankruptcy on the part of the city. He did this by drastically cutting services. His catchphrase during this period (still current 1983) was **How'm I doing?** He would call it out as he ranged round New York. 'You're doing fine, Ed,' the people were supposed to shout back. Clearly he did not have to quote anyone to launch this kind of phrase but an old song with the title was disinterred in due course. Unfortunately for him, Koch's achievements in NYC did not carry him forward to the State Governorship as he had hoped.

A 1979 cartoon in the *New Yorker* showed a woman answering the phone and saying to her husband: 'It's Ed Koch. He wants to know how he's doin'.' A booklet of his wit and wisdom used the phrase as its title and included: 'You know how I always ask everybody how am I doing? Well, today I asked myself, and the answer was "Terrific".'

Bunnies can (and will) go to France

Jeremy Thorpe (*b*.1929) was a flamboyant Liberal politician who became leader of his party but then had to resign in 1976 because a former male model called Norman Scott spread rumours that the two of them had had a homosexual affair. It was further alleged that Thorpe had plotted to have Scott murdered, though this charge was overturned at the Old Bailey in 1979.

In an earlier bid to defuse the situation Thorpe had allowed publication of a letter he had written to Scott on 13 February 1961. It ended: '**Bunnies can (and will) go to France**. Yours affectionately, Jeremy. I miss you.' Scott explained the 'bunnies' reference as referring to him as a frightened rabbit – this was how Thorpe had described him on the night he had seduced Scott. The saying became part of the folklore surrounding the scandal.

The upshot was, however, that the House of Commons lost one of its better speakers. In a memorable jibe at Harold Macmillan's 'Night of the Long Knives' in 1962, he told the House: **Greater love hath no man than this, that he lay down his friends for his life.**

Jack Dempsey (with Gene Tunney), 1926: 'Honey, I forgot to duck.'

R. A. Butler: 'The art of the possible.'

Nikita S.
Khruschev,
above: 'We w
bury you.'

Sir Hartley Shawcross: 'We are the
masters now.'

Hugh Gaitskell, *above*: 'Fight and fight and fight again.'

Enoch Powell with letters of support, 1968: 'Like the Roman, I seem to see . . .'

Mandy Rice-Davies: 'Well, he would, wouldn't he?'

A short, sharp, shock

When the British Home Secretary, William Whitelaw, addressed the Conservative Party Annual Conference in October 1979, he outlined a 'new' form of punishment for young offenders. It was characterised by the phrase **a short, sharp, shock**. Whitelaw was not the first Home Secretary to invoke this description – a number of his predecessors had done so. All of them might have done better to acknowledge its source: W. S. Gilbert's lyric for *The Mikado* (1885):

To sit in solemn silence in a dull, dark dock,
In a pestilential prison, with a life-long lock,
Awaiting the sensation of a short, sharp, shock,
From a cheap and chippy chopper on a big black block.

A play by Howard Brenton and Tony Howard, produced at the Royal Court Theatre, London, in 1980 took the phrase as its title, having been originally called *Ditch the Bitch* (by way of reference to Prime Minister Margaret Thatcher).

No such thing as a free lunch

This old American expression, meaning 'There's no getting something for nothing' dates back to the mid-nineteenth century. Flexner puts an 1840s date on the supply of free lunch – even if no more than thirst-arousing snacks like pretzels – in saloon bars. This was not strictly speaking 'free' because you had to buy beer to obtain it.

The idea was given a new lease of life in the late 1970s by the economist Milton Friedman. Indeed, the saying was sometimes attributed to him by virtue of the fact that he published a book, wrote articles and gave lectures incorporating the phrase **There is no such thing as a free lunch.** When Margaret Thatcher in the UK and then Ronald Reagan in the US attempted to embrace, up to a point, Friedman's monetarist thinking, the phrase was trotted out by their acolytes (in Thatcher's case, specific instructions were given for ministers to drop it into their speeches).

On your bike

Newly appointed Employment Secretary, Norman Tebbit (*b.*1931) addressed the Conservative Party conference on 15 October 1981. He related how he had grown up in the 1930s when unemployment was all around: '[My father] did not riot. He got on his bike and looked for work. And he kept on looking till he found it.'

This gave rise to a pejorative catchphrase 'on your bike' (or **get on your bike**) from the lips of Mr Tebbit's opponents and gave a new

249

twist to a saying which Partridge dated from *c*.1960, meaning 'go away' or 'be off with you'.

Tebbit later pointed out that he had not actually been suggesting that the unemployed should get on their bikes and look for work but claimed to find the catchphrase 'fun'.

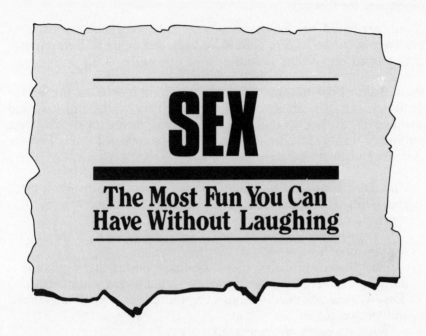

SEX

The Most Fun You Can Have Without Laughing

'THAT was **the most fun I've had without laughing**' is how the Woody Allen character compliments the Diane Keaton character in the film *Annie Hall* (1977). As a description of sex it is clearly derived from the old expression 'The most fun you can have with your clothes on', as applied to non-sexual enjoyment.

The second half of the twentieth century witnessed another swing of the pendulum towards permissiveness – not so much in the performance of sex (though in so far as it is possible to monitor sexual activity there was perhaps more of it) as rather in the public discussion of it.

At the beginning of the century, matters were largely as typified by an entry in the diary kept by Alice, Lady Hillingdon (1857–1940).[62] In 1912, she wrote:

I am happy now that Charles calls on my bedchamber less frequently than of old. As it is, I now endure but two calls a week and when I hear his steps outside my door I lie down on my bed, close my eyes, open my legs and think of England.

In the form **Close your eyes and think of England**, this compares with the reported advice to a woman about to be raped (which I have

251

heard attributed to the first Viscount Curzon, though I have no evidence in support): **She should lie back and enjoy it.** Both phrases have passed into sexual folklore.

Polly Adler (1900–62) was a notable madam in New York during the 1920s and 30s. She finally closed her New York bordello in 1945 and spent part of her twilight years writing memoirs which were published in 1954.[1] Among the titles she rejected was 'Forever Adler'. And then:

> One day I happened to be spraying a rose-bush in my back yard, and Dora [Maugham] . . . was profoundly impressed by this spectacle of suburban domesticity.
> 'I wonder what the cops would say,' she mused, 'if they could see you now.'
> 'Oh,' I said, 'probably they'd be disappointed that my home is not a house.' Dora's reaction to this remark was so unusual . . .
> 'Eeyow!' she squealed. 'Hold everything! . . . Turn that around and you've got it!'
> 'What on earth are you talking about?'
> 'The perfect title for your book . . .'
> So far as I was concerned, I told her, it was the most inspired piece of thinking anyone had done in a garden since the day Isaac Newton got conked by an apple.

So **A House is not a Home** it was.

John Profumo (*b*.1915) was the Secretary of State for War in Harold Macmillan's Government. In March 1963 rumours began to harden that he had been carrying on with a girl called Christine Keeler who had also been sharing her favours with the Soviet military attaché, Colonel Vladimir Ivanov. Ostensibly because of the security risks involved, parliamentarians got into a right old tizzy and Profumo made a personal statement before the House of Commons on 22 March which included the declaration: **There was no impropriety whatsoever in my acquaintanceship with Miss Keeler.** This was a lie and Profumo later had to resign.

IT *IS* A MORAL ISSUE thundered *The Times* on 11 June and, indeed, it was more because of Profumo's lie to the House than because of his sexual carryings-on that he had to go. On 13 June, Lord Hailsham, Leader of the House of Lords, in an explosive TV interview, said: 'A great party is not to be brought down because of a squalid affair between a woman of easy virtue and a proven liar.' On

13 July, Harold Macmillan stated: 'I was determined that no British Government should be brought down by the action of two tarts.'

Out of the scandal emerged the intriguing personality of Mandy Rice-Davies (*b.*1944), a friend of Christine Keeler's. When Stephen Ward, the ponce-figure in the Profumo Affair, was charged under the Sexual Offences Act, Rice-Davies was called as a witness during the preliminary Magistrates Court hearing on 28 June. Questioned about the men she had had sex with, she was told by Ward's defence counsel that Lord Astor – one of the names on a list – had categorically denied any involvement with her. To this she replied, chirpily: **Well, he would, wouldn't he?**

The court burst into laughter and the expression passed into the language, frequently resorted to – as a good catchphrase ought to be – because it is bright, useful in various circumstances and tinged with innuendo.[76]

In 1977, George Simenon (*b.*1903), the novelist and creator of 'Maigret', made an astonishing claim: **I have made love to 10,000 women.** In an interview with the Zurich newspaper *Die Tat*, he explained: 'I contend that you know a woman only after you have slept with her. I wanted to know women – I wanted to learn the truth.' When asked if he was sure of the figure, Simenon said he had gone back and checked. However, in 1983, his wife was quoted as saying 'We've worked it out and the true figure is no more than twelve hundred.' Most of these were prostitutes.

Also in 1977, a former Miss Wyoming, Joyce McKinney (*b.*1950) was charged in an English court with kidnapping Kirk Anderson, a Mormon missionary and her ex-lover. She allegedly abducted Mr Anderson to a remote country cottage where he was chained to a bed and forced to make love to her. **I loved Kirk so much**, Miss McKinney declared to a stunned court, **I would have skied down Mount Everest in the nude with a carnation up my nose.**

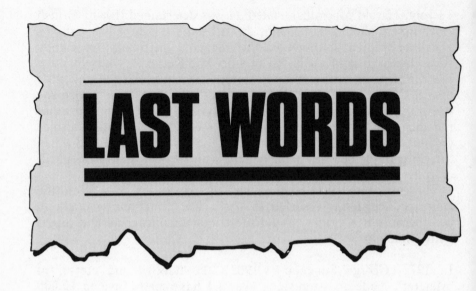

LAST WORDS

IT is an opportunity seized by few people these days to say something memorable on their deathbeds. Perhaps it has just gone out of fashion; or perhaps modern methods of treatment mitigate against the long drawn out death which allows more time for deathbed meandering? Noel Coward managed a typical **Goodnight, my darlings** the night before he died; Churchill's verbal inventiveness finally deserted him; but Edith Cavell rose to the occasion before her execution. Often there has been confusion between actual final words and deathbed words which may not have been the last spoken:

Nancy, Lady ASTOR (1879–1964)

The first woman MP to take her seat in the House of Commons, the American-born Lady Astor, uttered her last word – her husband's name 'Waldorf' – the day before she died. However, during her terminal illness she was visited by her son, the Hon Sir John J. ('Jakie') Astor:[30] 'I sat beside her for a bit and then she opened her eyes and saw I was there. She looked me straight in the face and said, "Jakie, **is it my birthday or am I dying?**" – which was quite a difficult one to answer. So I said, "A bit of both, Mum".'

254

Samuel BUTLER (1835–1902)

The author of *Erewhon* and *The Way of all Flesh* departed with what at first seems a curious saying on his lips: **Have you brought the chequebook, Alfred?** Although Butler knew he was dying, he was attempting to buy the freehold of a house in Hampstead. Having put the question to Alfred Cathie, his servant and friend, he took off his spectacles and put them down on a table, saying: 'I don't want them any more.' His head then fell back and he died.

Erskine CHILDERS (1870–1922)

The British-born author and Irish patriot joined the Republican Army after the establishment of the Irish Free State. He was captured by Free State soldiers, court-martialled and executed on 24 November 1922 but not before getting a delay of an hour to see his last sunrise, shaking hands with the firing squad, and shouting: **Take a step or two forwards, lads. It will be easier that way.**

Isadora DUNCAN (1878–1927)

The exponent of modern dance died in Paris while setting off to test-drive a Bugatti. Her long scarf got caught in the spokes of a wheel. Her last words: **Adieu, mes amis, je vais à la gloire.**

Charles FROHMAN (1860–1915)

In J. M. Barrie's play *Peter Pan* there is the line: 'To die will be an awfully big adventure.' When the American producer of the play, Charles Frohman, was coming to Britain on a visit he was drowned when the *Lusitania* was torpedoed by the Germans on 7 May 1915. In the twenty minutes it took the ship to sink he tried to console those near him with a paraphrase: **Why fear death? It is the greatest adventure in life.** How do we know what he said? There was a considerable number of survivors from the ship. The actress Rita Jolivet was one of these and passed on Frohman's remark in an interview. Barrie wrote: 'His last words . . . were really, I feel sure, "Death will be an awfully big adventure." '

O. HENRY (1862–1910)

Turn up the lights, the author said, **I don't want to go home in the dark.** Henry (real name W. S. Porter) was quoting the words of a popular song of the day 'I'm Afraid to go Home in the Dark'. However, there is some difference of opinion as to what he actually said. A nurse who was with him reported his words differently: 'Put up the shades, I don't want to go home in the dark.'

255

Henry JAMES (1843–1916)

The novelist's cry: 'So **here it is at last, the distinguished thing**' sometimes given as his last words were clearly not that and not even, in a sense, his. On 2 December 1915, James had a stroke and later told a friend that as he collapsed he heard a voice making this exclamation. He did not die until 28 February.

Cecil RHODES (1853–1902)

The gist of what the colonial financier and stateman said before he breathed his last on 26 March 1902 was **So little done, so much to do**, though this is sometimes quoted with the phrases reversed. It was a theme that had obviously preoccupied him towards the end of his life. He said to Lord Roseberry: 'Everything in the world is too short. Life and fame and achievement, everything is too short.'

His very last words were rather more prosaic: 'Turn me over, Jack.'

'SAKI' (H. H. Munro) (1870–1916)

In the fog of dawn on 14 November 1916 near Beaumont-Hamel, Corporal Munro – in peacetime the short story writer, 'Saki' – was shot dead by a German sniper. During a brief pause in an advance one of his men had lit up, and Munro had just yelled: **Put that bloody cigarette out!**

Gertrude STEIN (1874–1946)

The American author and poet had a quirky end, as was to be expected of her. There are several versions of what she said. One is: 'What is the question? . . . What is the question? . . . If there is no question, there is no answer.' In Donald Sutherland's biography (1951), however, we find this variation: **What *is* the answer? . . . In that case, what is the question?**

Dylan THOMAS (1914–53)

The Welsh poet made a boast to his girlfriend, Liz Reitell, after a drinking bout in New York: **I've had eighteen straight whiskies. I think that's the record.** These were not his last words although he went into a coma shortly afterwards and died. His biographers have subjected the boast to much scrutiny and have watered it down to a mere four or five whiskies. He often exaggerated.

Acknowledgements

I have been much helped in the preparation of this book by suggestions and information obtained from: Barry Day, the late Alan Melville, Sally Moore, Vernon Noble, Godfrey Smith, Martin Thomas QC, the Oxford Word and Language Service, as well as others mentioned in the text.

While gathering material for my BBC Radio programme *Quote . . . Unquote* (since 1976) I have had valuable access to the BBC's Sound Archives, Gramophone Library and Central Reference Library in London.

My thanks are also due to the authors and publishers of the following books (from some of which I have quoted). The numbers refer back to places in the text where information from the books has been used:

1 Adler, Polly, *A House is not a Home* (Heinemann, 1954).
2 Amery, L. S., *My Political Life* (Vol.3) (Hutchinson, 1955).
3 Armstrong, Neil *et al.*, *First on the Moon* (Little, Brown & Co., 1970).
4 Baker, Carlos (ed.) *Ernest Hemingway Selected Letters 1917–1961* (Granada, 1981).
5 *Bartlett's Familiar Quotations* (Macmillan, 1968 & 1980).
6 Barnes, John, and Middlemas, Keith, *Baldwin* (Weidenfeld & Nicholson, 1969).
7 Bernstein, Carl, and Woodward, Bob, *All the President's Men* (Quartet Books, 1974).
8 Bradlee, Ben, *Conversations with Kennedy* (Norton, 1975).
9 Burnam, Tom, *The Dictionary of Misinformation* (Futura, 1978).
10 Burnam, Tom, *More Misinformation* (Lippincott & Crowell, 1980).
11 Butler, David, and Sloman, Anne (eds), *British Political Facts 1900–75* (Macmillan, 1975).
12 Butler, Lord (R. A.), *The Art of the Possible* (Penguin Books, 1973).
13 Carpenter, Humphrey, *W. H. Auden* (George Allen & Unwin, 1981).
14 Churchill, Randolph S., and Gilbert, Martin, *Winston S. Churchill* (Vol.1–) (Heinemann, 1966–).
15 Churchill, Winston S., *Great Contemporaries* (Fontana Books, 1959).
16 Churchill, Winston S., *The Second World War* (Vols. 1–6) (Cassell, 1948–54).
17 Colson, Charles W., *Born Again* (Hodder & Stoughton, 1976).
18 *The Concise Oxford Dictionary of Proverbs* (OUP, 1982).
19 Cooke, Alistair, *Six Men* (The Bodley Head, 1977).
20 Dempsey, Jack, *Autobiography* (W. H. Allen, 1977).
21 Edelman, Maurice, *The Mirror: A Political History* (Hamish Hamilton, 1966).
22 Feiling, Keith, *The Life of Neville Chamberlain* (Macmillan, 1946).
23 Fleming, Ian, *Casino Royale* (Jonathan Cape, 1953).

24 Flexner, Stuart Berg, *I Hear America Talking* (Simon & Schuster, 1979).

25 Flexner, Stuart Berg, *Listening to America* (Simon & Schuster, 1982).

26 Flexner, Stuart Berg, and Wentworth, Harold, *Dictionary of American Slang* (Thomas Y. Crowell, 1975).

27 Foot, Michael, *Aneurin Bevan 1897–1945, 1945–60* (Granada, 1975).

28 Freedland, Michael, *Al Jolson* (Abacus, 1975).

29 Grey of Fallodon, Viscount, *Twenty-five Years* (Hodder & Stoughton, 1925).

30 Grigg, John, *Nancy Astor* (Sidgwick & Jackson, 1980).

31 Halliwell, Leslie, *The Filmgoer's Book of Quotes* Mayflower, 1978).

32 Hamilton, Willie, *My Queen and I* (Quartet Books, 1975).

33 Hart-Davis, Rupert, and Lyttelton, George, *The Lyttelton Hart-Davis Letters* (Vol.2) (John Murray, 1979).

34 Heller, Joseph, *Catch-22* (Corgi Books, 1962).

35 Hillary, Sir Edmund, *Nothing Venture, Nothing Win* (Hodder & Stoughton, 1975).

36 Hill, Frank Ernest, and Nevins, Allan, *Ford: Expansion and Challenge* (Scribner's, 1957).

37 Hills, Denis, *The White Pumpkin* (George Allen & Unwin, 1975.

38 Hoving, Thomas, *Tutankhamun–The Untold Story* (Hamish Hamilton, 1979).

39 Hunt, Sir David, *An Ambassador Remembers* (Peter Davies, 1975).

40 Ismay, Lord, *The Memoirs of Lord Ismay* (Heinemann, 1960).

41 Jackson, Robert, *The Chief* (Harrap, 1959).

42 James, Robert Rhodes (ed.), *Churchill Speaks* (Windward, 1981).

43 Jenkins, Roy, *Asquith* (Collins, 1964).

44 Joffre, *The Memoirs of Marshal Joffre* (Geoffrey Bles, 1932).

45 Lesley, Cole, *The Life of Noel Coward* (Penguin Books, 1978).

46 Liberace, *Liberace* (W. H. Allen, 1973).

47 Liddy, G. Gordon, *Will* (Sphere Books, 1981).

48 Macmillan, Harold, *Pointing the Way 1959–1961* (Macmillan, 1972).

49 *The Macquarie Dictionary* (Macquarie Library, 1981).

50 Manchester, William, *American Caesar* (Hutchinson, 1978).

51 McClaine, Ian, *Ministry of Morale* (George Allen & Unwin, 1979).

52 Mao Tse-tung, *Quotations from Mao Tse-Tung* (Foreign Languages Press, Peking, 1972).

53 Martin, George, *Madam Secretary–Frances Perkins* (Houghton Miflin Company, 1976).

54 Morgan, Ted, *Somerset Maugham* (Jonathan Cape, 1980).

55 Morris, William & Mary, *The Morris Dictionary of Word and Phrase Origins* (Harper & Row, 1972).

56 Nicholson, Vivian and Smith, Stephen, *I'm Going to Spend, Spend, Spend* (Jonathan Cape, 1977).

57 Nixon, Richard M., *The Memoirs of Richard Nixon* (Sidgwick & Jackson, 1978).

58 Orwell, George, *The Collected Essays, Journalism & Letters* (Vols.1–4) (Penguin Books, 1970).

59 *The Oxford Dictionary of Quotations* (OUP, 1953 & 1979).

60 Page, Martin, *Kiss Me Goodnight, Sergeant Major* (Hart-Davis, 1973).

61 Partridge, Eric, *Dictionary of Slang and Unconventional English*

(Routledge & Kegan Paul, 1970).
62 Partridge, Eric, *Dictionary of Catch Phrases* (Routledge & Kegan Paul, 1977).
63 Payn, Graham, and Morley, Sheridan *The Noel Coward Diaries* (Little, Brown & Co., 1982).
64 Polykoff, Shirley, *Does She . . . Or Doesn't She?* (Doubleday, 1975).
65 Ponsonby, Arthur, *Falsehood in War-Time* (George Allen & Unwin, 1928).
66 Puzo, Mario, *The Godfather Papers* (Heinemann, 1972).
67 Raw, Charles (etc.) *Do You Sincerely Want to be Rich?* (Penguin Books, 1972).
68 Rees, Goronwy, *A Chapter of Accidents* (Chatto & Windus, 1972).
69 Rees, Nigel, *Book of Slogans and Catchphrases* (Unwin Paperbacks, 1984).
70 Rees, Nigel, *Slogans* (George Allen & Unwin, 1982).
71 Rees, Nigel, *Very Interesting . . . But Stupid!* (Unwin Paperbacks, 1980).
72 Reith, Lord (J. C. W.), *Into the Wind* (Hodder & Stoughton, 1949).
73 Reitlinger, Gerald, *The Final Solution* (Vallentine Mitchell, 1953).
74 Remy, *Ten Years with de Gaulle* (Paris, 1971).
75 Repington, C. A. C., *The First World War 1914–18* (Constable, 1920).
76 Rice-Davies, Mandy, *Mandy* (Michael Joseph, 1980).
77 Robertson, Patrick, *The Guinness Book of Film Facts and Feats* (Guinness Superlatives, 1980).
78 Rose, Kenneth, *George V* (Weidenfeld & Nicolson, 1983).
79 Rosten, Leo, *Hooray for Yiddish!* (Elm Tree Books, 1983).
80 Rothel, David, *Who Was That Masked Man?* (A. S. Barnes & Co., 1976).
81 Safire, William, *On Language* (Times Books, 1980).
82 Safire, William, *Safire's Political Dictionary* (Ballantine, 1980).
83 Schlesinger, Arthur M., *Robert Kennedy and his Times* (Ballantine, 1979).
84 Schlesinger, Arthur M., *A Thousand Days* (Andre Deutsch, 1965).
85 Sherriff, R. C., *No Leading Lady* (Gollancz, 1968).
86 Sidey, Hugh, *A Very Personal Presidency* (Andre Deutsch, 1968).
87 Sorensen, Theodore C., *Kennedy* (Hodder & Stoughton, 1965).
88 Stuart, William H., *The Twelve Incredible Years* (M. A. Donohue & Co., 1935).
89 *Supplement to the Oxford English Dictionary, A*, 3 vols. (OUP, 1972–).
90 Taylor, A. J. P., *Beaverbrook* (Hamish Hamilton, 1966).
91 Taylor A. J. P., *English History 1914–45* (OUP, 1965).
92 Thomas, Hugh (ed.), *The Establishment* (Anthony Blond, 1959).
93 Tynan, Kenneth, *Curtains* (Longman, 1961).
94 Walker, Alexander, *Sex in the Movies* (Pelican Books, 1968).
95 Wheeler-Bennett, Sir John (ed.), *Action This Day* (Macmillan, 1969).
96 Williams, Philip, *Gaitskell* (Jonathan Cape, 1979).
97 Wilson, Harold, *The Labour Government 1964–70* (Weidenfeld & Nicholson, 1971).
98 Windsor, The Duke of, *A King's Story* (Cassell, 1951).

Picture Credits

260

Between pages 200 and 201

A Child Weeping	Topham Picture Library (Will Dyson)
The Price of Petrol . . .	British Museum (Zec)
Whose Finger?	British Museum
Top People . . .	*The Persuasion Industry*
General de Gaulle	BBC Hulton Picture Library
Orson Welles, *The Third Man*	Kobal Collection
Sean Connery as James Bond	Keystone Press Agency
Clark Gable and Vivien Leigh,	
Gone With the Wind	BBC Hulton Picture Library
Greta Garbo	Kobal Collection
Ingrid Bergman and Humphrey Bogart,	
Casablanca	Topham Picture Library
Al Jolson	BBC Hulton Picture Library

Between pages 216 and 217

Martin Luther King	Associated Press
Nurse Edith Cavell	Popperfoto
Stop Me and Buy One	Birds Eye Walls Ltd
Mao Tse-tung	Keystone Press Agency (Paul Raffaele)
Votes for Women	Museum of London

Between pages 248 and 249

Jack Dempsey and Gene Tunney	BBC Hulton Picture Library
R. A. Butler	Popperfoto
Sir Hartley Shawcross	Topham Picture Library
Khruschev	Keystone Press Agency
Hugh Gaitskell	Topham Picture Library
Enoch Powell	Topham Picture Library
Mandy Rice-Davies	Topham Picture Library

Index of Sayings

Adieu, mes amis, je vais à la gloire 255
Affluent society 42
After you've met one hundred and fifty Lord Mayors, they all begin to look the same 4
Alianza para Progreso 78
Alive and well and living in 43
Alliance for progress 74
All Americans are deaf, dumb and blind 40
All animals are equal, but some are more equal than others 89
All dressed up and no place to go 49
All Human Life is There 162
All I have, I would have given gladly not to be standing here today 80
All over by Christmas 122
All Quiet on the Western Front 168
All reactionaries are paper tigers 206
All the way with LBJ 80
All this will not be finished in the first one hundred days 75
All we want is the facts, ma'am 139
Am in Market Harborough. Where ought I to be? 17
And so, my fellow Americans, ask not what your country can do for you: ask what you can do for your country 76
And so we say farewell . . . 176
And this certainly has to be the most historic phone call ever made 83
Angry young man 43
Any club that would have me as a member, I don't want to belong to 24
Any gum, chum? 128
Any man who hates dogs and babies can't be all bad 20
Anyone for tennis? 134-6
Any publicity is good publicity 60
Anything you say will be taken down and may be given in evidence 46
Archaeologist is the best husband, An 18
Are we downhearted – No! 32
Are you now or have you ever been a member of the Communist Party? 234
Are you sitting comfortably . . . then we'll begin 136
'Arf a mo, Kaiser! 30
Ars Gratia Artis 20
Art of the possible 223
At a stroke 153

At 60 miles an hour the loudest noise in this new Rolls-Royce comes from the electric clock 193
At the eleventh hour on the eleventh day of the eleventh month 34
Avoid 'Five O'Clock Shadow' 196

Back to Normalcy 66
Back to square one! 136
Backs to the wall 34
Ban the Bomb 214
Banzai! 131
Because it's there 11
Believe it or not! 44
Be Prepared 59
Berlin by Christmas 28
Bertie! 4
Best Prime Minister we have? 223
Better red than dead 214
Big Apple 44
Big Brother is Watching You 89
Bigger bang for a buck, A 235
Big One, The 194
Black is beautiful 215
Black Power 215
B.O. 194
Bolshevism run mad 227
Bombs away with Curt LeMay 213
Boneless Wonder, The 100
Born with a gift of laughter and a sense that the world was mad 91
Boys in the back-rooms, The 126
Breakfast of Champions 195
Bridegroom on the wedding cake, The 24
Britain Can Take It 124
Britain will not be involved in a European war this year, or next year either 119
Broad, sunlit uplands, The 100
Brotherhood of man under the fatherhood of God, The 241
Brute force of monopoly 156
Buck stops here, The 70
Bugger Bognor! 5
Bunnies can (and will) go to France 248
Burn, baby, burn! 170
Burn your bra 215
Business as usual 29
Bust King George in the snoot 225
Butler did it!, The 45

262

Call Me Madam 169
Can *you* tell Stork from butter? 195
Careless Talk Costs Lives 124
Catch 22 92
Chief business of the American people is business, The 67
Close your eyes and think of England 251
Come now, [and] let us reason together 81
Come on, you sons of bitches! Do you want to live forever! 34
Come up and see me some time 177
Come with me to the Casbah 177
Comin' in on a Wing and a Prayer 131
Comment is free, but facts are sacred 157
Communism with a human face 241
Contemptible little army 30
Corridors of Power 169
Crisis? What crisis? 154
Cross of Lorraine is the heaviest cross I have had to bear, The 105
Cult of personality 236

Daddy, what did *you* do in the Great War? 32
Daily Express is a bloody awful newspaper, The 10
Damn you England 25
Date which will live in infamy, A 69
Dead birds don't fall out of nests 108
Dear boy 18
Deep Throat 48
Desiccated calculating machine 232
DEWEY DEFEATS TRUMAN 71
Diamond is forever, A 195
Discussing Ugandan affairs 63
Does she . . . or doesn't she? 195
Domino Theory 211
Do not fold, spindle or mutilate 51
Do not pass 'Go' 52
Don't forget the diver 136-7
Don't get mad, get even 238
Do you sincerely want to be rich? 209
Dragged kicking and screaming into the twentieth century x
Drinka Pinta Milka Day 196
Drop the gun, Looey! 178

East is Red, The 240
Eat your heart out 53
Effete corps of impudent snobs, An 243
EGGHEAD WEDS HOURGLASS 159
Eight-ulcer man on a four-ulcer job and all four ulcers working, An 71
Ein Reich, Ein Völk, Ein Führer 117
Elementary, my dear Watson! 92
Empty taxi arrived at 10 Downing Street, and when the door was opened Attlee got out, An 106

England and America are two countries separated by the same language 40
Enosis! 234
Establishment, The 49
Every day and in every way I am getting better and better 44
Every other inch a gentleman 25
Everything you always wanted to know about sex but were afraid to ask 50
Everywhere the glint of gold 13
Exporting is fun 148
Extremism in the defence of liberty is no vice 240

Fair shares for all 231
Family that prays together stays together, The 50
Female of the species is more deadly than the male, The 93
Fifty million Frenchmen can't be wrong 51
Final solution 127
Fire Next Time, The 170
First casualty when war comes is truth, The 29
First World War 26
5-4-3-2-1 178
Float like a butterfly, sting like a bee 222
Food shot from guns 197
Forgive but never forget 78
For God's sake look after our people 12
For Whom the Bell Tolls 170
France has lost a battle, but France has not lost the war! 165
Frankly, my dear, I don't give a damn 179
Free at last, free at last, thank God Almighty, we are free at last! 192
Free the Chicago 7 215
From Land's End to John of Gaunt 110
From Stettin in the Baltic to Trieste in the Adriatic, an iron curtain has descended across the Continent 107
Full-hearted consent of the Parliament and people 153

Gentlemen, I am sorry for keeping you waiting like this – I am unable to concentrate 5
George Davis is innocent, OK 60
Germany calling, Germany calling! 131
Geronimo! 131
Get on your bike 249
Gnomes of Zurich 239
Goddamn the whole friggin' world and everyone in it but you, Carlotta 20
God protect me from my friends 51
Gone for a Burton 197
Good fences make good neighbours 94

Good evening Mr and Mrs North America and all the ships at sea. Let's go to press! 137

Goodnight, my darlings 254

Good . . . to the last drop 66

Go placidly amid the noise and haste 48

Go to Hell, Babe Ruth – American, you die 131

Go to it! 125

Go to work on an egg 197

Grace under pressure 78

Great Britain . . . has lost an Empire and not yet found a role 239

Greater love hath no man than this, that he lay down his friends for his life 248

Greatest Motion Picture Ever Made, The 179

Greatest thing since sliced bread, The 61

Great Leap Forward 206

Great silent majority of my fellow Americans 84

Great Society 80

Greeks had a word for it, The 52

Guilty men 124

Guinness is good for you 198

Guns or butter 228

Had we lived, I should have had a tale to tell 12

Hang the Kaiser! 35

Happiness is . . . 53

Hard Day's Night, A 171

Has anyone here been raped and speaks English? 162

Have a banana 198

Have a nice day 58

Have you brought the chequebook, Alfred?. 255

Hearts and minds 211

He can't fart and chew gun at the same time 81

Heineken refreshes the parts other beers cannot reach 198

He Kept Us Out of the War 66

Hello, sailor! 137

Hello, sucker! 51

He marks – not that you won or lost/But how you played the game 220

He missed the bus 122

He mobilised the English language and sent it into battle 78

Here it is at last, the distinguished thing 256

Here on 11 November 1918 succumbed the criminal pride of the German Reich, vanquished by the free peoples which it tried to enslave 115

Here's a pretty kettle of fish 6

Here's Johnny! 138

Here we will stand and fight; there will be no further withdrawal 130

He sat so long upon the fence that the iron has entered into his soul 144

He's not as nice as he looks 106

He was against it 67

He will drown everything with HP sauce 151

Hey, hey, LBJ, how many kids did you kill today? 212

Him bad man, kemo sabe! 138

His Majesty's Government looks with favour upon the establishment in Palestine of a national home for the Jewish people 145

History is bunk 21

Hitler Has Only Got One Ball 125

Hi-yo, Silver 138

Honey, I just forgot to duck 220

Hoobert Herver 111

House is not a Home, A 252

How can you govern a country which produces 246 different kinds of cheese? 165

How can they tell? 67

How is the Empire? 5

Howls of anguish 247

How many divisions has *he* got? 227

How'm I doing? 248

How odd/ Of God/ To choose/ The Jews 95

Hundred days of dynamic action 151

I always thought I was Jeanne d'Arc and Buonaparte – how little one knows oneself 165

I am a Ford not a Lincoln 85

I am as strong as a bull moose 66

I am just going outside. I may be some time 12

I am not a crook 84

I am not going to speak to the man on the bridge and I am not going to spit on the deck . . . 146

I am ready to meet my Maker. Whether my Maker is ready for the ordeal of meeting me is another matter 109

I am the greatest 221

I cannot and will not cut my conscience to fit this year's fashions 234

Ich bin ein Berliner 79

I cry all the way to the bank 23

I desire the Poles carnally 87

If anything can go wrong, it will 56

I felt like the moon, the stars, and all the planets had fallen on me 70

If I had to choose between betraying my country and betraying my friend, I hope I should have the guts to betray my country 96

264

If It's Tuesday, This Must be Belgium 62

If you can't ride two horses at once, you shouldn't be in the circus 227

If you can't stand the heat, get out of the kitchen 70

If you know a better 'ole, go to it 125

If they'd stuffed the child's head up the horse's arse they would have solved two problems at once 19

I, General de Gaulle 164

I guess that'll hold the little bastards 111

I have a dream 190

I have felt that the Suez Canal was flowing through my drawing room 143

I have found it impossible to carry the heavy burden of responsibility and to discharge my duties as King as I would wish to do without the help and support of the woman I love 8

I have made love to 10,000 women 253

I have nothing to offer but blood, toil, tears and sweat 101

I have promises to keep 94

I have a secret plan to end the war 84

I have seen the future and it works 224

I have to tell you now that no such undertaking has been received, and that consequently this country is at war with Germany 120

I Like Ike 71

Illegitimi non carborundum 53

I'll make him an offer he can't refuse 90

I loved Kirk so much . . . I would have skied down Mount Everest in the nude with a carnation up my nose 253

I Love New York 199

I'm a cop 139

I'm an optimist, but I'm an optimist who takes his raincoat 150

I'm as mad as hell, and I'm not going to take this anymore 180

I'm going to spend, spend, spend, 25

I'm only here for the beer 199

Imprisoned in every fat man a thin one is wildly signalling to be let out 50

I'm so bored with it all 109

I must down to the seas again 92

I must get out of these wet clothes and into a dry Martini 17

I myself have always deprecated . . . appeals to the Dunkirk spirit 150

In a hierarchy every employee tends to rise to his level of incompetence 210

Include me out 112

I never see any home cooking – all I get is fancy stuff 10

In My Way 171

In Place of Strife 242

In the country of the blind the one-eyed man is king 45

In the future everyone will be famous for fifteen minutes 15

In the name of God, go! 124

In war, resolution; in defeat, definance; in victory, magnanimity; in peace, goodwill 108

Iron Curtain 106

Iron Lady 154

I said to the man who stood at the Gate of the Year, 'Give me a light that I may tread safely into the unknown' 9

I say it's spinach 61

I seem to hear a child weeping! 156

I shall go to Korea 72

I shall not seek, and I will not accept, the nomination of my party for another term as your President 81

I shall return 129

I should have stood in bed 221

Is it a book that you would even wish your wife or your servants to read? 22

Is it my birthday or am I dying? 254

Is it true . . . Blondes have more fun? 194

I sleep each night a little better . . . because Lyndon Johnson is my President 81

Is Paris burning? 132

Is the name of the game 57

Is Your Journey Really Necessary? 125

It beats . . . as it sweeps . . . as it cleans 199

I thought . . . 199

It is better to die on your feet than to live on your knees 227

IT *IS* A MORAL ISSUE 252

It is still pretty exciting to be English 19

It is the last territorial claim which I have to make in Europe 117

It'll play in Peoria 245

It makes me sick, sick, sick way down inside 234

It's a bird! 139

It's all part of life's rich pageant 181

It's a plane! 139

It seemed like a good idea at the time 181

It's Superman! 139

I think it is about time we pulled our finger out 10

It wiggles, it's shapely and it's name is Ainsley Gotto 243

I've been to the mountain top 192

I've got his pecker in my pocket 81

I've had eighteen straight whiskies. I think that's the record 256

I've looked on a lot of women with lust. I've committed adultery in my heart many

265

times. God recognises I will do this and forgives me 86
I want to be alone 181
I want you all to stonewall it 84
I was a seven stone weakling 204
I was only obeying orders 133
I went to Philadelphia and found that it was closed 20
I would walk over my grandmother . . . to get Nixon re-elected! 243

Jaw-jaw is better than war-war 147
Je vous ai compris 165
Jimmy Stewart for Governor, Reagan for best friend 87
Jimmy who? 86
Journey's End 171
Justice should not only be done, but should manifestly and undoubtedly be seen to be done 54
Just know your lines and don't bump into the furniture 18

Keep cool with Coolidge 67
Keep punching 221
Kill the other guy before he kills you 221
Kilroy was here 55
King's life is moving peacefully towards its close, The 5
Kristallnacht 119

Lafayette, we are here 33
La Grande Illusion 170
Lamps are going out all over Europe; we shall not see them lit again in our lifetime, The 27
Land fit for heroes, A 35
La réforme, oui; la chienlit, non 166
Less is more 16
Let a hundred flowers bloom 206
Let him twist slowly, slowly in the wind 245
Let's do the show right here in the barn! 182
Let's Get America Moving Again 238
Let the word go forth from this time and place 74
Let us go forward together 101
Let us never negotiate out of fear, but let us never fear to negotiate 75
Liberty is precious – so precious that it must be rationed 224
Licence to print . . . money, A 162
Life begins at forty 56
Life is not meant to be easy 41
Life is unfair 78
Life's better with the Conservatives . . . don't let Labour ruin it 236
Light at the end of the tunnel 212

Like a vicarage tea-party 64
Like being savaged by a dead sheep 247
Like the Mississippi it just keeps rolling along 105
Like the Roman, I seem to see 'the River Tiber foaming with much blood' 242
Little local difficulties 147
Little old lady from Dubuque, The 157
Live Now, Pay Later 56
Lloyd George knew my father 230
Long and the Short and the Tall 172
Long, hot summer 62
Look, Stranger 172
Lost generation, A 56
Love in a Cold Climate 173
Love it or leave it 211
Love means not ever having to say you're sorry 182
Lower than vermin 232
Lunatic fringe 66
Lunatics have taken over the asylum 209

Make Love, not War 216
Man you love to hate, The 53
Martini, shaken, not stirred, A 183
May the Force be with you 184
Mean Streets 173
Me Tarzan, you Jane 184
Moderation in the pursuit of justice is no virtue! 240
Moon and Sixpence, The 174
More stars than in Heaven 20
More than half the children in my class never had any boots 150
More will mean worse 15
Most fun I've had without laughing, The 251
Most important thing in the Olympic Games is not winning but taking part 219
Mousetrap, The 173
Mr Balfour's poodle 144
My face looks like a wedding-cake left out in the rain 16-17
My friends 68
My husband and I 9
My lips are sealed 146
My name's Friday 139
My name is Jimmy Carter and I'm running for President 86

Nation shall Speak Peace unto Nation 156
Nattering nabobs of negativism 243
Navy's here, The 122
Never Again 128
Never-ending battle for truth, justice, and the American Way, A 139
Never give a sucker an even break 20
Never in the field of human conflict was so

much owed by so many to so few 104
Never miss an opportunity to relieve your-
self; never miss a chance to sit down and
rest your feet 4
New Deal 68
NIBMAR 247
Nice guys finish last 220
Nice one, Cyril 200
Night and Fog 127
Night is your friend. The 'V' is your sign,
The 127
Night of the Long Knives, The 116
No comment 47
No more coals to Newcastle, no more Hoares
to Paris 5
No more Mr Nice Guy 241
Non! 166
Nostalgia isn't what it used to be 175
Not a penny off the pay, not a minute on the
day 216
Not bloody likely! 38
Not in a thousand years 247
Not while I'm alive he ain't 233
Nothing over sixpence 201
Now she is like the others 165
Now the trumpet summons us again 76
Nuts! 132

Of Human Bondage 174
Oh, Calcutta! 173
OK, Houston, we have had a problem here
. . . Houston, we have a problem 14
Old soldiers never die. They just fade away
71
One look at you, Mr Hitchcock, and I know
who made it 40
One look at you, Mr Shaw, and I know
there's famine in the land 40
One picture is worth ten thousand words 158
One Step Forward, Two Steps Back 224
On les aura! 33
Only connect! 96
Only her hairdresser knows for sure 196
Only the names have been changed to protect
the innocent 139
Only thing we have to fear is fear itself, The
68
On the whole I'd rather be in Philadelphia 20
O O O O that Shakespeherian Rag – 95
Opera isn't over until the fat lady sings, The
58
Oral contract is not worth the paper it's
written on, An 113
Our long national nightmare is over 86
Our reporter made an excuse and left 160
Out of the closets and into the streets 216
Out of their tiny Chinese minds 247

Overpaid, overfed, oversexed and over here
128
Over the moon/ Sick as a parrot 58
Over There 128
Over the top 30

Parliamentary leper 151
Patriotism is not enough; I must have no
hatred and bitterness towards anyone 31
Peace for our time 118
People can have [the Model T in] any colour
so long as it's black 21
Perpendicular expression of a horizontal
desire 40
Phoney war 121
Play it again, Sam 184
Policeman isn't there to *create* disorder, the
policeman is there to *preserve* disorder, The
113
Political power grows out of the barrel of a
gun 205
Portrait is a remarkable example of modern
art, The 108
Pound . . . in your pocket, The 152
Power to the People 216
Power without responsibility – the preroga-
tive of the harlot through the ages 145
Praise the Lord and Pass the Ammunition
131
Pretty amazing! 10
PRICE OF PETROL HAS BEEN
INCREASED BY ONE PENNY – official
160
Public Enemy Number One 59
Put a tiger in your tank 201
Put that bloody cigarette out! 256

Quaecunque 157
Quarrel in a faraway country between people
of whom we know nothing 118

Randy – where's the rest of me? 87
Razor's Edge, The 174
Regardless of what they say about it we are
going to keep it 82
Return to Normalcy with Harding 66
Road to Wigan Pier, The 174
Room at the Top 174
Rose is a rose is a rose is a rose 91
Rugged individualism 67
. . . Rule OK 60
Running dogs! 207
Russians with snow on their boots 29

Safety First 226
Say it with flowers 202
She could eat an apple through a tennis

racquet 19
Sheep in sheep's clothing, A 106
She should lie back and enjoy it 252
Short, sharp, shock 249
Show me a good loser and I'll show you a loser 220
Second Front Now 130
See you later, alligator 140
Sick as a parrot/ Over the moon 58
Sieg Heil! 117
Sighted sub, sank same 129
Situation excellente. J'attaque 34
Sixty-four dollar question, The 140
Smack of firm government, The 235
SMALL EARTHQUAKE IN CHILE. NOT MANY DEAD 159
Smoke-filled room, A 225
Social Contract 246
Sock it to me 140
Softly, Softly 174
Soldier of the Great War. Known unto God, A 36
So little done, so much to do 256
Some of my best friends are Jews 54
Something must be done 6
Son of a bitch isn't going to resign on me, I want him fired, The 70
Speak for England 120
Speak softly and carry a big stick 65
Spirit of Dunkirk will once again carry us through to success, The 150
STICKS NIX HICKS PIX 159
Stop – Look – Listen 226
Stop me and buy one 202
Stop the World I Want to Get Off 175
Strange how potent cheap music is 18
Sun Also Rises, The 170
Sun sinks slowly in the West, The 177
Symbolic of the desire of our peoples never to go to war with one another again 118

Take a step or two forwards, lads. It will be easier that way 255
Tall, Dark and Handsome 62
Terminological inexactitude 99
That's one small step for a man, one giant leap for mankind 1
That's the way the cookie crumbles 185
That's the way it crumbles, cookie-wise 185
That this house will in no circumstances fight for its King and Country 115
Their Name Liveth for Evermore 36
There ain't gonna be no war 147
There are some of us, Mr Chairman, who will fight and fight and fight again to save the Party we love 237
There is no alternative 154

There is no reason to attack the monkey when the organ grinder is present 233
There is no right to strike against the public safety by anybody, anywhere, at any time 67
There is no Soviet domination of eastern Europe and there never will be under a Ford administration 86
There is no such thing as a free lunch 249
There seems to be something wrong with our bloody ships today 33
There's less in this than meets the eye 17
There was no impropriety whatsoever in my acquaintanceship with Miss Keeler 252
There will be no whitewash in the White House 84
They are going to be squeezed as a lemon is squeezed – until the pips squeak 35
There, but for the grace of God goes God 106
They shall grow not old, as we that are left grow old 97
They shall not pass 32
They shoot horses, don't they? 61
Things were done better in my day 7
Third Man, The 174
This country needs . . . good plumbers . . . 85
This country of ours, which we love so much, will find dignity and greatness and peace again 19
This is the greatest week in the history of the world since the Creation 83
This is the operative statement. The others are inoperative 245
This is the city 139
This tightly knit group of politically motivated men 152
This was their finest hour 104
This week's deliberate mistake 142
Through a dark glassly . . . 110
Tired and emotional 63
'T' is silent – as in Harlow, The 16
To come on like gangbusters 136
Today is the first day of the rest of your life 62
Today . . ., Tomorrow the World! 117
Tomorrow is another day! 180
Tonic water by you-know-who . . . 202
Top People take *The Times* 161
Tora-tora-tora 128
To save the town, it became necessary to destroy it 213
Tranquillity Base here – the Eagle has landed 13
Troops that can advance no farther must, at any price, hold on to the ground they have conquered and die on the spot rather than

give way 28
Truth is the glue that holds government together 85
Turn on, tune in, drop out 217
Turn up the lights . . . I don't want to go home in the dark 255
Two Cultures, The 170
Two things should be cut: the second act and the child's throat 19

Unacceptable face of capitalism 153
. . . Until I discovered Smirnoff 199
Until a shrimp learns to whistle 236
Up there, Cazaly! 221
Up, up and awa-a-a-ay! 138

Vast wasteland, A 162
Very rich are different from you and me. Yes, they have more money, The 21
Very gallant gentleman, A 12
Very sad death – eaten by missionaries, A 110-11
Very well, alone 124
Victory has a hundred fathers but defeat is an orphan 78
Village tyrant, A 246
Vive l'Algérie française! 165
Vive de Gaulle! 166
Vive le Québec libre 166
Votes for women 217

Wait and see 143
Wake up, England! 4
Wake up there! 17
WALL STREET LAYS AN EGG 159
Walls Have Ears 125
War to end wars, The 34
War is too serious a business to be left to the generals 31
Weaned on a pickle 24
We are not amused 3
We are today in the midst of a cold war 231
We are the masters now! 229
We came in peace for all mankind 14
We have won the war: now we have to win the peace 34
Week is a long time in politics, A 149
Weeks rather than months 151
We have ways and means of making you talk 185
We knocked the bastard off! 13
Well may he say 'God Save the Queen', because nothing will save the Governor-General 247
Well, he would, wouldn't he? 253
We must guard against the acquisition of unwarranted influence, . . . by the

military-industrial complex 72
We must love one another or die 97
We're eyeball to eyeball and the other fellow just blinked 238
We're more popular than Jesus now 22
We shall fight on the beaches, we shall fight on the landing grounds, we shall fight in the fields and in the streets, we shall fight in the hills; we shall never surrender 103
We should bomb them into the Stone Age 213
We stand today on the edge of a New Frontier 73
We will bury you 235
We wuz robbed! 221
What a way to run a railroad! 209
What did that produce? The cuckoo clock 178
What if the child inherits my beauty and your brains? 39
What *is* the answer? . . . In that case, what is the question? 256
What is the secret of Schh. . .? 202
What's good for General Motors is good for the country 234
What's a nice girl like you doing in a joint like this? 58
What this country needs is a good five cent cigar 224
When a great many people are unable to find work, unemployment results 67
When I hear the word 'Culture' I reach for my revolver 228
When the going gets tough, the tough get going 238
When you got it, flaunt it 202
Where Were you When the Lights Went Out 175
Which twin has the Toni? 203
White heat of the technological revolution, The 151
Who he? 157
Who's Afraid of Virginia Woolf 175
Who is in charge of the clattering train? 155
Whole Fleet's lit up, The 111
Who, whom? 224
Whose finger . . . on the trigger? 160
Why don't we put on a show! 182
Why fear death? It is the greatest adventure in life 255
Why not the best? 86
Will the real — — —, please stand up! 142
Wilson's Wisdom Wins Without War 66
Wind of change is blowing through this continent, The 148
Winning isn't everything, it's the only thing 220

Win this one for the Gipper 87
With appalling frankness 146
With regard to the problem of Sudeten
　Germans, my patience is now at an end 118
Wonderful things 13
Work expands so as to fill the time available
　for its completion 210
World must be safe for democracy, The 66
Would you be shocked if I put on something
　more comfortable? 185
Would you buy a used car from this man? 82

Yeah-yeah-yeah 142
Yesterday, a shaft of light cut into the
　darkness . . . 79
Yes, We Have No Bananas 198
You ain't heard nothin' yet 186
You are Mr Lobby Lud – I claim the
　Westminster Gazette prize 158
You ask, what is our aim? I can answer in
　one word: victory 101
You dirty rat! 186
You don't even [need to] do your teeth with
　the light on. You can do it in the dark 114

You don't have to do anything. Not a thing.
　Oh, maybe just whistle 180
You don't want no pie in the sky when you
　die 222
You have used every cliché except 'God is
　Love' and 'Please adjust your dress before
　leaving' 143
You must have seen a lot of changes in your
　time? 10
You 'orrible little man 17
You're going out a youngster – but you've got
　to come back a star! 186
You're never alone with a Strand 203
Your Country Needs You! 27
Your King and Country need you 27
You see things; and you say 'Why?' But I
　dream things that never were; and I say
　'Why not?' 40
You too can have a body like mine 203
You've never had it so good 148
You will send a Foreign Secretary . . . naked
　into the conference chamber 233
You won't have Nixon to kick around any
　more 83